Humanitarian aid, genocide and mass killings

Manchester University Press

HUMANITARIANISM
Key debates and new approaches

This series offers a new interdisciplinary reflection on one of the most important and yet understudied areas in history, politics and cultural practices: humanitarian aid and its responses to crises and conflicts. The series seeks to define afresh the boundaries and methodologies applied to the study of humanitarian relief and so-called 'humanitarian events'. The series includes monographs and carefully selected thematic edited collections which will cross disciplinary boundaries and bring fresh perspectives to the historical, political and cultural understanding of the rationale and impact of humanitarian relief work.

Islamic charities and Islamic humanism in troubled times
   Jonathan Benthall

Calculating compassion: Humanity and relief in war, Britain 1870–1914
   Rebecca Gill

Humanitarian intervention in the long nineteenth century
   Alexis Heraclides and Ada Dialla

Donors, technical assistance and public administration in Kosovo
   Mary Venner

Humanitarian aid, genocide and mass killings

Médecins Sans Frontières, the Rwandan experience, 1982–97

Jean-Hervé Bradol and Marc Le Pape

Manchester University Press

The right of Jean-Hervé Bradol and Marc Le Pape to be identified as the authors of this work has been asserted by them in accordance with the Copyright, Designs and Patents Act 1988.

Published by Manchester University Press
Altrincham Street, Manchester M1 7JA
www.manchesteruniversitypress.co.uk

British Library Cataloguing-in-Publication Data
A catalogue record for this book is available from the British Library

Library of Congress Cataloging-in-Publication Data applied for

ISBN 978 1 7849 9305 4 hardback
ISBN 978 1 5261 1551 5   paperback

First published 2017

Typeset by Out of House Publishing
Printed in Great Britain
by CPI Group (UK) Ltd, Croydon, CR0 4YY

Contents

List of maps		*page* vi
Acknowledgements		viii
Abbreviations		ix
	Introduction: through the eyes of field teams' members	1
1	From the persecution of Kinyarwanda speakers in Uganda to the genocide of Rwandan Tutsis	14
2	Rwandan refugee camps in Tanzania and Zaire, 1994–95	43
3	The new Rwanda	66
4	Refugees on the run in war-torn Zaire, 1996–97	102
	Epilogue: the effectiveness of aid in the face of repeated mass atrocities	126
	Select bibliography	139
	Index	144

Maps

0.1 The Great Lakes region. Edited by authors from Évaluation conjointe de l'aide d'urgence au Rwanda, *Étude I. Perspective historique. Facteurs d'explication* (London: ODI, 1996), p. 13.   *page* 7

1.1 Internally displaced Rwandans. MSF archives, July 1993.   18

1.2 Humanitarian issues in Rwanda. Edited by authors from Secrétatariat permanent du Comité de Crise, Problématiques humanitaires in Rwanda, Kigali, 3 March 1994.   19

1.3 Burundian refugee camps in Rwanda. Edited by authors from Secrétariat du Comité de Crise (projet C.E.E) and UNHCR, Kigali, 1993.   21

1.4 Kigali City. Edited by authors from A. Guichaoua, *Les crises politiques au Burundi et au Rwanda (1993–1994)* (Paris: Karthala, 1995), p. 524.   30

1.5 RPF's movements from April to July 1994. Edited by authors from Évaluation conjointe de l'aide d'urgence au Rwanda, *Étude III. L'aide humanitaire et ses effets* (London: ODI, 1996), p. 30.   37

2.1 Rwandan refugee camps, Ngara district (Tanzania). Edited by authors from Évaluation conjointe de l'aide d'urgence au Rwanda, *Étude III. L'aide humanitaire et ses effets* (London: ODI, 1996), p. 35.   45

2.2 Rwandan refugee camps, Goma (Zaire). Edited by authors from Évaluation conjointe de l'aide d'urgence au Rwanda, *Étude III. L'aide humanitaire et ses effets* (London: ODI, 1996), p. 39.   48

2.3 Rwandan refugee camps, Bukavu (Zaire). Edited by authors from Évaluation conjointe de l'aide d'urgence au Rwanda, *Étude III. L'aide humanitaire et ses effets* (London: ODI, 1996), p. 43.   51

3.1 MSF field teams in the Great Lakes region, August 1994. Edited by authors from MSF, ZARWABUTA 31 August 1994, Paris, 1994.   71

3.2   Kibeho camp. Edited by authors from L. Binet, *The Violence of the New Rwandan Regime 1994–1995* (Paris: MSF, 2005), p. 8.   85
4.1   Movements of Rwandan refugees in Zaire, 1996–97. Edited by MSF from Map 10.3 Rwandan and Burundian refugee movements, 1994–99 in UNHCR, *The State of World's Refugees: Fifty Years of Humanitarian Action* (Geneva: Oxford University Press, 2000), p. 270.   108

Acknowledgements

We warmly thank Claudine Vidal, Fabrice Weissman, Judith Soussan, Rony Brauman, Michael Neuman, all members of CRASH (Centre de réflexion sur l'action et les savoirs humanitaires, Fondation Médecins Sans Frontières), for their careful and critical reading of this work. We are grateful to those in charge at MSF Paris for allowing free access to archives. Caroline Serraf organised the translations, which were proofread and edited by Ros Smith-Thomas. They are warmly thanked. Gwendolyn Blin, archivist, was a precious help in researching the texts contained in the bibliography. We are also grateful to Sarah Imani who designed the maps that accompany some of the chapters of the book. We hope our research does justice to the work of MSF personnel, especially the Rwandan staff, who contributed in the assistance programmes in the Great Lakes region – at the cost of their lives for some.

Abbreviations

ACT	Action by Churches Together
ADFL	Alliance of Democratic Forces for the Liberation of Congo/Zaire
AICF	Action Internationale Contre la Faim/International Action against Hunger
AMREF	African Medical and Research Foundation
ASRAMES	Regional Association for the Supply of Essential Medicines
CARE	Cooperative for Assistance and Relief Everywhere
CDC	Centers for Disease Control and Prevention
CDR	Coalition for the Defence of the Republic
CHK	Central Hospital of Kigali
COOPI	Association Cooperazione Internazionale
CRASH	Centre de réflexion sur l'action et les savoirs humanitaires (Fondation MSF)
CTC	cholera treatment center
DHS	Demographic and Health Surveys
DRC	Democratic Republic of Congo
FAR	Forces Armées Rwandaises
FIDH	Fédération internationale des droits de l'homme
HRW	Human Rights Watch
ICRC	International Committee of the Red Cross
ICTR	International Criminal Tribunal for Rwanda
IDP	Internally Displaced Person
IFRC	International Federation of Red Cross and Red Crescent Societies
IOC	Integrated Operations Center
IOM	International Organization for Migration
IRIN	Integrated Regional Information Network (UNDHA)
JEEAR	Joint Evaluation of Emergency Assistance to Rwanda

MdM	Médecins du Monde (Doctors of the World)
MDR	Mouvement Démocratique Républicain (Republican Democratic Movement)
Merlin	Medical Emergency Relief International
MRND	Mouvement Républicain National pour la Démocratie et le Développement / National Republican Movement for Democracy and Development
MSF	Médecins Sans Frontières
NGO	non-governmental organisation
NMOG	Neutral Military Observers Group
OAU	Organisation of African Unity
OCHA	Office for the Coordination of Humanitarian Affairs
ODA	Official Development Administration (UK)
ODI	Overseas Development Institute
OFDA	Office of US Foreign Disaster Assistance
Oxfam	Oxford Committee for Famine Relief
PVOs	Private Voluntary Organizations
RANU	Rwandese Alliance for National Unity
RCN	Réseau Citoyens/Citizen's Network
RPA	Rwanda Patriotic Army
RPF	Rwandan Patriotic Front
RRWF	Rwandese Refugee Welfare Foundation
SCHR	Steering Committee for Humanitarian Response
SPD	Special Presidential Division
UN	United Nations
UNAMIR	United Nations Assistance Mission for Rwanda
UNDHA	United Nations Department of Humanitarian Affairs
UNHCHR	United Nations High Commissioner for Human Rights
UNHCR	United Nations High Commissioner for Refugees
UNICEF	United Nations Children's Fund
UNPO	Unrepresented Nations and Peoples Organization
UNREO	United Nations Rwanda Emergency Office
UNSC	United Nations Security Council
USAID	US Agency for International Development
VOA	Voice of America
WFP	World Food Programme
WHO	World Health Organization
ZCSC	Zairian Camp Security Contingent

Introduction: through the eyes of field teams' members

In 1994 and during the years that followed, humanitarian workers found them-selves first-hand witnesses to genocide and mass killings, not only in Rwanda but also in those countries with which it shares a border. Unprecedented in the history of humanitarian action since decolonisation, the experiences of these aid workers remain just as much of an exception now as they were in the 1990s.

The year 2014 marked the twentieth anniversary of the genocide of the Rwandan Tutsis. The political and moral shockwaves engendered by the extermination of this people acted as a catalyst for major changes to the way the international com-munity reacted to situations of extreme crisis. A particularly tragic demonstration, the events in Rwanda served to expose the inability of states and international insti-tutions to put an end to the most radical acts of mass violence – as had been the case in other post-Cold War conflicts in countries such as the former Yugoslavia, Sudan, Chechnya and Angola. By the same token, they also revealed the flaws in international aid agencies' operating procedures with their failure not only to deliver appropriate and timely aid but also to prevent the siphoning off of a not-insignificant proportion of this aid into the war economy.

As preparations for the commemoration ceremonies got underway, the two authors of this book were in no doubt that they would be questioned about Médecins Sans Frontières' humanitarian operations and strategies, not only in Rwanda before, during and after the April to July 1994 genocide, but also in neighbouring Burundi, Zaire and Tanzania where Rwandan refugees had sought refuge. It is rare indeed that humanitarian workers find themselves first-hand witnesses to identifiable indi-viduals (soldiers and militiamen) slaughtering large numbers of civilians and former combatants (prisoners and the wounded) as aid is almost invariably delivered to war victims some distance from the scene of actual massacres. Their role consists more commonly in providing assistance to survivors fleeing in search of refuge and assis-tance, frequently across borders supposedly safe from armed aggression. In cases where humanitarian workers do find themselves working in situations of wholesale slaughter, the perpetrators and their leaders aspire to anonymity and so commit their crimes out of the sight of such inconvenient witnesses and their pursuit of the truth. Nevertheless, humanitarian aid agencies and national and international institutions, such as the media, and human rights and religious organisations, are sometimes able to glean information from local sources – whether during or after the killings – that can help to identify them. Both before and during the 1990s, the authors of this book had occasion to visit Rwanda and the countries around it. In 1994, sociologist Marc Le Pape was a researcher at the Centre National de la Recherche Scientifique and at the École des Hautes Études en Sciences Sociales, and medical doctor Jean-Hervé Bradol was employed as desk officer for Rwanda at Médecins Sans Frontières (MSF) headquarters in Paris. We began to work together in 1995, our collaboration inspiring a mutual interest in each other's disciplines.[1] Humanitarian doctor Bradol began to take part in a process to develop critical thinking on humanitarian medical action, while sociologist Le Pape was appointed to MSF France's Board of Directors in 1998. He remained a member until 2008.

In 2014, before the genocide commemoration, we asked ourselves if we were capable of answering three very specific questions about Rwanda and the Great Lakes region during the period 1990 to 1997.

Where were MSF's teams working?

What work were they involved in?

Which of the obstacles they encountered became the subject of debate, and which of these went on to be made public?

It soon became clear that we did not have the data we would need to answer these questions and produce a detailed and overarching account that would differ from the commemorative writings and texts whose sources have in the main been selected and edited to confirm the generally critical attitude to humanitarian action. This realisation inspired us to launch our investigations and write this book.

Research sources and the principle of the 'close-up observation'[2]

Our approach is underpinned by the multitude of different environments framing our observations of MSF's actions. Our investigations included several countries where Kinyarwanda-speaking peoples live, either as exiles, refugees or residents

---

[1] J.-H. Bradol contributed to a special issue of *Les Temps Modernes* entitled 'Les politiques de la haine [The Politics of Hatred]. Rwanda, Burundi 1994–1995'. Cl. Vidal and M. Le Pape oversaw the issue. See *Les Temps Modernes*, 583 (July–August 1995), 126–48.

[2] This expression comes from an article by Carlo Ginzburg published under the title 'Microhistory: two or three things that I know about it'. Applied to an event or, even more significantly, any historical process, 'a close-up observation permits us to grasp what eludes a comprehensive viewing, and vice versa.' We subscribe fully to the 'vice versa', and we therefore wish to elaborate, within the limits of our sources, the sort of 'comprehensive viewing' that influenced the MSF associations from 1990–1997, since they paint a picture that is indiscernible to the close-up look. C. Ginzburg, 'Microhistory: two or three things that I know about it', *Critical Inquiry*, 20:1 (1993), 10–35.

whose families date back to the colonial era. We looked at Kinyarwanda-speaking people in Rwanda itself, as well as in Uganda, Zaire (now the Democratic Republic of Congo), Tanzania and Burundi. While our research covered several teams and field operations active simultaneously in each of the countries, our goal was not to review the entirety of the humanitarian programmes implemented in all of these countries.

From the outset, we adopted a detailed, circumscribed analysis of archives and other sources and a scale of observation to afford us an understanding of aid pro-gramme management and practices. Our research initially focused on a given team's working environment and negotiations, which we then used as a basis to track mes-sages sent from field teams to in-country heads of mission and then to desk officers and managers at headquarters. The following questions guided our choice of scales of observation and data. How were MSF's activities implemented in an environment of mass murder, military operations, political upheavals and forced population dis-placements? In these types of situations, what were the salient or reference points that aid workers called on to guide their actions?

We worked with the archives at MSF headquarters in Paris and consulted docu-ments from the MSF movement's various operational sections.[3] We became familiar with part of these archives thanks to the work of Laurence Binet who, seeking to retrace the history of the dilemmas that have marked the public positions adopted by the MSF movement, sorted and compiled them into separate studies. The first four (publication started in 2004) covered the Great Lakes region during and after the genocide of Rwandan Tutsis.[4] We looked at several series of documents, begin-ning with the situation reports sent regularly by field teams to the head office of the MSF section in charge of operations and assessment missions.[5] Recipients of situation reports varied according to the period and the degree of coordination established between sections but also to lines of accountability and division of tasks between departments at head offices. At times of serious crisis, messages divided into standardised sections were exchanged on a daily basis. Some report-writers focused on contacts and interviews with local authorities, commenting on decisions and directives and evaluating the consequences on existing programmes. They also described and analysed the deadly incidents occurring at sites where MSF was deliv-ering aid. Seeking to respond to such events, they wrote to head offices to propose

---

[3] The names of MSF personnel appear in the documents we studied and cite. However, we have chosen not to reproduce them. In making this choice, we hope to avoid the consequences of individual accusations and the justifications they would trigger. Which is not to say that such discussions are of no value in general, but they are of very little interest in the context of our study.

[4] Laurence Binet undertook this work at the MSF Centre de Réflexion sur l'Action et les Savoirs Humanitaires (CRASH). She created a website where case studies and a large number of archives are freely available. See http://speakingout.msf.org/en. Jean-Hervé Bradol and Marc Le Pape are also members of the CRASH team.

[5] Assessment missions are initiated by head offices in order to decide if action needs to be taken and what form it should take.

operational and media plans or, conversely, to express doubts over decisions desk officers and directors were asking them to implement. Field teams occasionally gave vent to their indignation, condemning the publication of interviews, press releases and reports critical of local political and military actors with whom they had established dialogue to enable them to do their work and ensure their access to refugees and displaced persons. It is important to note that, at the other end of the spectrum, policies of silence were also subject to criticism. Indeed, the archives reveal that, whereas several mission reports described systematic attacks or crimes committed against civilians, these were not made public. One such example is the following message a MSF communication officer in Paris sent in April 1997 referring to military operations conducted by Rwanda against Rwandan refugees in the South Kivu region of Zaire: 'Below you will find the report I told you about yesterday. This is an internal and confidential report. Please do not circulate it or cite any part of it that would allow MSF to be identified as the source, and do not take it with you if you go to the field!' The words 'NOT FOR RELEASE' were handwritten in capital letters.[6]

Medical data is also important to our study because it provides details of epidemiological studies on mortality and morbidity, for example, in refugee camps, hospitals and nutritional centres for children under the age of five years. It also includes records of day-to-day activities at hospitals, health centres and nutritional centres as well as summaries and charts included in reports sent regularly to head offices. These documents also provide information on the logistical aspects of medical programmes, such as the setting up of health centres, field hospitals, cholera treatment camps, sanitation and water provision, building durable facilities and repairing buildings.

Needless to say, MSF head offices generate masses of documents. We analysed messages sent to the field regarding the direction programmes were to take as well as other types of archives relating to the operations we wanted to examine: meeting reports, situation and strategy analyses, press releases and reports (both public and private) containing field data. Choosing to focus on reports that included summarised eyewitness accounts and observations during times of extreme violence, the same question appears over and over again: how should we react and what action should we take in such circumstances?

Our research led us to look beyond MSF's archives and eyewitness accounts and we were able to consult works from previously unexplored sources. One example is Arnaud Royer's thesis on 'The twin destiny of Burundian and Rwandan refugees in the African Great Lakes region since 1959'. As well as the post he held at the United Nations High Commissioner for Human Rights (UNHCR) at the

---

[6] The report that was not to be released concerned the assessment mission conducted in South Kivu at the end of March 1997. The document, which became public knowledge within the MSF movement on 16 April 1997, related executions of Rwandan refugees encouraged to leave the forest with the promise of humanitarian aid. Soldiers from Rwanda were responsible for these deadly operations.

time of the events, he used his expertise as a sociologist to describe the United Nations (UN) agency's operations in the Great Lakes region and the agency's archives were one of the main sources for his research.[7] We should also mention the research commissioned by the Danish Ministry of Foreign Affairs in 1994 and carried out by fifty-two researchers and consultants. An assessment of humanitarian operations, their research involved studies of all the countries in the Great Lakes region following the genocide of Tutsis in Rwanda.[8] One looked at 'humanitarian aid and its effects' in Tanzania and Zaire during the period April 1994 to July 1995 and, with its analysis of the aid provided to refugees in these two countries, it affords access to a wide range of mainly hitherto unpublished data, documents, interviews and research. Providing a comprehensive and a close-up observation of relief operations conducted by military contingents, local and international non-governmental organisations (NGOs) and UN agencies, the study also gives insight into logistical assistance and its cost.[9]

Other 'close-up observations' are provided by those with first-hand experience of the horrific events that unfolded in the Great Lakes region. We examined three types of eyewitness accounts: those recorded and sometimes published at the time by humanitarian workers and journalists; those compiled later by scholars, activists, tribunals and researchers; and those written post-facto by or with the participants and witnesses directly involved in the events.[10] Regarding the validity of eyewitness accounts, there are three different approaches: 'a neutral position' that examines them on a case-by-case basis; 'systematically doubting them until they have proven to be above suspicion'; and 'accepting them without question', i.e. as long as there is no reason to disbelieve them.[11] We have opted for the case-by-case approach. In other words, we take into account the circumstances in which they were delivered, the intentions of the authors, narrative patterns and any evidence of truth produced by their authors. We should explain that we use eyewitness accounts – not to fill in gaps left by the archives, nor to endorse or condemn the witnesses – but to comprehend their ordeals and how they lived through them.

---

[7] A. Royer, 'De l'exil au pouvoir, le destin croisé des réfugiés burundais et rwandais dans la région des Grands Lacs africains, depuis 1959' [From exile to power: the twin destiny of Burundian and Rwandan refugees in the African Great Lakes region since 1959] (Sociology thesis, University of Paris I, 2006).

[8] J. Borton, 'Doing Study 3 of the Joint Evaluation of Emergency Assistance to Rwanda: the team leader's perspective', in A. Wood *et al.* (eds), *Evaluating International Humanitarian Action: Reflections from Practitioners* (New York: Zed Books, London: ALNAP, 2001).

[9] See J. Borton, E. Brusset and A. Hallam, *Humanitarian Aid and Effects, Study III of The International Response to Conflict and Genocide: Lessons from the Rwanda Experience. Joint Evaluation of Emergency Assistance to Rwanda* (London: ODI, 1996).

[10] See F. Lagarde, *Mémorialistes et témoins rwandais (1994–2013)* [Rwandan Chroniclers and Witnesses (1994–2013)] (Paris: L'Harmattan, 2013). He has compiled and analysed eyewitness accounts by Rwandan people published between 1994 and 2013.

[11] P. Engel, 'Faut-il croire ce qu'on nous dit?' [Should we believe what we're told?], *Philosophie*, 88 (2005), 63–4.

And lastly, we consulted reports and public positions adopted by international NGOs (medical or otherwise), International Committee of the Red Cross (ICRC), UNHCR and other UN agencies present in the Great Lakes region between 1990 and 1997. We endeavour to show that, as a general rule, the MSF teams cooperated with other organisations, feeling free to criticise them while negotiating scope of action, discussing security measures and sharing information.

As of April 1994 and during the months of the Tutsi genocide, several international press publications took a close interest in the African Great Lakes region, which resulted in a number of investigative reporters spending time (sometimes as much as several years) working on the topic. Now accessible online, the articles we consulted were published by *Libération* and *Le Monde* in France, the *New York Times* and the *Washington Post* in the United States, the *Guardian* in the UK and *Le Soir* in Belgium. We therefore frequently refer back to the very articles humanitarian organisation managers were reading while they directed operations.

Since 2012, François Lagarde from the University of Texas in Austin has been compiling texts written on Rwanda from 1990 on. Four volumes of his work are freely available on the Internet.[12] The list of authors, details of their qualifications and the themes they address facilitate identification of the subjects and the approaches adopted. These bibliographies, ordered according to analytical categories, provide valuable guidance through an abundance of publications. The first volume, gathering documents published between 1990 and 2011, devotes a section to forty-two eyewitness accounts provided by humanitarian workers. The following volumes do not feature this category, but humanitarian activities are nonetheless represented under other sections such as 'Refugees', 'Genocide', 'Traumas' and 'Health', etc. What emerges from the series is that the relationship between political, military and humanitarian action has been the subject of many political science publications. There are also several studies on the humanitarian aid itself. These analyse the results of international aid and how coordination mechanisms functioned in Rwanda and in neighbouring Uganda, Tanzania, Burundi and Zaire where Kinyarwanda-speaking peoples live. A modest body of research looks at the specific techniques of humanitarian medical aid, such as mobile field hospitals and treatment of psychological trauma. A number of publications describe humanitarian workers' views on the social, political and cultural contexts where they operate. More rare are texts where humanitarian workers discuss aspects of their individual experiences as well as their thoughts from an ethical and political standpoint. A small number of works examine the links between humanitarian action, the promotion of human rights and international criminal justice. This bibliographical venture serves to demonstrate that few academic publications trace the history of humanitarian action in terms of the experiences of one or more teams actually working in the field.

---

[12] www.univ-paris1.fr/ufr/iedes/recherche-et-valorisation-umr-ds/afrique-des-grand-lacs/.

Map 0.1 The Great Lakes region

Milestones in the recent history of Rwanda

It is important to recall certain milestones in recent Rwandan history. These concern events, policies and realities that will help readers to understand the contexts where MSF was working and identify the standpoints in the prevailing interpretative patterns, particularly among the organisations (humanitarian and otherwise) present in the Great Lakes region. This introduction offers an initial overview of these elements and each chapter provides a detailed historical context to the humanitarian operations that took place.

We would like to start with a geographical outline of Rwanda in the late 1980s. This mountainous and small country of 26,338 sq. km was then home to a population of around 7,150,000 (according to a census published in 1991), 93 per cent of them rural dwellers. Average density was over 250 inhabitants per sq. km, one of the highest in Africa. High demographic growth resulted in a serious shortage of farmland and, despite the impressive and recognised know-how of the country's peasant farmers, the constantly growing population was jeopardising food security. Emigration to Rwanda's larger neighbours could have eased this enormous land pressure, but post-independence political history rendered it impossible. In the early 1990s, Rwanda was one of the poorest countries in the world.

At the turn of the nineteenth century, Rwanda was a kingdom dominated by a Tutsi dynasty. The population was mostly made up of Hutu farmers and a minority of Tutsi herdsmen. Everyone spoke the same language, inhabited the same lands and was guided by the same ethos of the sacred. The sovereign governed through chiefs of royal lineages, forming an aristocracy whose power extended over herdsmen and farmers alike. First colonised by Germany, the country was placed under Belgian mandate in the wake of the First World War. The colonial authorities and Catholic Church, which had acquired a monopoly over education, elected to educate chiefs from the Tutsi aristocracy and they were receiving a specific training. However, these religious schools were also opened to Hutu seminarists, granting them access to secondary studies.

During the 1950s, a Hutu elite, also educated in the seminaries, instigated campaigns denouncing the privileges held by the Tutsi oligarchy. This was a time when identity cards issued by the colonial government mentioned the bearer's social category defined in ethnic terms and, according to this criterion, 17.5 per cent of Rwandans were Tutsi. The year 1959 saw the creation of political parties in the run-up to local elections, which would the following year give a large majority to groups supporting the demands of Hutu leaders. In the autumn of 1959, groups of Hutu peasant farmers committed acts of violence – murder, arson and looting – against Tutsi chiefs and their deputies. So began the Tutsi exodus, with tens of thousands Tutsis fleeing to neighbouring countries as the violence against them increased. On 28 January 1961, the monarchy was overthrown and the Republic was established with the consent of the Belgian authorities. Rwanda finally proclaimed independence on 1 July 1962.

Tutsi guerrillas based in Burundi launched a series of raids on Rwanda. Although they did not meet with any military success, the authorities consistently retaliated by committing massacres that caused a huge number of deaths within the Tutsi population. In early 1973, violent campaigns were waged against Westernised Tutsi social groups. Students were expelled from educational institutions, employees of government offices and private companies were ordered to leave their jobs, homes were burned down and murders were committed in certain prefectures. These campaigns were designed to create the unrest that Minister of Defence General Juvénal Habyarimana used as a pretext to seize power on 5 July 1973, triggering yet another exodus of Tutsis to neighbouring countries.

The Second Republic set up a single ruling party, the Mouvement Révolutionnaire National pour le Développement [National Revolutionary Movement for Development] (MRND), of which all Rwandans became members at birth. The country was in the iron grip of the government, augmented by the MRND, which exerted control via committees set up at every territorial level and in all secular and religious institutions. On 1 October 1990, the Rwandan Patriotic Front (RPF), a party founded by Rwandan Tutsis born in exile, attacked Rwanda from Uganda. The offensive was driven back by the Forces Armées Rwandaises [Rwandan Armed Forces] (FAR) with the help of Zairian and French troops. From then on, French military aid proved decisive in warding off the total defeat of an inexperienced Rwandan army facing rebels whose leaders had been among the victors of the Ugandan civil war when they fought alongside President Museveni. Pogroms against the Tutsis began in northern prefectures. In June 1991, a new constitution introduced a multi-party system and a number of opponents were freed. However, violence swept through the country. In 1992 and 1993, the RPF resumed its attacks on northern Rwanda with increasing success, committing deadly acts of violence against civilians that prompted the flight of hundreds of thousands of Hutu to the south of the country. Political crime spiralled with assassinations of local and national leaders, incitement to ethnic hatred in the media, the repeated slaughter of Tutsis and acts of violence committed by militias established by the various parties. International pressure resulted in the signing of a peace treaty (the Arusha Accords) between the RPF and the Rwandan government in Arusha, Tanzania, on 4 August 1993. In October, the UN Security Council (UNSC) created the United Nations Assistance Mission for Rwanda (UNAMIR), tasked with 'helping to implement' the treaty. Leaving behind a small group of military advisers, the French army withdrew from Rwanda.

On 6 April 1994, a regional summit on the crises in Rwanda and Burundi was held in Tanzania's Dar-es-Salaam. That same evening, the plane transporting Rwandan president Juvénal Habyarimana and Burundian president Cyprien Ntaramyira was shot down around 8.30 p.m. as it returned to Kigali. During the night, a group of putschists took advantage of the confusion in the wake of President Habyarimana's assassination to seize power, assassinate anyone likely to oppose them (including the Prime Minister and three other ministers), order massacres of Tutsis in the capital and northern prefectures and impose an interim government that assumed office three days later. RPF troops immediately resumed their offensive. On 12 April, the interim government launched its genocidal policy, using radio broadcasts to announce that Tutsi civilians now had to be 'attacked' (i.e. killed) throughout Rwanda. On 21 April, the UNSC adopted resolution 912, which reduced UNAMIR forces to just 120 civilians and 150 soldiers.

The war ended in victory for the RPF on 4 July 1994 as troops swept into the capital and hunted down the FAR. On 18 July a ceasefire was declared and a new government, whose membership was based on the Arusha Accords, was formed and sworn in the next day.

MSF operations in the Great Lakes region

MSF settled in the region in 1980 to respond to a famine in north-eastern Uganda. When the organisation first delivered aid in Rwanda in 1982, it was barely ten years old. Founded in Paris in 1971, MSF set itself the goal of bringing together 'exclusively doctors and health sector workers' in order to 'provide assistance to victims of natural disasters, collective accidents and armed conflict'.[13] In practise, its first concrete actions consisted in sending paramedics and doctors to work for various organisations in other countries.[14] When MSF sent French volunteers to Rwanda in 1982, it was responding to requests from UNHCR, the French ambassador to Rwanda and the Rwandan Red Cross. At the time of MSF's very first operations in Rwandan refugee camps in Uganda (1984), its professional and political independence was still taking shape in terms of its emergency and 'refugee' aid operations as well as its more long-term 'technical assistance'. Its programmes grew steadily in the 1980s as new national sections were set up in Belgium, Switzerland, Spain and the Netherlands.

Before war broke out in Rwanda in 1990, MSF was operating in Zaire (now the Democratic Republic of Congo), Rwanda, Burundi, Tanzania and Uganda. In Rwanda, MSF provided the Ministry of Health with expertise in nephrology, while in neighbouring Burundi MSF's European doctors occupied administrative posts as medical health officers tasked with implementing the national public health plan at provincial level. The teams running these technical assistance operations also dealt with emergencies, such as the campaign to vaccinate the entire population of Burundi against meningitis in 1992.

New skillsets appeared, both at head office and in the field: recruiter, logistician, mechanic, administrator, medical coordinator, vaccination and nutrition coordinator and desk officer. All the head offices' departments and satellite units were mobilised to support the teams deployed in the Great Lakes region.[15] This ensured that the teams were supplied with staff, cash and standard ready-to-use kits assembled in MSF logistics centres. They were also provided with epidemiological expertise for field surveys (population numbers, mortality rates, malnutrition prevalence,

---

[13] MSF, Charter, 1971, Board of Director archives, Paris.

[14] See A. Vallaeys, *Médecins Sans Frontières. La biographie* (Paris: Fayard, 2004), pp. 127–50.

[15] The satellite units are institutions created by MSF benefiting from a degree of autonomy so they can develop specific areas of expertise. During the missions to the Great Lakes region in the 1990s, three satellite units were particularly closely involved: the two logistics centres and the epidemiology research and training unit (Épicentre). See Cl. Vidal and J. Pinel, 'MSF satellites: a strategy underlying different medical practices', in J.-H. Bradol and Cl. Vidal (eds), *Medical Innovations in Humanitarian Situations: The Work of Médecins Sans Frontières* (New York: MSF-USA, 2011).

descriptions of epidemics, effectiveness of antibiotics and antimalarial drugs). Field teams participated in putting together the written and audio documents and videos needed for communication in the field as well as at the European head offices. During this period, the MSF teams in Rwanda used a range of systems to communicate, from oral and written using radio (including telex), landline and satellite phones with fax machines.

Managers at the European head offices were not always in agreement, even if, according to MSF's European Council established in 1988, they were supposed to coordinate. The fact is that they each enjoyed operational and political autonomy and, as a result, many different voices spoke for MSF in the public sphere. Members of teams in the field and at Paris headquarters spontaneously answered journalists' questions, official press releases were sent out by the head offices of MSF's national sections, articles were published in the press and interviews were given to the media by various European MSF managers. The many spokespeople in MSF's network were so geographically scattered yet simultaneously active that for instance it makes it difficult, if not impossible, to establish which staff member from which section, from which head office or from where in the field, actually took the decision to label as genocide the widespread slaughter committed in Rwanda in April 1994.

In concrete terms, MSF's decision to launch activities was taken in response to requests from other aid organisations such as when UNHCR asked for help with providing aid in the Rwandan refugee camps in Uganda in 1984, or governments, as in 1982 when the French ambassador in Kigali asked the organisation to assist Kinyarwanda-speaking people deported from Uganda to Rwanda. Decisions to launch operations were also taken by field teams and managers at MSF's European head offices, including in response to information garnered from journalists, workers from other aid organisations, local authorities (official and rebel) and leading figures and inhabitants in the affected regions. For example, when the crisis in Burundi caused by President Ndadaye's assassination (1993) began, the first offers of help arrived not only from Europe but also from neighbouring countries. When the decision to deliver aid was taken, a written proposal detailing the actions that had been chosen and the resources required to implement them was sent to the authorities. If and when agreement was reached, the MSF head offices dispatched the necessary international staff, equipment and funds.

During the 1980s and 1990s, MSF's financial resources primarily stemmed from contracts signed with European and American public aid institutions. However, during this period funds raised from individual donors were becoming a major source of income for the organisation, a phenomenon that the war and genocide in Rwanda helped to accelerate. MSF's expenditure in 1994 reached new heights: 88 million francs of MSF France's overall budget of 430 million francs was allocated to the 'Rwandan crisis' between 6 April and 31 December 1994 and to its repercussions in Zaire and Tanzania. Between 1 July and early September, the MSF movement spent a total of 165.5 million francs on aid programmes for refugee and displaced

Rwandans. Thanks to private funding, work in the refugee camps and Rwandan hospitals could begin as soon as the authorities gave the green light, without having to wait for approval from public institutional donors. In the late 1980s, greater access to European and American public funds enabled MSF to recruit increasing numbers of national staff to deliver health care and assistance. National and international personnel reported to field coordinators and, at the national level, to heads of mission. Heads of mission reported to the desk officers at their European head offices, who in turn reported to operations directors.

The study

Our investigations begin with MSF's first provision of aid to Rwanda in 1982 and end in late 1997. Although mass violence did not disappear from the Great Lakes after this date, 1997 was the last year that the sheer scale of the massacres committed against the Kinyarwanda-speaking peoples set them apart from other groups in the region also affected by political violence.

In the first chapter, we look at the years 1980 to 1994, which are divided into four periods and start with the provision of aid to Rwandan Tutsi exiles in Uganda during the 1980s. We then examine how MSF, between October 1990 and April 1994, delivered assistance to people internally displaced within Rwanda after fleeing the military advance of Tutsi exiles (led by the RPF) and to the 260,000 Burundian refugees living in camps as of October 1993. Next we look at the period of the genocide and the medical assistance the organisation provided – during which time more than 200 of MSF's Rwandan employees were executed. And to finish, we analyse the call for armed intervention in Rwanda and, more specifically, the French military operation launched mainly in south-west Rwanda in June 1994.

The second chapter focuses on the Rwandans who began fleeing their country in April 1994 and ended up in vast camps, notably in Tanzania and Zaire. Humanitarian organisations and UNHCR were quick to step into action. MSF's assistance mainly focused on the frequent health emergencies, especially when the camps first opened. Events required taking decisions of a political nature as the refugees included those who had led and carried out the Tutsi genocide in Rwanda. The archives show that MSF field teams and head offices soon came to realise that these leaders continued to exert their influence over those who had sought refuge in the camps. Aid workers in the field found themselves forced to choose between pulling out from the camps and delivering medical aid; they either had to abandon their relief to avoid supporting those responsible for the genocide, or carry on providing assistance to civilians who could in no way bear the burden of collective guilt.

The third chapter explores what happened in Rwanda after the RPF's military victory in July 1994. Mandated by the UN, the French army controlled the south-west of the country until late August. Camps sheltering Hutus Rwandans fleeing the rebel offensive had sprung up in the region and the health situation was disastrous. From

November 1994 to April 1995, the new Rwandan army used force to close the displaced persons' camps, which resulted in the massacre of several thousand people. The MSF teams involved in getting the country's hospitals and health centres back into working order were witness to the repression the new government inflicted on certain districts. Meanwhile, MSF provided medical aid in Rwanda's overpopulated prisons, where mortality rates were catastrophic.

The fourth chapter focuses on Rwandan refugees in Zaire. Between 1994 and 1996, all international attempts to persuade them to return failed. In October 1996, Rwanda and the movements opposing President Mobutu launched a military offensive in east Zaire and then advanced towards Kinshasa. How were the refugees affected by this offensive? How did they react? A great many of them were repatriated to Rwanda, whereas countless others fled into the interior of Zaire. This chapter examines the humanitarian operations deployed during this period – from the destruction of the refugee camps in October and November 1996 to the final wave of refugees who walked 2,000 km to the border between Zaire and Congo-Brazzaville to escape their pursuers.

The final chapter puts the spotlight on some of the problems humanitarian workers had to tackle in the situations described above. We focus on three issues that all humanitarian workers working in places where mass violence was being committed were forced to address:

How to comprehend, in the midst of an emergency, the political and social dynamics unique to each situation of extreme violence?
How to avoid falling victim to or becoming accomplices of criminal forces?
How to remain effective in such situations?

1

From the persecution of Kinyarwanda speakers in Uganda to the genocide of Rwandan Tutsis

In October 1982, MSF set up operations for the first time in Rwanda after Ugandan President Milton Obote expelled 40,000 Kinyarwanda speakers (Hutus and Tutsis) deemed hostile to the government.[1] Rwanda called them 'Kinyarwanda-speaking Ugandans' and opposed their entry into its territory.[2] At the request of the UNHCR, MSF began providing in cooperation with the Rwandan Red Cross medical services to these refugees who had just settled on the outskirts of Akagera Park in north Rwanda. In 1986, Yoweri Museveni assumed the presidency and most of them were able to return to Uganda. In January 1984, again at the request of the UNHCR, MSF set up operations in eight camps in south-west Uganda – where part of the Kinyarwanda-speaking population had been forcibly transferred[3] – providing preventive and curative care to 104,000 people and training local staff. Political and humanitarian activities were intertwined in these camps. The Rwandese Refugee Welfare Foundation (RRWF) was created in 1979 and the following year became a political movement called the Rwandese Alliance for National Unity (RANU). From 1981 to 1986, some of the young Tutsis belonging to RANU joined Museveni's guerrilla war against the regime of Milton Obote, who had been persecuting the Kinyarwanda-speaking population. After the rebellion's victory in 1985, guerrilla of Rwandan descent held high positions in the new Ugandan government. Fred Rwigema, future founder and president of the RPF, became Secretary of Defence and later an adviser to President Museveni while Paul Kagame was appointed head of Military Security. As part of the aid they provided to refugees, MSF's international staff worked alongside Rwandan colleagues, some of whom went on to become leaders of the RPF that was founded in 1987.

In the Rwanda of the late 1980s, the political situation was not the only cause for concern. The deteriorating economic conditions took a dramatic turn during 1988

---

[1] In power from 17 December 1980 to 27 July 1985.

[2] A. Guichaoua, 'Migrants, réfugiés et déplacés en Afrique centrale et orientale', in A. Guichaoua (ed.), *Exilés, réfugiés, déplacés en Afrique centrale et orientale* (Paris: Karthala, 2004), p. 119.

[3] MSF, Annual evaluation of the MSF programme in Rwandan displaced persons camps, 1986.

and 1989 when famine struck the south of the country. In addition to the vagaries of climate, a drought that had persisted since 1984, the famine served to underline the final gasps of a national economic model focused on food self-sufficiency. Rwanda's inhabitants had doubled in twenty years, and the population density was one of the highest in the world. In a country where 90 per cent of families were involved in agriculture, the average size of family farms had shrunk to less than one hectare. Such small plots meant many families were no longer able to produce enough food for their needs and 50 per cent of Rwanda's children under the age of five were already suffering from chronic malnutrition.[4]

RPF's first military offensive

In October 1990, negotiations between Uganda and Rwanda on the return of the refugees appeared to have stalled. In Uganda, the role played by Kinyarwanda-speakers in Museveni's regime sparked xenophobic political rhetoric. The RPF then decided to launch an armed attack on Rwanda and invaded from Uganda on 1 October.[5] This led to the displacement of thousands of people within Rwanda as well as another wave of several thousand Rwandans seeking refuge in Uganda. Already working in Uganda, MSF teams carried out an exploratory mission with the aim of providing medical aid to the 7,000 Rwandan refugees who had fled to the south-west of the country after this latest offensive. Operations (preventive and curative care, water supply and sanitation) were initiated at Nakivale camp in Mbarara. At the same time, a team from Brussels was sent to Rwanda to provide support to health centres in municipalities in Byumba prefecture in the north-east of the country where war-displaced populations had assembled and another from Uganda to the rebel-held area in north Rwanda. While RPF leaders in Kampala had responded to requests for a meeting without any sense of urgency, during an encounter they declared the need for medical supplies, particularly for war surgery. On 20 October 1990, MSF representatives accessed the rebel-held area through Mirama Hills without meeting any obstacles on the Ugandan side. Officers of the rebellion's military wing across the border prohibited visitors from entering both the area and their field hospital and declined all offers of medical assistance:

> He [commander Furuma from the rebellion], then, proposed to visit a small dispensary, Nyabwishongwezi [municipality de Muvumba, prefecture de Byumba], 15 km S-W of border post, which was run by Spanish Catholic sisters. The Sisters were anxious about their fate. They wanted to go out, we assure them we would do everything to get them out. Furuma promised their safe passage to the border.

---

[4] P. Verwimp, *Agricultural Policy, Crop Failure and the 'Ruriganiza' Famine (1989) in Southern Rwanda: A Prelude to Genocide?* (Leuven: Discussion paper series, Department of Economics, Katholieke Universiteit, 2002).

[5] The RPF's military wing was called the Rwandan Patriotic Army (RPA). To make the text easier to read, the acronym RPF will be used to designate both the military and political wings of the rebel force.

The Sisters dispensary is the only medical structure in the area. It was in good state and covering the basic medical need for the +/- 10.000 Hutus farmers living there prior the rebel invasion. At that time, the Sisters had 150 consultations/a day. Since the rebel attack, half of the population left and consultations dropped to a mere 20 patients/a day. When we returned, we insisted to meet some of RPA [Rwandan Patriotic Army, the military branch of the rebellion] medical staff, but our proposition was turned down. We were still not allowed to visit their field hospital.[6]

To prevent the rebel force from advancing, Kigali received support from Belgian, French (Operation Noroit) and Zairian troops, whose intervention enabled the FAR to regain lost ground. The Belgian and Zairian troops quickly left the country, while the French army dug in to prop up the regime militarily. In 1991, calm appeared to be restored. In March, a ceasefire agreement was signed in N'sele, a neighbourhood of Kinshasa, and in November 1991 the school and employment quota system limiting the number of Tutsis who could gain access to educational programmes and jobs was dropped. The first multi-party Rwandan government was formed in December and, following an amnesty law adopted that same month, massive numbers of political prisoners were released.

Despite advances in the political negotiations, pogroms against Tutsis had resumed in Gisenyi prefecture in 1990 and spread to Kigali, Ruhengeri and Byumba prefectures in 1991. In March 1992, massacres of Tutsis, fomented by extremist authorities, intensified to such an extent in Kigali-Rural prefecture (Bugesera) that several human rights organisations warned in a report published in March 1993 that the scale of the persecution of Tutsis raised the question of whether 'genocide' would be an appropriate characterisation.

Testimony established that many Rwandans have been killed for the sole reason that they were Tutsi. The question remains whether the designation of some members of the Tutsi ethnic group as a target for destruction demonstrates an intention, in the sense of the Convention [on the Prevention and Punishment of the Crime of Genocide, 9 December 1948] to destroy this group or a part of it because of its members' ethnicity.

   While the casualty figures established by the Commission are significant, they may be below the threshold required to establish genocide.[7]

In August 1992, a Neutral Military Observers Group was dispatched by the Organisation of African Unity (OAU) to monitor the ceasefire. That same month,

[6] MSF, Confidential, Médecins Sans Frontières – Holland, Exploratory Mission to Rwanda, General and security situation report & Follow-up, Amsterdam, June 1990.
[7] International Federation for Human Rights (Paris), Inter-African Union for Human Rights (Ouagadougou), Africa Watch (New York, Washington, London), International Centre for Human Rights and Democratic Development (Montreal), 'Report of the International Commission of Investigation on Human Rights Violations in Rwanda since 1 October 1990. 7–21 January 1993' (Paris, March 1993), p. 29.

Tutsis were massacred in Kibuye prefecture. In January 1993, new killings of Tutsis and political opponents erupted in Gisenyi, Ruhengeri, Kibuye and Byumba prefectures. In February 1993, a further RPF offensive launched from Uganda led to a significant increase in the number of displaced persons in the country, and those who had already fled during the first stages of the war in 1990 moved further south. Kisaro, Kinihira, Buyoga and Tumba camps in Byumba prefecture emptied out and all of MSF's facilities and equipment were destroyed or looted. Everything had to be rebuilt from scratch, but on a much larger scale in new camps. The authorities now spoke about one million displaced persons throughout the country, with many settling in or around the capital.

Negotiations were initiated in Tanzania in March 1993 and culminated in a new ceasefire agreement. Rwanda's political geography was now taking shape: in the north, a strip of land along the Ugandan border spanning part of Byumba and Ruhengeri prefectures was controlled by the rebels, the south and capital remained under government authority, and lastly, the agreement called for the belligerents to create a demilitarised buffer zone between the government- and rebel-held areas. Although a large percentage of displaced persons had found refuge among the population in the rest of the country, others had settled in camps. In Ruhengeri prefecture, the sites were small, accommodating from 500 to 3,000 people. As a result, rather than working in the displaced persons camps, MSF focused on providing support to hospitals, health posts and health centres located near these small camps, particularly in the municipalities of Mukingo, Nyakinama, Cyabingo and Ruhondo. In Byumba prefecture, 155,000 people were crowded into ten camps: Rusine, Nyacyonga 1 and 2, Mugambazi, Bugarura, Bidudu, Gikoma 1 and 2, Kiziguro and Gituza. Conditions were appalling. Epidemics, particularly malaria and dysentery, were decimating a population living in makeshift shelters and weakened by malnutrition, with insufficient access to drinking water and a lack of latrines. MSF supplied water to the displaced, built latrines, sprayed insecticide in shelters, vaccinated refugees against measles, provided primary health care that included treatment of infections, organised mass malaria treatment campaigns, treated thousands of children suffering from acute malnutrition and set up epidemiological surveillance. Despite their best efforts, the teams were unable to bring the number of deaths below the disaster threshold for many months. For example, in the Nyacyonga and Rusine camps, mortality rates in June 1993 were eight and five out of 10,000 people per day, respectively.[8] Severe acute malnutrition was rampant and the intensive nutritional rehabilitation centres were treating thousands of children, particularly in Nyaconga camp (June 1993).

---

[8] MSF-Holland, Amsterdam, Internal-confidential, 'The displaced in Rwanda, Smaller numbers, bigger disaster', 22 June 1993. During the 1990s in Africa, the situation was considered normal when the mortality rate stood at around 0.3 to 0.5 deaths per 10,000 people per day. The situation is considered to be an emergency above one death per 10,000 people per day and a disaster above two. See the Sphere Project, *Humanitarian Charter and Minimum Standards in Disaster* (Oxford: Oxfam Publishing, 2000), p. 260. The first draft was circulating in 1998.

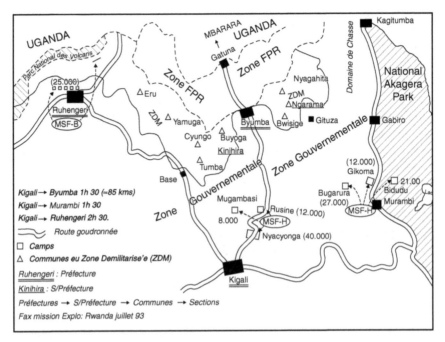

Map 1.1 Internally displaced Rwandans

In addition to the health disaster in the displaced persons camps in the government-held area, humanitarian workers had two other causes for concern: the absence of international aid in the rebel-controlled area and its insufficiency in the buffer zone between the belligerents. MSF decided to support several health posts and centres in the buffer zone in Ruhengeri prefecture and also attempted to gain a better understanding of the health situation and the state of health centres in the Byumba prefecture buffer zone. Some of the displaced persons had returned to live in the prefecture while many others were travelling back and forth between their refuge in the government area and their fields in the buffer zone. During an exploratory mission in July 1993, peasant farmers told MSF staff they could no longer take up permanent residence in the buffer zone due to killings perpetrated by rebel soldiers.[9] Earlier in the year, in March, an exploratory mission had been sent from Uganda to the RPF-controlled area in the north of Ruhengeri and Byumba prefectures, entering Rwanda through the Gatuna border post. The region was almost deserted and fields were left abandoned. The few remaining inhabitants had been displaced from where they lived and transferred to rebel-controlled Gishambashi, Butaro, Gitare and Rugamara. RPF representatives claimed that the population had been grouped together to facilitate

---

[9] J.-H. Bradol, co-author of this book, took part in the mission.

Map 1.2 Humanitarian issues in Rwanda

access to education and health care. The MSF team decided not to set up operations in these camps in the RPF-held area because the two camps where the health situation was most critical, Gitare and Rugamara, were set to close in the near future. People living in them were supposed to return to their hillside homes, once the belligerents signed an agreement. MSF wanted to conduct another exploratory mission from Kigali in July 1993 to glean more information about the health situation in the RPF-controlled area. Both warring parties granted authorisation, thanks to the mediation of a Senegalese officer in the OAU's Neutral Military Observers Group (NMOG).[10] On the way to their Mulindi headquarters, the rebels ordered the MSF team to turn back, even though they were travelling with the NMOG convoy.

Arrival of Burundian refugees in October 1993

On 4 August 1993, the signing of the Arusha Accords between the government and opposition in Tanzania raised hopes of peace. The agreement called for the RPF to join a national unity government, its armed wing to integrate the FAR and French troops that had intervened in support of the Habyarimana regime to leave

---

[10] Captain Mbaye Diagne was killed by an RPF's mortar in Kigali on 31 May 1994.

the country. Resolution 872 of the UNSC authorised a contingent of peacekeepers, scheduled for arrival in the autumn.[11] The troops numbered 1,260 by the end of December. But this glimmer of hope was short-lived. The negative signal came from the neighbour, sometimes said to be the 'twin brother'. In October 1993, a small group of Tutsi soldiers in Burundi assassinated President Melchior Ndadaye, the country's first democratically elected Hutu president.[12] Militias of the parties that had supported the president began massacring Tutsis. The army, also supported by militias, then launched its own round of massacres against the Hutu population. In late October and early November, some 700,000 Burundians, for the most part Hutus, sought refuge in Rwanda, Tanzania and Zaire. Around 260,000 Burundian refugees joined the 352,000 internally displaced persons from Rwanda already living in camps at a time when 900,000 peasant farmers were still supposed to be receiving food aid following the famine of 1988 and 1989. In March 1994, more than one and a half million people were receiving food aid in a country of some seven million inhabitants, according to the Crisis Committee's Permanent Secretariat.

The Rwandan authorities, UN agencies (UNHCR, World Food Programme (WFP)), the Red Cross movement (Rwandan Red Cross, Belgian Red Cross, International Federation and International Committee), international NGOs (Action Internationale Contre la Faim, Oxfam, Médecins Du Monde, MSF, etc.), and churches and their aid organisations (Caritas, for example) were overwhelmed by the magnitude of the task. Burundian refugees were now experiencing the same health disaster as the Rwandan displaced. How can the limited effectiveness of the aid provided in the camps be explained? First, it is important to note that the disaster occurred in populations already vulnerable from both a socio-economic and a physiological perspective. One indicator illustrates this double deficit: approximately one out of two Rwandan children and one out of three Burundian children suffered from chronic malnutrition, according to nationwide Demographic and Health Surveys (DHS) conducted in Rwanda in 1992 and Burundi in 1987.[13] The food provided in the camps was unfit for consumption. It consisted of corn kernels supplied by the UN WFP that were hard as stone, with no mills available to grind them into flour. Moreover, no provision was made for the type of food adapted to young children's nutritional rehabilitation. While children under the age of five only accounted for about one-fifth of the population, they died at twice the rate of the general refugee

---

[11] United Nations Security Council, S/RES/872, 5.1993.

[12] The army in Burundi was led by Tutsi officers. The two previous presidents, Jean-Baptiste Bagaza (1976–87) and Pierre Buyoya (1987–93) were Tutsi officers who assumed power after coups d'état. As in Rwanda, most of the population was Hutu. Neighbouring Rwanda carefully watched the assumption to power of a democratically elected Hutu president.

[13] B. Barrère et al., *Demographic and Health Survey of Rwanda, 1992* (Kigali and Maryland: Republic of RwandaNational Population Office and Macro International Inc Calverton, 1994). L. Segamba et al., *Demographic and Health Survey of Burundi, 1987* (Bujumbura and Maryland: Ministry of the Interior, Population Department and Institute for Resource Development, 1988).

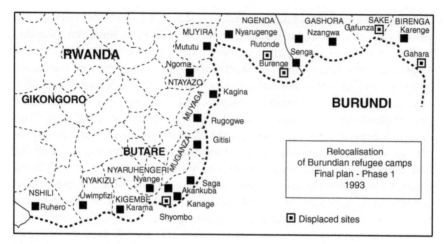

Map 1.3 Burundian refugee camps in Rwanda

population. In addition, the WFP's food supplies and its distributions were both irregular and insufficient. The Rwandan Red Cross was responsible for distributing food and misappropriated part of it. From November 1993 to February 1994, rations in Burenge and Nzangwa camps (Bugesera, Kigali-Rural prefecture) provided on average fewer than 1,500 calories per person per day and were sometimes less than 1,000 calories over periods of several weeks.[14] Standards in effect at UN specialist agencies recommended a food ration of at least 2,000 calories per person per day. Civil servants present in the camps and aid agencies misappropriated food aid intended for displaced Rwandans and Burundian refugees by manipulating lists of beneficiaries.

To treat severe acute malnutrition in children, protocols at the time required at least one month's inpatient care and therapeutic foods were not nearly as effective as they would be ten years later. Mothers were often put off by the lengthy hospitalisation and the treatment's limited impact on their children's condition. In Burenge camp in the municipality of Gashora (Kigali-Rural prefecture), the percentage of children who were cured after their stay in the intensive nutritional centre was 11 per cent in December 1993 and 34 per cent in January 1994. During these same months, the percentage of children abandoning treatment was 70 per cent and 51 per cent, respectively.[15] Whenever a camp opened, the most common deadly infectious disease would be an outbreak of bloody diarrhoea caused by a bacterium (*Shigella dysenteriae* type 1). One out of four refugees could be struck by the epidemic, increasing

---

[14] C. Cambrezy et al., *Évaluation du programme d'aide nutritionnelle et alimentaire auprès des réfugiés burundais au Rwanda, Intervention de MSF dans les camps de Burenge, Nzangwa et Masa, October 1993 – March 1994* (Paris: Epicentre, 1994).

[15] C. Cambrezy et al, *Évaluation du programme d'aide nutritionnelle et alimentaire*, p. 11.

to one out of two among children under the age of five. The case fatality ratio reached around 5 per cent among patients aged under fifteen and over forty-five, compared to about 2 per cent among other patients.[16] These bacterial strains reacted very aggressively on contact with the digestive tract, aggravating patients' nutritional status. Furthermore, they were often resistant to the antibiotics used – ampicillin, cotrimoxazole, chloramphenicol and nalidixic acid – and required ciprofloxacin, the price of which was exorbitant as it was not available in generic form at the time. This mismatch between available drugs and the resistance of microorganisms responsible for the most serious infections and parasitic diseases also occurred with the *Plasmodium falciparum* strain of malaria, one of the leading causes of death in the camps. Chloroquine, the main antimalarial drug used, was ineffective in one-third and sometimes one-half of all cases. Medical organisations such as MSF, whose main task in these situations is to fight infections, were unable to deliver. The camps' water supply (clear and chlorinated) fell short of what was needed. In Burenge, Nzangwa and Masa camps (Bugesera, Kigali-Rural prefecture), from November 1993 to March 1994, the amount of water necessary for drinking, cooking and personal hygiene varied between five and ten litres per person per day, depending on the week and the camp.[17] A programme is considered successful when it delivers at least fifteen litres of treated water per person per day.[18]

Two other factors contributed to the aid organisations' ineffectiveness. They had divided the work among themselves by area of expertise, such as food provision, water supply, preventive and curative care, sanitation, shelter and epidemiological surveillance, and some of the organisations had acted as cluster leads in areas for which they did not have the requisite skills. As a result, whole areas of responsibility were neglected for weeks, and even months, on end. These shortcomings were difficult to remedy for lack of alternatives, even though the European Union's food aid coordinator and the medical aid coordinator, a UNICEF doctor, were quick to identify them. Furthermore, aid organisations chose their priorities for implementing key activities on the basis of a standard plan, applicable in all circumstances, rather than adapting to the specific situation of a given camp at a specific time. For example, when a high number of deaths resulted from co-existing scourges of dysentery and malnutrition after the opening of a camp, aid organisations wishing to comply with a standard response plan may have prioritised building latrines. Possibly the right decision in other circumstances, this had little chance of preventing deaths in the short term. The resources used to improve sanitation could have been, during the same period, allocated to increasing isolation centres for patients with diarrhoea

---

[16] C. Paquet *et al.*, 'Une épidémie de dysenterie à *Shigella Dysenteriae* type 1 dans un camp de réfugiés au Rwanda', *Cahier Santé*, 5 (1995), 183.

[17] Cambrezy *et al.*, *Évaluation du programme d'aide nutritionnelle et alimentaire*, 12.

[18] The Sphere Project, *Humanitarian Charter and Minimum Standards in Disaster*, p. 11.

and nutritional rehabilitation centres for the youngest children. In one of the few camps where projects were implemented to respond to the actual health situation (Nzangwa), i.e. prioritising hospitalisation, the crude mortality rate fell to below two deaths per 10,000 people per day by the end of November.[19] In comparison, the same target was not reached in Burenge and in most of the Burundian refugee camps until February 1994. Among the 260,000 Burundian refugees who arrived in Rwanda in the autumn of 1993, it can be estimated that, by reviewing the variation in mortality rates as a function of time, some 10,000 died during their first three months in the camps (November and December 1993 and January 1994), a mortality rate ten times higher than normal.[20] MSF considered publicly condemning the ineffectiveness of aid in the Rwandan displaced persons camps, but never did – aside from the few press interviews given by MSF Holland's coordinator. An almost identical health disaster in the Burundian refugee camps led Action Internationale Contre la Faim [International Action against Hunger] (AICF) and MSF to hold a press conference in Paris a few months later, on 2 December 1993, during which they denounced the deficiencies of the food aid provided to people in the camps.

Deterioration in public safety after the Arusha Accords

The insinuation of extremist militants into the aid system was palpable at all levels. In November 1993, the manager of MSF's operations in the Burundian refugee camps in Kibungo prefecture fired two Rwandan employees because they were militia members terrorising the area around Gahara camp (municipality of Birenga). The doctor responsible for public health in Kigali-Rural prefecture, home to large Burundian refugee camps in Bugesera (specifically Nzangwa and Burenge camps in the municipalities of Gashora and Negenda), told the Paris Operations Manager the reasons for his hostility towards MSF during a joint field visit: 'You employ Tutsis, our enemies.'[21] These Tutsis had been hired by MSF in the camps and received an allowance so they could live within the local community. Fearing for their lives because of the large numbers of militiamen near the camps, they demanded to be housed on MSF premises in Karama. Bungalows and sanitary facilities were built for this purpose on its plot.

While the teams' attention was focused on the health disaster and the failures of the aid organisations in the camps, the country's political situation was deteriorating. On the night of 17 November 1993, some forty local officials from the president's MRND party were assassinated immediately after winning the municipal by-elections supervised by the United Nations in the buffer zone in Rwanda's northeast Ruhengeri prefecture. All the political factions, including the RPF, had

[19] P. Vial, 'Évaluation de la réponse de la communauté internationale à l'urgence Burundi. October 93 – March 94' (Paris: MSF, June 1994).

[20] MSF, 'Crude mortality rate, refugee camps, Butare' (MSF Holland, 1993).

[21] Interview in January 1994 with J.-H. Bradol, co-author of this book.

run candidates in these elections. In Kigali, militia members opposed to the sharing of power organised 'ghost city' days to block the political process initiated by the Arusha Accords, which called for RPF representatives to join the parliament, government and army. On 8 January 1994, an MSF Tutsi employee seized by militiamen at a roadblock set up in the capital during one of these 'ghost city' days only escaped with her life because of the intervention of one of her foreign colleagues. UN peacekeepers just a few metres away witnessed the attack but made no effort to help.[22]

In February 1994, all the international relief organisations, which included AICF, ICRC and MSF, worked together to prepare for a large influx of wounded patients in Kigali's dispensaries and hospitals. MSF set up the equipment, such as tents and water tanks, that would be needed to open a triage centre at the entrance to the CHK, Kigali's largest public hospital. On 21 February, Félicien Gatabazi, Minister for Public Works and Infrastructure, Secretary-General of the Social Democratic Party and a supporter of the Arusha Accords, was assassinated by a group of armed men after being ambushed near his home. On 22 February, Martin Bucyana, chairman of the Coalition for the Defence of the Republic (CDR) and fierce opponent of the Arusha Accords, was lynched by a mob in Butare. Around thirty-seven people died and 150 were injured during an outbreak of violence sparked by these murders. MSF treated twenty-five of the injured at the CHK.[23]

Scheduled for 23 February, the swearing-in ceremony of the parliament and 'broad-based' transition government, i.e. including the RPF, was once again postponed because of the violence. The same day, a convoy of peacekeepers taking RPF representatives from their Mulindi headquarters to Kigali was attacked. Implementation of the Arusha Accords was suspended and the country's institutions were in such disarray that the parliament had not even been able to adopt the finance act for 1994.

In March, MSF team managers in the capital were particularly alarmed when a 'civil self-defence plan', which included the arming of militia members belonging to the president's MRND party, was brought to their attention. The resumption of large-scale hostilities between government and rebel forces seemed inevitable. But with the awareness of danger came a certain fatalism fed by prejudices that had influenced their analysis of events ever since MSF's work began with Kinyarwanda-speaking populations in the early 1980s. In most cases, the conflict was attributed to ancestral inter-ethnic hatred between Hutus and Tutsis, an interracial conflict between Bantus and Hamites or a class conflict between aristocrats (Tutsis) and their servants, as evidenced by various accounts: 'These different races are easy to recognise and not only by their physical appearance.'[24] 'The Bahutus [Hutus] were their serfs.'[25]

[22] MSF, Programme Manager, 'Report on Rwanda visit, 3 January 1993 to 19 January 1994' (Paris, January 1994).

[23] AFP, 'Nouveau report sine die de l'installation des institutions de transition' (Kigali, 2 February 1994).

[24] MSF, 'Rwandan refugee camp project, Uganda', 1987.

[25] MSF, 'Kiaka II Mission report, November 1985 to May 1986, Uganda', 1986.

Recounting his visit to the region in March 1994, the Deputy Operations Director in Paris told the Board of Directors: 'No one is giving thought to the political issues, such as the right to asylum, why people are fleeing, or the nature of the huge conflict between Hutus and Tutsis.'[26] The judgement was harsh but not without justification; the MSF teams were so absorbed in the technical aspects of treatment and aid provision that they did not always take the time to look beyond the clichés handed down from colonial historiography to understand the context in which they were operating. But some volunteers did go into the field with documents that opened up new perspectives, such as the book edited by Jean-Loup Amselle and Elikia M'Bokolo, available at the Paris headquarters documentation centre.[27] For their part, MSF managers in the capital followed the political developments closely, well aware that these never failed to hinder relief operations and to cause numerous casualties, inevitably resulting in medical aid organisations being called in to assist.

April 1994: beginning of the genocide and departure of aid organisations

In early April 1994, MSF teams were deployed in all prefectures except Kibuye. In the north (Ruhengeri, Byumba), they provided preventive and curative medical care in internally displaced persons camps where the health disaster was just ending – at the cost of thousands of lives. In the southern prefectures of Kibungo, Kigali, Butare and Gikongoro, the teams were still struggling to reduce mortality rates to near-normal levels in the Burundian refugee camps. MSF rented a large number of offices and warehouses in the cities of Kigali and Butare to support and coordinate activities, with the teams departing from these sites every morning to work in the camps. MSF teams were also working in all of Rwanda's neighbouring countries – Uganda, Tanzania, Zaire and Burundi – in response to population displacements (Burundian refugees in Zaire and Tanzania, for example), health emergencies (outbreak of endemic sleeping sickness in Uganda, collapse of public health services in Zaire) and internal armed conflicts in some of these countries (Burundi, Uganda, Zaire). The teams received assistance from MSF staff in Nairobi, Kenya, who provided logistical support to their colleagues deployed in east and central Africa. Over several months, the teams had been witnessing an increasing number of violent acts perpetrated by the various forces: the RPF, operating in the northern prefectures of Ruhengeri and Byumba and in Kigali with several hundred men in the parliament, the FAR, and militias belonging to the political parties controlling the rest of the country. Between the belligerents were peacekeepers under the command of Canadian General Romeo Dallaire, but their ability to intervene was hindered by the UN mandate, which, despite the deteriorating situation, especially in Kigali, prohibited the use of force.

---

[26] MSF, 'Minutes of the Board of Directors meeting', Paris, 25 March 1994.
[27] J.-L. Amselle and E. M'Bokolo (eds), *Au cœur de l'ethnie. Ethnies, tribalisme et état en Afrique* (Paris: La Découverte, 1985).

Around 8.30 p.m. on 6 April, the aeroplane carrying Rwandan President Juvénal Habyarimana and Burundian President Cyprien Ntaryamira back from Tanzania was shot down during its descent to Kigali airport, and the following morning saw the first murders of Tutsis and political leaders who supported the RPF's integration into national institutions. Members of the presidential guard assassinated Prime Minister Agathe Uwilingiyimana and three ministers while ten Belgian peace-keepers attempting to assist the Prime Minister were disarmed and executed by Rwandan army soldiers. The first clashes between national and rebel armed forces took place outside the parliament, where rebel troops were stationed in compliance with the Arusha Accords. From their houses, the MSF teams witnessed the loot-ing of neighbourhood homes and attacks against their residents. The streets were so unsafe that the staff decided against going to work. Hunted residents sometimes asked for refuge in MSF houses and, while some were taken in, others were refused out of fear of being killed along with them when the militias would come to search their homes. There was even greater concern for the many Belgian and French staff members. Some in the government were accusing Belgium of being involved in the attack against the presidential plane and France had been the main military ally since 1990 of those who were committing the massacres, making them fear rebel reprisals against French citizens.

On 7 April, a Tutsi family sought refuge in an MSF house in Murambi in Byumba prefecture. The militiamen were not long in coming. 'The group was threatening to attack the house if we refused to turn the man over. A few minutes later, he went to the gate, hands in the air ... Behind us, Godefroid, one of our guards, was taken away. We yelled that he was one of our staff, but no one listened. The man who sur-rendered was beaten to death with clubs and machetes.'[28]

The team decided to evacuate with the surviving women and children to an orphanage in Murambi a few kilometres away. They hid under a tarpaulin on a lorry that joined a convoy of other MSF vehicles escorted by three unarmed UN soldiers. Looting of MSF's facilities began right after the convoy left the premises. On 9 April, militiamen came to the orphanage where some 120 Tutsis had taken refuge. They confiscated an MSF lorry and took them by force to Kiziguro parish, where they had assembled hundreds of people to await execution. Members of the team's interna-tional staff decided to leave for Tanzania.

In Bugesera (Kigali-Rural prefecture), the killings had begun on the evening of 7 April near the MSF residence in Karama. On 8 April, the teams working in the Burundian refugee camps decided to cross over the border a few kilometres away to Kirundi province in Burundi. The convoy that arrived at the Rwandan border post included foreigners, among them Rwandan Tutsis and many Zairians. The Rwandan soldiers refused to let the Tutsis enter Burundi and negotiations ensued. Faced with

---

[28] MSF, 'Extract from the coordinator's diary – Murambi, April 1994', *Ins and Outs, MSF Holland internal newsletter* (June 1994).

the soldiers' refusal, the border about to close and approaching nightfall, an argument broke out between the team members. Some advocated bribing the soldiers and absolutely refused to enter Burundi without the Tutsis, even if it meant spending the night at the border post. Others did not think it wise to try to bribe the soldiers, preferring to ensure the safe passage of those authorised to cross the border, even if that meant leaving their Tutsi colleagues behind. After heated discussion, the team managers decided that the foreign staff – about fifty people, including twenty-five Zairians – would cross the border: 'At 5:15 p.m. A. [a logistician with the international staff] is still negotiating, but just for four Tutsis women who are going to be killed. The customs officials still flatly refuse. A. even resorts to shouting, creating a very tense situation and briefly disrupting the negotiations.'[29]

The Tutsis returned to Rwanda in MSF's vehicles. On 9 April, some Tutsi employees left the Bugesera area and managed to reach Butare. On 10 April, soldiers and militiamen began looting MSF facilities and equipment in the Burundian refugee camps and, on 11 April, militia members attacked the team's facilities in Karama with the help of two Rwandan MSF employees. According to accounts by several members of staff, the militiamen and soldiers separated MSF personnel and executed the Tutsis: 'Given the situation, it was difficult to determine how many people were killed, but we estimate that around 20 of them were MSF France staff.'[30] The bodies were buried in a common grave. The soldiers evacuated to Zaire those of MSF's Zairian employees who had not already left for Burundi.

On 8 April, the ICRC visited several of Kigali's neighbourhoods and reported seeing hundreds of bodies as well as an influx of casualties at the CHK. On 9 April, the Rwandan Red Cross and the ICRC, which were transporting injured patients to health centres in Kigali, shared their assessment of the situation with the other aid organisations. According to their estimates, several thousand people had already died in the capital and some 400 bodies were piled up in the CHK morgue.[31] Taking advantage of a brief lull, the MSF teams implemented the plan that had been prepared in late February and set up a triage centre at the CHK using the tents, water tank and supply kits already on-site. Supporting the Ministry of Health's Rwandan doctors, the MSF teams began to care for the wounded with the help of European cooperation doctors. There were some fifty seriously injured patients waiting for surgery, but the surgical teams were overwhelmed and there was a shortage of resources such as anaesthetics and transfusion and surgical supplies. MSF teams were at the ready at Kigali airport and in Kenya, Uganda, Burundi and Europe to provide further supplies and personnel. On 10 April, in view of the general lack of security, the murder the previous day reported in an ICRC communiqué of some

---

[29] MSF, 'Logistician with the international staff in Bugesera, Rwanda Mission for MSF-France, Activity Report', April 1994, p. 3.

[30] MSF, 'Memorandum on the destruction of the MSF France camp, Isar Karama Base in Nzangwa', Butare, 20 April 1994.

[31] AFP, 'Des milliers de morts à Kigali selon le délégué du CICR', Kigali, 8 April 1994.

of the Tutsi patients receiving treatment at the CHK and the possibility of using air assets provided by foreign militaries, the decision was taken to evacuate MSF's international staff. Bodies were strewn along the road from the city centre to the airport and a woman was killed right in front of the vehicles the staff were travelling in. On 11 April, fighting continued between government and rebel forces outside the parliament building where 600 RPF soldiers were stationed. The following day, evacuations of foreigners came to an end and the foreign soldiers assigned to this task left the country.

On 13 April, Tutsi refugees fleeing Gisenyi prefecture arrived in Zaire's Goma region. The MSF team coordinator sent her assessment of the refugees to the Amsterdam headquarters: 'In some cases, their arms were hanging, almost detached from their shoulders. They had received machete blows to the head ... The stories we are hearing from Rwanda can be called nothing less than genocide; the Hutus are clearly committing a systematic massacre of Tutsis.'[32]

On 15 April, after the international team had already left the region, 2,800 people – including several MSF employees – were massacred at the Saint Joseph Centre in Kibungo. Only forty survived, one an MSF staff member.[33] According to his account, soldiers had kidnapped, raped and decapitated an MSF nurse. The killers also murdered two drivers and the White Father [Missionary of Africa] from the traditional medicine centre in Barre where the MSF team had once lived. They then looted aid organisation facilities in the Burundian refugee camps. Large-scale killings had not yet begun in Butare because of opposition from the prefect, Jean-Baptiste Habyarimana, and military officials. The MSF team continued its operations by replacing Belgian staff with employees of other nationalities and, on 15 April, they provided surgical supplies to Kabgayi Hospital in Gitarama prefecture where around one hundred injured patients were receiving treatment.

Opening of surgical activities in Kigali

On 13 April, a team that had left Bujumbura in an ICRC convoy arrived in the government-held area of Kigali to replace the teams evacuated on 11 April. While the former teams' equipment and professional qualifications had been tailored to the requirements of refugee and displaced persons camps, the new team was made up of the staff needed to set up a surgical facility in a war zone.[34] They arrived in the capital with a surgical kit containing enough supplies for 300 procedures, expecting to be resupplied by road from Bujumbura. On 14 April, the ICRC and MSF visited the CHK, where MSF had intended to set up operations. After their visit, the team abandoned its plans to work in the hospital.

[32] MSF, 'Fax from MSF Holland Zaire to Amsterdam desk, 13 April 1994', ZRE/455.dsk, Gisenyi, April 1994.
[33] AFP, 'Près de cent membres du personnel rwandais tués depuis mi-avril, selon MSF', Paris, 13 May 1994.
[34] J.-H. Bradol served as the team's coordinator.

In the days leading up to our visit, there had been up to 1,000 corpses in the hospital morgue. As we visited, there were 400 bodies still in the morgue. Between this observation and quick conversations with the few wounded Tutsis who had been spared, it became all too clear that the hospital was being used as a slaughterhouse.[35]

In agreement with the ICRC, MSF's surgical team decided to work at the field hospital that the ICRC was setting up on land adjacent to its delegation's offices on Kyovu Avenue. Due to the nature of its mandate and operations, the ICRC knew the Rwandan authorities far better than MSF. To save time and facilitate negotiations between humanitarian organisations and the interim government's civilian and military representatives, MSF decided to be represented by the ICRC and place its team under the coordination of the delegation head, Philippe Gaillard. On the same day, Rwandan radio station Radio-Television Libre des Mille Collines announced that the Red Cross was transporting enemies of the Republic disguised as fake casualties.[36] The consequences were not long in coming: 'Early in the afternoon of 14 April, armed militiamen in Kigali shot dead in the presence of soldiers six wounded patients Rwandan Red Cross volunteers were evacuating to the field hospital set up the previous day by the ICRC.'[37]

The ICRC received assurances from the interim government concerned with gaining international recognition that it would give instructions to militiamen and soldiers not to attack ambulances belonging to the Rwandan Red Cross and ICRC field hospital. On 15 April, Rwandan state radio broadcast messages supporting ICRC activities and Red Cross ambulances displayed under their windscreens a photocopy of a pass signed by Augustin Bizimungu, the army's new chief of staff. A Rwandan army colonel acted as liaison officer between humanitarian organisations and government forces, militias and military units.

On 15 April, during a visit to a religious institution in the district of Gikondo, the team found dozens of smouldering, almost completely burnt bodies. They then went to a market where casualties had been reported, only to be told by the militiamen that there was no need to move them as they were in the process of killing them. Before letting the ambulance go, they checked to make sure there were no Tutsis hiding under the vehicle. Through the open windows of houses, the ambulance staff could see militiamen conducting thorough searches of every home in the neighbourhood. During this period, it was occasionally possible to transport Tutsi women and children by ambulance but almost never Tutsi men. Staff had to negotiate daily at each and every militia checkpoint. This meant showing the authorisations provided by the military authorities, pointing out that the militiamen would receive care if they themselves were injured, identifying who it was easiest to engage

[35] J.-H. Bradol, 'Rwanda, avril-mai 1994, limites et ambiguïtés de l'action humanitaire', *Les Temps Modernes*, 583 (August 1995), 130.

[36] J.-P. Chrétien, *Rwanda, les médias du génocide* (Paris: Karthala, 2000).

[37] ICRC, *Press release* 94/16, Geneva, 14 April 1994.

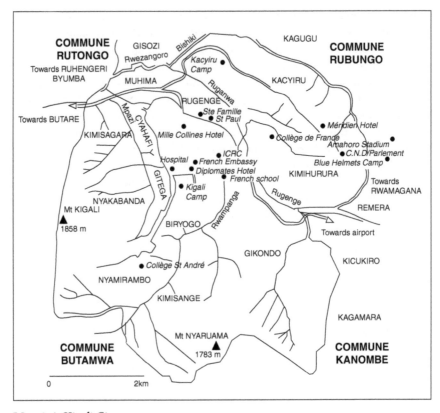

Map 1.4 Kigali City

with, appeasing them by trying to establish some kind of rapport, buying them beer and cigarettes, etc. The whole process was dangerous, especially since the killers consumed large quantities of alcohol and narcotics. The best time to pass the check-points was early in the morning while they were still groggy from the previous day's massacres and a night of drinking.

On 18 April, the RPF launched a mortar attack on the Radio-Television Libre des Mille Collines building and two injured journalists came to the field hospital for treatment. The same day, state radio broadcast once again messages support-ing the work of the Red Cross, and the convoy heading to Bujumbura for logistics purposes passed through the various roadblocks without incident. On 19 April, the field hospital team in Kigali organised a convoy to evacuate wounded patients from Amahoro stadium, where a contingent of peacekeepers was also stationed. The RPF was in the process of taking control of the area. The peacekeepers had negotiated a ceasefire, but as soon as the convoy crossed the front line, gunfire broke out. The operation was nevertheless carried out successfully without causing any casualties.

But armoured personnel carriers would have been required to continue evacuating the wounded without loss of life and the peacekeepers did not have enough of them.

In Kigali, MSF's plan was to operate on both sides of the city, including in rebel-controlled districts. During the evacuations of foreign nationals, an MSF team had stayed at Kigali airport for several days, hoping to return later to the city to care for the wounded. But the lack of security prevented them from doing so. A few days later, another team flew in from Nairobi and, like the other team, was unable to travel between the airport and city centre. It would take several weeks before another MSF surgical team, travelling overland from Uganda, could set up operations in the private King Faisal Hospital in the rebel-held part of the city. This team worked in partnership with the ICRC until the city came under the full control of the RPF.

The humanitarian organisations' main activities involved the delivery of care and relief in religious institutions, orphanages and schools sheltering vulnerable people who telephoned the ICRC delegation for help, triage of injured patients and the transport of those requiring surgery to the field hospital. Institutions sheltering Tutsis could not defy militiamen or soldiers for long. During the humanitarian teams' almost daily visits to the Sainte-Famille complex, patients told them that militiamen came at other times of the day with the express purpose of killing certain people. At times, staff at the ICRC delegation and field hospital witnessed killings just a few metres away. Some of the hunted people tried to take refuge in the hospital:

> The fugitive was soon grabbed from behind by another group ... and after his pursuers caught him, they started violently attacking him with a machete ... We screamed like people possessed ... Seeing us coming in large numbers, the assailants stopped in their tracks and retreated a few metres. We seized the opportunity and evacuated the victim. He had serious wounds to his neck and face and one of his arms was half-severed.[38]

What could staff do in this situation, with patients who had completed treatment but could not return to where they came from because there was such a high risk of being killed? After an initial period of indecision, during which some patients were sent back to institutions incapable of standing up to soldiers and militiamen, the field hospital annexed adjacent homes. So a field hospital became a place of refuge too. A Tutsi family from Gisenyi was concealed at the rear of the facility, even though none of them were injured or sick. The wounded were not harassed by militiamen inside the ICRC field hospital in Kigali, even though the security situation remained unpredictable. Some Rwandan staff were suspected of drawing up lists of patients and colleagues with the intention of passing the information to the killers. The atmosphere was tense in the sense that, each time someone new arrived, everyone was obsessed with one simple question – because the answer separated those

---

[38] R. Caravielhe, *Ou tout, ou rien. Journal d'un logisticien* (Presses de Lunel, 2002), pp. 50–2. Caravielhe, an MSF staff member, was responsible for logistics at the ICRC field hospital.

who were going to die from those who were not – Tutsi or Hutu? This atmosphere pervaded every detail and every moment of daily life. At any time, in any situation, even the most trivial, anyone could be accused by anyone else of being a Tutsi or a Tutsi supporter. The humanitarian teams had to carefully test the water with each and every new encounter. Was this someone who supported the killers or somebody indifferent to the fate reserved for Tutsis and opponents, a fatalist resigned to the victims' fate, or someone who could be counted on to rescue those trying to survive? There were many surprises and, of course, behaviours did not always conform to what people said they believed. Genocide perpetrators could turn out to be obliging while individuals claiming the highest ethical standards could turn into criminal informants when given the opportunity. Erratic feelings and behaviours were widespread. Added to the endless suffering, they lent society an air of collective madness, as an American surgeon in the ICRC field hospital wrote to his friends back home: 'I've lost my sense of humor. I'm beginning to feel a certain distance. People are beginning to look as insects. Bad sign.'[39]

Above all, rescuing people required knowing how to instantly spot the improbable chinks of a remaining iota of humanity in the midst of both the order and disorder of an extermination campaign. Too few or too many biases against a person or situation could prove fatal. It was clearly impossible to live through such events without committing errors of judgement that others paid for dearly. The militiamen never kidnapped or killed patients or staff members at the field hospital on Kyovu Avenue. But roundups and executions were commonplace elsewhere, particularly at the CHK, Kabgayi Hospital (Gitarama prefecture) and Nyarushishi camp (Cyangugu prefecture). The dilemma was as simple as it was cruel: agree to support the work carried out in these facilities at the risk of being caught up in a spiral of violence or refuse to work and deprive those trying to survive there of outside help. When the genocide perpetrators were defeated in early July, thousands of Tutsis were still alive in those places the ICRC had continued to support, despite the horrors that had taken place there.

Spread of massacres to Butare

The Butare team working in the Burundian refugee camps consisted of nineteen Belgian nationals, who had to leave the country precipitously when militiamen and soldiers made specific threats against Belgian citizens – rumours and extremist media accused them of being complicit in the assassination of President Habyarimana. Massacres had begun in neighbouring prefecture Gikongoro on 7 April and, on 13 April, the team learned that killings were beginning in the south of Butare prefecture, particularly in the municipality of Nyakizu near the Burundian border, where Rwandan employees of AICF, the Belgian Red Cross and MSF had been killed. An increasing number of Tutsi employees in Butare were asking to be evacuated

---

[39] J. Sundin, 'Kigali's wound, through a doctor's eyes (experiences of a Red Cross doctor in Kigali, Rwanda)', *Harper's Magazine* (1 August 1994).

to Burundi. From 13 April to 22 April, an emergency coordinator from Amsterdam organised the evacuations to Burundi:

> Along the 50 kilometres from Butare to the border, there were four or five checkpoints. We saw people being killed at some of the checkpoints and bodies piled up along the side at others ... The day after my arrival, MSF's Tutsi employees asked to leave the country because they were afraid for their lives. I didn't know anything about the situation ... I saw the despair in their eyes and thought they must have good reason to fear for their lives ... I had an argument with the logistician, who wanted nothing to do with it ... Another time, when we arrived at the border, the car was surrounded by Hutus with knives and machetes ... The border guard wouldn't let us pass ... I offered him money, but he refused ... In Butare, two priests joined our convoy ... One of them walked up to the border guard and started talking to him about Jesus ... and the guy said, 'Okay, let them pass'.[40]

On other occasions, it was impossible to protect people in danger and the MSF international staff witnessed killings: 'A guard and a soldier armed with clubs were smashing a civilian's head in.'[41]

MSF set up a surgical unit in Kayanza Hospital in Burundi to treat injured Tutsis who managed to cross the border. On 16 April, the team and Caritas organised a convoy from Butare to rescue wounded victims reported in Kibeho (Gikongoro prefecture). When they arrived at the site, the relief workers had to turn back under pressure from militiamen who threatened to kill them. Back in Butare, they met Zairians who had witnessed the massacres in Kibeho and had seen the MSF cars approaching the site. They reported that some 2,000 Tutsis, including all the wounded, had been assembled in the church and slaughtered by militiamen and soldiers. In Butare prefecture, some in the administration, who included the Tutsi prefect, tried to stop the killings. The prefect was dismissed on 17 April and murdered, along with his wife and children.[42] On 19 April, the Head of State, Prime Minister, several members of the interim government and extremist political party leaders arrived in Kigali and encouraged the killings. The presidential guard flew in during the night of 20 April while the militiamen were bussed in earlier in the day.[43]

The militia and military set up more checkpoints. MSF vehicles, like those of other aid organisations, were stopped and searched. Passports were demanded and hostility against Belgians and sometimes against 'whites' in general was manifest. The militiamen viewed the ICRC and MSF as supporters of the Tutsis and the RPF. At the University Hospital in Butare some fifty men, women and children, almost all of them with machete wounds (severed hands and legs, multiple injuries), awaited treatment.

[40] 'Interview with an MSF Holland manager sent to Butare from 13–22 April 1994' in Binet, *Génocide des Rwandais Tutsis 1994* (Paris: MSF, 2003), pp. 22–3.

[41] 'Interview with an MSF Holland manager sent to Butare from 13–22 April 1994', p. 24.

[42] A. Guichaoua, *Rwanda 1994. Les politiques du génocide à Butare* (Paris: Karthala, 2005).

[43] Guichaoua, *Rwanda 1994*.

A number of mutilated bodies had been taken to the morgue. On the wards, relations were strained between Ministry of Health staff, most of whom supported the interim government or could not defy its orders, and MSF staff, including Tutsis who had come to help with the growing number of patients. In order to improve relations with the hospital staff, MSF decided to pay a bonus to the ministry personnel (4,000 Rwandan francs for a nurse and 10,000 for a doctor). Patients who received treatment did not dare leave the hospital for fear of being immediately killed.

On 22 April, the Butare team went to Saga 1 and 2 camps for Burundian refugees. The MSF houses were in flames and the team requested permission to evacuate its staff, but a crowd of armed militiamen vehemently refused. One of their leaders said, 'If you're here to rescue Tutsis, we're going to kill them anyway and we'll kill you too'.[44] The next day, the team found out from its Zairian staff what had happened after they left: 'They checked ID cards, then the MSF employees were separated into Tutsis, Hutus and Zairians. The Interahamwe handed out machetes and guns to MSF's Hutu staff and told them to kill their Tutsi colleagues.'[45]

On 22 and 23 April, while the MSF team was working on the wards, 150 patients and five MSF staff members were massacred behind Butare University Hospital. Disregarding attempts to negotiate, militiamen killed a Hutu nurse who was seven months pregnant; her crime, in their eyes, was bearing a child with a Tutsi husband. On 24 April, the international staff on the Butare team left Rwanda for Bujumbura where they made statements to the press demanding international military intervention to evacuate the Tutsis to a secure area. On 21 April, the UNSC had adopted resolution 912, which reduced the size of the peacekeeping force in Rwanda from around 2,100 to 270 soldiers, provoking a profound sense of abandonment and despair. MSF reacted publicly to this announcement as follows:

> As the United Nations withdraws from the country, the people of Rwanda risk sinking into oblivion ... MSF is thus urging the international community to take every possible measure to ensure that the belligerents respect civilians as well as all health personnel and facilities and provide full access to victims.[46]

Between 3 and 17 May, MSF conducted a survey in Burundi to compile information on the situation in Bugesera (Kigali-Rural prefecture). The team interviewed Rwandan Tutsi refugees in Bugnari camp and Burundi Hutus in Gatare and Ceru camps who had returned to their country after fleeing advancing RPF forces. The information was collected from Rwandan and Burundian Hutus and Tutsis who had been employed by MSF in Burundian refugee camps in the Bugesera area and who had just arrived in Burundi. The international staff had left on 8 April, and the

---

[44] 'Interview with the MSF Belgium medical coordinator in Butare until 24 April 1994' in Binet, *Génocide*, p. 25.
[45] 'Interview with the MSF Belgium medical coordinator in Butare until 24 April 1994', the term Interahamwe referred to the MNRD militia. It gradually became a generic term referring to civilians involved in the massacres.
[46] MSF, Press release, Paris and Amsterdam, 22 April 1994.

goal was to understand what had happened to the personnel in MSF facilities and in these camps during the period 7 April to 17 May 1994. Their accounts prompted yet another concern: violence committed by the RPF, particularly against Burundian refugees. Staff members and refugees, some with bullet wounds, had just arrived from Rwanda as the team began the one-on-one interviews. Respondents related that, on 13 May, the RPF had attacked Nzangwa camp (municipality of Gashora), which was sheltering thousands of Burundian Hutu refugees. According to their account, 'The [RPF] soldiers trapped the refugees (women, children and men) by handing out saucepans and promising food. They (3,000 people) were then locked in the mosque and food storage room and slaughtered'.[47]

The collecting of witness statements had been standardised by MSF's legal adviser and this procedure was used to record accounts of crimes witnessed by MSF national and international staff. On 7 June, the testimony from MSF staff was sent to the rapporteur for the UN Commission on Human Rights and the UN Secretary-General as well as representatives of the UNSC's Member States.[48] The report chiefly presented testimony on the extermination of Tutsis by Rwandan government militiamen and soldiers in an effort to prove the genocidal nature of the events and to be better prepared to support the proposal put forward by René Degni Segui, Special Rapporteur for the UN Commission on Human Rights, calling for the creation of an international criminal court to bring the genocide perpetrators to justice.

RPF violences against the Rwandan population and humanitarian workers

By mid-May, MSF teams were working in the majority of Rwanda's prefectures (Kigali, Kigali-Rural, Ruhengeri, Byumba and Gitarama), the main border regions of Zaire (Goma, Bukavu and Uvira), Burundi (Kayanza, Ngozi and Kirundo) and Tanzania (Ngara) where hundreds of thousands of refugees had fled. Meanwhile, the security of the ICRC and MSF teams in Kigali was deteriorating:

> In Kigali itself our situation was most uncomfortable. In the middle of May one of our food convoys was deliberately targeted by the RPF as it was leaving Kigali for Gitarama. For an hour and a half, our delegates Pierre Gratzl, François Conrad and Ian Stefanski came under a hail of bullets and mortars. Pierre Gratzl was wounded in the stomach by an exploding shell. General Dallaire saved him by dispatching two armoured vehicles to the spot at our request. Pierre Gratzl underwent an operation in our hospital and that day I learned a new word – laparotomy. At the same time, mortar fire launched by the RPF fell on the ICRC delegation, leaving two dead and five wounded. In June, two shells launched by the RPF hit the emergency room in the field hospital, killing seven patients and wounding about ten others.[49]

[47] MSF, 'Report by MSF-France medical coordinator', *Témoignages*, Paris (May 1994).
[48] F. Bouchet-Saulnier and P. Salignon, 'Génocide au Rwanda – Témoignages' (MSF Paris, June 1994).
[49] P. Gaillard, ICRC head of delegation in Rwanda from 1993 to 1994, 'Rwanda 1994: La vraie vie est absente (Arthur Rimbaud)' Talk given at the International Museum of the Red Cross and Red Crescent, Geneva, 18 October 1994.

In late April, MSF set up from Uganda several new programmes in the RPF-controlled area in north Rwanda. One team launched operations in Gitare in Ruhengeri prefecture and in Byumba prefecture in the town of the same name. In June, the Byumba team manager began sending Brussels headquarters information about the RPF's actions: 'The former head of the Byumba hospital and his wife and three children were killed two weeks ago ... I also issued a protest about a lieutenant striking a 16-year-old girl with a steel pipe inside the hospital.' In his messages to headquarters, he described the incidents: 'interrogating patients at gunpoint, the nightly infiltration of RPF security service members in the hospital who come armed for this kind of activity and the disappearance of at least two patients ... a nurse who has worked for us since the beginning disappeared in late May'.[50]

Ten years later, the team manager still remembered the barely veiled threats made to him by the RPF: 'They were targeting us. They said I was top of the list ... if your brakes fail on the road, you might be the victim of a terrible accident ... One time in Nyanza, I saw them threaten the ICRC representative. They pointed a rocket launcher at him.'[51] During a visit to the field, MSF Belgium's General Director noted the teams' lack of preparation for the RPF's escalating violence against non-combatants: 'This lack of experience and clear instructions is leading to mistakes that sometimes end in tragedy, such as when two armed guards taken along for security reasons jumped out of the MSF car to coldly slaughter two pedestrians, simply because they looked "suspicious"'.[52]

The violence committed by the RPF was not limited to the Bugesera area and Byumba prefecture. On 24 June, MSF informed the press of the RPF's forced evacuation on 23 June of 35,000 civilians living in the region between Gitarama and Butare toward the south of Kigali-rural prefecture (Bugesera). The MSF Communications Director from Brussels was in the area: 'Conditions were horrifying, with absolutely no organisation or assistance. People were literally dying along the side of the road. They were forced to walk under exhausting and dreadful conditions.'[53]

The routed Rwandan army nevertheless remained dangerous in the region, as MSF reported to the press:

> This morning, at 9.45 a.m. on 1 July, a Rwandan army helicopter attacked a Médecins Sans Frontières car five km from the town of Nyamata in Bugesera. Two rockets were fired from a low altitude (25 m) at a white car clearly identified by the MSF humanitarian logo. No other vehicle was on the road at that specific time. The rockets missed the vehicle by just a few metres.[54]

[50] MSF, 'Report by the Byumba team manager to MSF Brussels', Rwanda, 20 June 1994.
[51] 'Interview with the MSF Belgium coordinator in Byumba and Bugesera from May to September 1994' in Binet, *Génocide*, p. 45.
[52] MSF Belgium Executive Director, 'Un contexte éclaté, un nouveau mandat?', *Contact* (MSF Belgium in-house magazine) 29 (July–August 1994), 7–8.
[53] 'Interview with the MSF Belgium Communications Director' in Binet, *Génocide*, p. 61.
[54] MSF, 'Médecins Sans Frontières attaqué par un hélicoptère de l'armée rwandaise', Press release, Brussels, 1 July 1994.

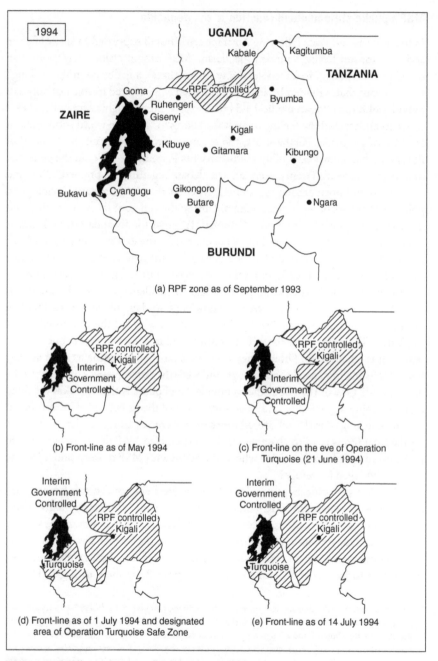

(a) RPF zone as of September 1993

(b) Front-line as of May 1994

(c) Front-line on the eve of Operation Turquoise (21 June 1994)

(d) Front-line as of 1 July 1994 and designated area of Operation Turquoise Safe Zone

(e) Front-line as of 14 July 1994

Map 1.5 RPF's movements from April to July 1994

MSF's public statements in reaction to the genocide

In the months and years following April 1994, MSF staff expressed a sense of failure and guilt for not having sounded the alarm: 'MSF cannot claim – any more than the United Nations – to have said at any time: "there's a genocide in the making". I never heard that.'[55] Remembering that back then MSF viewed its role not only as a provider of humanitarian medical aid but also as a 'human rights sentinel' makes it easier to understand the feeling of guilt for failing to warn the world sooner about the 'risk of genocide'. Furthermore, the organisation had received the Council of Europe Parliamentary Assembly Human Rights Prize in 1992. Could the genocide have been foreseen? Twenty years on, the debate regarding its premeditation and planning is still open among researchers, whether they be historians, sociologists, political scientists or legal practitioners. During the different trials of political and military authorities, International Criminal Tribunal for Rwanda (ICTR) judges did not accept the prosecutor's line of reasoning, i.e. the existence of an agreement to commit genocide allegedly hatched before 7 April 1994 among the defendants themselves and with other figures. Of course legal truth and historical truth do not always concur.[56] But it is clear in this case that the evidence gathered by the ICTR provides the most extensive source of knowledge to date informing the timeline of decisions and measures taken by the individuals who led the extermination of the Tutsis. The other cause for self-criticism found in MSF's archives concerns the nature of the massacres. Should they have been labelled genocide as soon as they began? Was the label used soon enough and were the consequences of using it fully understood? One of the issues the 'genocide' label poses is that it makes breaking with neutrality a possibility, and neutrality is one of the principles of humanitarian action. A feeling of malaise hovered more or less consciously over the discussions on the legal terms used to characterise the events. Had MSF done enough to help endangered people to flee, those who had worked with MSF or been under its care or who had asked for refuge?

When the genocide began, aid workers in the field concentrated mainly on attracting world attention to Rwanda. Global diplomatic efforts and media coverage at that time were focusing on Nelson Mandela's election in South Africa and the siege of Gorazde by Slobodan Milosevic's troops in the former Yugoslavia. On 13 April, a Canadian television crew and a Sigma news service photographer received permission to join an ICRC convoy travelling from Bujumbura to Kigali. During

---

[55] 'Interview with the MSF Belgium Executive Director', in Binet, *Génocide*, p. 13. In 1993, two reports, one published by several organisations, including the FIDH (International Federation for Human Rights), and the other by the United Nations human rights special rapporteur M.B.W. Ndiaye, had stressed that the nature of the attacks being perpetrated against the Tutsis met the relevant Convention articles' definition of the crime of genocide (Convention on the Prevention and Punishment of the Crime of Genocide, articles 2 and 3).

[56] Cl. Vidal, 'Le fait d'"entente en vue de commettre le génocide". Entre le judiciaire et l'historique au Rwanda', *L'Afrique des Grands Lacs: Annuaire 2014–2015* (Paris: L'Harmattan, 2015), 269–86.

an international meeting on 12 April, MSF also decided to send journalists as much information as possible about the massacres and provide them with logistical support. Several foreign correspondents were already in Kigali, including one from Agence France Presse as well as a photographer and a reporter from *Le Figaro*, to whom MSF lent a car and driver. The ICRC head of delegation, in a break with the traditional reserve of his organisation's representatives, made an increasing number of public statements to publicise the extent of the killings, while refusing to use the term 'genocide':

> At the time, the ICRC contributed more to media coverage and provided more information than possibly ever before in its 130 years of existence. On 28 April 1994, some three weeks after the genocide had begun, the Committee called on the governments concerned and Security Council members to take every possible measure to put an end to the massacres. The words used, such as 'systematic carnage' and 'extermination of a large percentage of the civilian population', left no doubt as to what was happening.[57]

The term 'genocide' made its appearance in MSF's internal communications after being used on 13 April by the Goma team who had treated and interviewed surviving Tutsi refugees in Zaire. But there was a precedent that advised caution. Three years earlier, some MSF members had used the term in press statements to describe the Iraqi army's repression in Kurdistan in 1991 and this had initiated an internal controversy at the time. The MSF team had become part of the ICRC delegation in the government-held area in Kigali and, during the first few weeks, left the initiative for making public statements to the ICRC. Moreover, during the first two weeks after the attack against the presidential aeroplane, the organisation's presence was limited to Kigali and Butare (a prefecture so far unaffected by the massacres), so it was difficult to conclude with any certainty whether an entirely new phenomenon was taking place. Was it a nationwide campaign to exterminate all Tutsis or another manifestation of an old phenomenon recurrent since 1959 – pogroms against Tutsis limited to particular regions? After the massacre of wounded patients at Butare University Hospital on 23 April, it became clear that the term 'genocide' was in fact warranted because this prefecture had been one of the few places not yet affected by the massacres. On 28 April, the President of MSF Belgium stated in *De Morgen*: 'The Rwanda crisis is no longer a crisis; it's a genocide.' This did not mean, however, that public statements by the organisation's members had become wholly consistent. In many cases, they used a contradictory combination of terms, such as 'chaos', 'inter-ethnic massacres' and 'genocide'. The nature of the international reaction was discussed far more than the labelling of the event. The President of MSF Belgium wrote in an

---

[57] Speech by Philippe Gaillard, ICRC head of delegation to Rwanda from 1993 to 1994 at the Genocide Prevention Conference, organised by Aegis Trust and the British Foreign Office, London, January 2002.

opinion column published on 28 April: In our day and age, it is unacceptable that the great powers ... are unable or do not even have the will required to incapacitate machetes and relatively light weapons.[58] Then, on 29 April, rather than demanding action against the genocide perpetrators, as the President had done the day before in *De Morgen*, the Operations Director in Brussels demanded in *La Wallonie*: 'that protected areas be set up where wounded victims would at least be respected and that humanitarian corridors be created'.[59] Putting these statements back in context requires remembering that, despite the failure of the international military intervention then under way in Somalia, the 'right to intervene' still received strong support from humanitarian organisations, including MSF. Again in *De Morgen*, the President of MSF Belgium came out in support of the 'right to intervene', specifying: 'Such is the definition of a "humanitarian intervention", which gives a State or a group of States the right to intervene in the internal affairs of a third State if the latter violates the rights of its citizens.'

MSF managers in Paris focused on how to devise a realistic (i.e. fast and effective) international action plan to rescue Tutsis and opponents who could still be saved. On 16 May, the MSF team manager who had been working with the ICRC in Kigali in the government-held area had returned to France and was invited to appear on the evening news of leading French TV channel TF1. During the interview, he said: 'The people who are carrying out massacres as we speak, who are implementing this planned and systematic policy of extermination, are financed, trained and armed by France.'[60] On 18 May, MSF addressed the President of France in an open letter published in *Le Monde*: 'How is it possible that France, with its "protégés", has no means of putting a stop to these massacres?'[61] A few days earlier, on 27 April 1994, Jérôme Bicamumpaka, Minister of Foreign Affairs for the interim government, and Jean Bosco Barayagwiza, a leading member of the CDR, had been received in the offices of both the French President and the Prime Minister. On 19 May, Bruno Delaye and Dominique Pin, civilian officers on the Africa desk in the French President's office, requested a meeting with the President of MSF, who attended with the team manager who had made the statements on TF1's evening news on 16 May. The MSF representatives went to the meeting with a specific goal in mind: to demand once again that French government officials pressure their allies to stop the killings. In response, the two diplomats expressed shock that their work in Rwanda could be called into question and boasted of the excellence of the diplomatic efforts that had led the belligerents to sign the Arusha Accords. They answered the demand for intervention to end the massacres by saying they could not get hold of their Rwandan allies on

[58] Réginald Moreels, 'Opinion sur la crise au Rwanda', *Le Soir* (6 May 1994). Published in *De Morgen* (28 April 1994).

[59] Georges Dallemagne, 'Rwanda – MSF témoigne: le génocide est en cours', *La Wallonie* (29 April 1994).

[60] Jean-Hervé Bradol, www.youtube.com/watch?v=4DCrkBjQiGc#t=42 (availability confirmed in September 2015).

[61] MSF, 'Lettre ouverte au Président de la République française', *Le Monde* (18 May 1994).

the telephone. Anxious to appease the two MSF representatives, Bruno Delaye and Dominique Pin offered to allocate an additional three million francs to aid organisations, even though that was not the subject of the meeting. They then invited the MSF President to meet with François Mitterrand, with the explicit goal of curtailing MSF's public statements on France's role. He declined the invitation, answering it was out of the question to meet with the French President to hear a repeat of the justifications he had just been given.

On 23 May, the *New York Times* published a letter written by MSF's International Secretary demanding that the UNSC take urgent steps to end the genocide: 'A targeted and clearly defined intervention by the United Nations is not an option for Rwanda; it's an obligation. If not, why teach history?'[62] In late May, MSF's Executive Director in Brussels met with the UNSC President in the hope that his presentation of the events witnessed by his teams would finally provoke a reaction equal to the severity of the events. In early June, an emissary from MSF Paris headquarters and the head of MSF's New York office met with Donald Steinberg of the United States National Security Council USSC. They urged the US administration to send a few armoured personnel carriers to peacekeepers in Kigali for the purpose of providing security during some of the evacuations of wounded victims to hospitals.[63] The vehicles were already in the region because of the American military operation in Somalia. The American official informed the two MSF representatives that this was not possible for administrative reasons. He went on to add that his administration refused to consider the ongoing killings as genocide and expressed his personal disappointment with this stance.

On 17 May 1994, the UNSC adopted resolution 918, which called for a ceasefire agreement, an end to the massacres and the deployment of 5,500 peacekeepers. On 8 June, resolution 925 took note of 'reports indicating that acts of genocide have occurred in Rwanda'. At press conferences in Paris and Brussels on 17 June 1994, MSF representatives made the following appeal ('You can't stop a genocide with doctors') to the UNSC: 'It is urgent to use every available means to stop the massacres, by supporting an immediate United Nations intervention that will take meaningful action against the killers and protect the survivors.' During the press conference, they stated: 'The genocide convention has been waiting since 1948 for States to adopt appropriate rules and create a court of law capable of ensuring their compliance.'[64] This position was controversial within MSF as the call to arms conflicted with the very principle of peaceful humanitarian action. On 18 June, Minister of Foreign Affairs Alain Juppe announced France's intention to address the UNSC and propose 'a targeted military intervention for humanitarian ends', dubbed 'Operation

[62] A. Destexhe, International Secretary of MSF, 'Rwandans die while the U.N. procrastinates', *New York Times* (23 May 1994).

[63] J.-H. Bradol.

[64] MSF, 'You can't stop a genocide with doctors', press kit, Paris (17 June 1994).

Turquoise'. With the exception of France, no other country agreed to lead an intervention. UN Secretary-General Boutros Boutros-Ghali, who had been demanding international military action to put an end to the massacres since late April, could not hide his anger with the UN Member States: 'I begged them to send troops ... Unfortunately, and I say this with the greatest humility, I failed. It's an outrage and I'm the first to say it.'[65] On 22 June, the UNSC (resolution 929) authorised the military operation, stressing the 'strictly humanitarian character of this operation which shall be conducted in an impartial and neutral fashion.'[66]

While the RPF did not agree to the return of French troops to Rwanda, the announcement that their main military ally would be returning raised hopes among the FAR and the militias. Due to the French State's political and military support to its Rwandan ally, the majority of aid organisations and most MSF sections came out against Operation Turquoise: 'Rather nobody than the French.'[67] In France, MSF stated that a UN intervention would have been preferable but priority should have been given to stopping genocide by all means available.

In reality, the French forces did nothing to arrest the leaders of the extermination campaign in south-west Rwanda where they had taken control. They were able to continue to order the killings and flee with their weapons to Zaire with impunity. But, it has to be said that, according to the ICRC head of delegation, surviving Tutsis in Nyarushishi camp (Cyangugu prefecture) would later be protected by French troops serving with Operation Turquoise.[68] By late June 1994, however, discussions on the specifics of an international military operation to rescue genocide victims already seemed futile. Hundreds of thousands of Tutsis and opponents had been killed by then, among them some 200 Rwandans who had worked with MSF.[69]

At the end of the war, MSF staff wavered between sorrow at the extermination of the vast majority of Rwandan Tutsis and the Hutus who had refused to take part in the genocide, joy at witnessing the defeat of the genocide perpetrators but fear of their control over refugee camps in neighbouring countries, hope that the massive violence committed by the victors against non-combatants would not continue past the few skirmishes inevitable in an immediate post-war period and lassitude at having to re-launch medical relief operations yet again obliterated by the resurgence of violence in April 1994.

---

[65] P. Lewis, 'Boutros-Ghali angrily condemns all sides for not saving Rwanda', *New York Times* (26 May 1994).

[66] Operation Turquoise, placed under French command, comprised 3,060 soldiers, including 508 from seven different countries (Senegal, Guinea-Bissau, Chad, Mauritania, Egypt, Niger and Congo).

[67] MSF Belgium Communications Director, *La Nouvelle Gazette* (21 June 1994).

[68] P. Gaillard, ICRC head of delegation in Rwanda from 1993 to 1994, 'Rwanda 1994: La vraie vie est absente (Arthur Rimbaud)', talk given at the International Museum of the Red Cross and Red Crescent, Geneva, 18 October 1994.

[69] This is a rough estimate. The real figures could be much higher. It is impossible to provide precise figures due to the deaths of some witnesses and the loss of records.

2

Rwandan refugee camps in Tanzania and Zaire, 1994–95

When hundreds of thousands of Rwandan refugees began flooding into Tanzania and Zaire in the spring and summer of 1994, MSF's management and field teams had two reasons to be concerned. Mortality rates in the vast camps set up in Tanzania and then Zaire were indeed catastrophically high at first. Before April 1994, it had taken several months for humanitarian organisations working with internally displaced people and Burundian refugees in Rwanda to lower the persistently high mortality caused by malnutrition and infections. Hence the concern about these influxes of refugees; would relief agencies be able to prevent further health catastrophes?

Running operations in the camps was the second reason for MSF's concern. Teams feared having to cooperate with the dignitaries responsible for the genocide of the Tutsis in Rwanda, thereby legitimising their power in the camps and being seen as or becoming their – albeit unwilling – accomplices.

Rwandan refugees in Tanzania, 1994–95

On April 1994, Rwandan refugees, the immense majority of them Hutus, began pouring into north-west Tanzania and, according to UNHCR, an estimated 250,000 had arrived by the beginning of May.[1] The refugees settled in Benaco (Ngara district, Kagera region), just sixteen kilometres from the Rwandan border. They had fled from advancing RPF fighters who were conducting an offensive from east Rwanda. 'The rebels, whose numbers grew to around 25,000 as the fighting continued, were sweeping through east Rwanda, moving south swiftly, but being careful to consolidate their advances.'[2]

---

[1] The figure of 250,000 was in fact an overestimate; 'the figure of 170,000 has since been adopted as more accurate'. See Borton *et al.*, *Humanitarian Aid and Effects*, p. 110.

[2] S. Vogel, 'Student of war graduates on battlefields of Rwanda; rebel leader ran a textbook operation', *Washington Post* (25 August 1994).

This first wave was made up mainly of refugees from Byumba and Kibungo prefectures where the genocide against the Tutsis had first started on 7 April. Among those to arrive were Jean-Baptiste Gatete, former mayor (*bourgmestre*) of Murambi, and Sylvestre Gacumbitsi, mayor of Rusumo (a commune on the border between Rwanda and Tanzania), both local orchestrators of the genocide. Sylvestre Gacumbitsi was not afraid to parade in public. According to an MSF report: 'Recognised leaders, like the burgomaster of Rusumo, walk along the roads taking the pulse of the camp … Nobody controls the camp except the Rwandese.'[3] On 28 August 1994, the BBC broadcast a documentary called *Journey into Darkness*, filmed by BBC correspondent Patrick Fergal Keane who had travelled to Rusumo in May to investigate the genocide. Gacumbitsi, by then firmly established in Benaco, agreed to be interviewed by the reporter and even allowed himself to be filmed. Years later, P. Fergal Keane testified against Rusomo's former mayor at the ICTR in Arusha, Tanzania.[4]

Working in Burundian refugee camps in Tanzania since 1993, MSF arrived in Benaco at the beginning of May 1994 and quickly set up activities to cope with the influx of refugees, using the town of Ngara as the rear base for its operations in the camps.

In a report dated 13 June, MSF queried the UNHCR's figure of 340,000 refugees in Benaco. Why this mistrust of official population numbers that the UN agency used to calculate aid requirements? MSF's real issue was in fact political rather than technical. Should the organisation accept estimates that had not been drawn up by UNHCR, but by Rwandan mayors who had participated in the genocide? MSF developed its own means so as not to have to and put Benaco's population at somewhere between 200,000 and 220,000.

This estimate was based on data from a nutrition survey carried out on 7 June and the results of a measles immunisation campaign during which 75,000 children aged six months to fifteen years were vaccinated. The epidemiologists based themselves on the assumption that the under-fifteen population constituted, in theory, 45 per cent of the total population.[5] It was therefore probable and plausible that the figure produced jointly by UNHCR and the former mayors overestimated the population of Benaco by at least 120,000 people. Yet food distribution was calculated on this overestimation and the Rwanda dignitaries took full advantage of it by diverting considerable amounts of food and selling it to Tanzanian traders.[6]

---

[3] MSF Holland, Emergency Team, 'Report on security and protection of Rwandese refugees in Kagera region, Tanzania, 27 August–13 September 1994', 30 September 1994. This report gathers testimonies and observations concerning Benaco camp.

[4] MSF Holland, *Breaking the Cycle: MSF Calls for Action in the Rwandan Refugee Camps in Tanzania and Zaire* (Amsterdam, 10 November 1994), p. 10 and the International Criminal Tribunal for Rwanda, *Prosecutor v. Sylvestre Gacumbitsi*, 17 June 2004, § 144.

[5] MSF, 'Situation report Ngara, Tanzania', 13 June 1994.

[6] About political and military leadership in the Rwandan refugee camps and about refugee numbers, see F. Terry, *Condemned to Repeat?* (London: Cornell University Press, 2002), pp. 186–91.

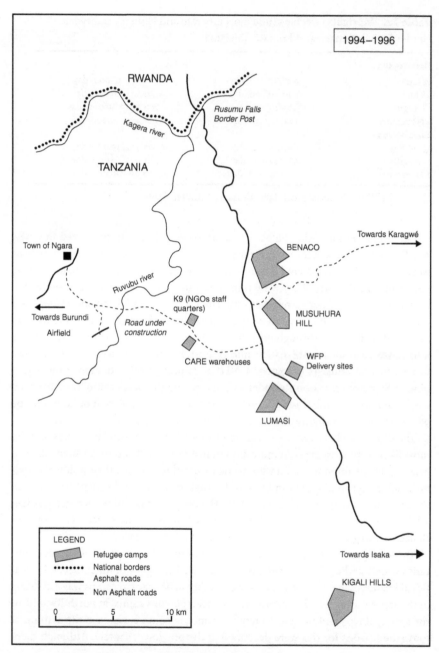

Map 2.1 Rwandan refugees camps, Ngara district (Tanzania)

Table 2.1 Mortality: weekly crude mortality rate and child mortality rate (under five) in Benaco and Lumasi, Tanzania

Benaco, 1994		
13 June	0.57/10,000/day	<5yrs 1.71/10,000/day
28 July	1.90/10,000/day	<5yrs 5.52/10,000/day
18 August	3.85/10,000/day	<5yrs 10.27/10,000/day
2 November	1.22/10,000/day	<5yrs 2.82/10,000/day
Lumasi, 1994		
15–30 July	1.19/10,000/day	<5yrs 3.32/10,000/day
18 August	1.85/10,000/day	<5yrs 6.13/10,000/day
2 November	0.29/10,000/day	<5yrs 0.81/10,000/day

Source: MSF epidemiological data, Benaco, Lumasi, 1994

On 8 June, some of the refugees in Benaco camp began to be moved to a new site, Lumasi, ten or so kilometres away. MSF set up a reception centre where arrivals were examined and registered. The refugees were organised according to their home communes in Rwanda. They were transferred in groups, by commune, under the leadership of the former communal authorities who ensured discipline among their 'constituents'. By 28 July, 63,000 people were living in Lumasi camp while 190,000 remained in Benaco. Throughout July and August, Rwandans continued flooding into Tanzania at such a rate that, by mid-August, Benaco's population had increased to 218,000, and Lumasi's to 87,000.[7] UNHCR confirmed this situation at the beginning of September: 17,000 Rwandans were crossing the border into Tanzania each week.[8] In mid-November 1994, UNHCR estimated the population of Lumasi to be 98,000 refugees (the figure also used by MSF) and of Benaco to be 260,000.[9]

The difference between the numbers produced by the Rwandan leaders and the most likely estimates gives an indication of just how much aid they were misappropriating. Huge amounts of aid were being diverted to support their political activities, including running their militias, or for their own personal benefit. The scale of the diversion is easy enough to calculate. The daily food ration per refugee was half a kilo (around 2,100 kilocalories), so the initial overestimate of 120,000 people in Benaco camp generated an extra sixty tonnes of food per day.

This misappropriation of food aid not only served the purposes of former dignitaries implicated in the genocide, it also deprived refugees of much-needed nutritional resources at a time when excess mortality in Tanzanian camps was escalating in the same way as it had in internally displaced persons camps in north Rwanda in the spring of 1993 and Burundian refugee camps in south Rwanda in the autumn of 1993 (the reasons for this were described in the previous chapter). Although there

[7] MSF, 'Sitrep Tanzania/Benako, Ngara', 16 August 1994.
[8] MSF, 'Situation of missions in Rwanda, Zaire and Tanzania, no. 13', 5 September 1994.
[9] MSF, 'Medical sitrep, Lumasi', 24 November 1994 and UNHCR, 'Health Coordination Meeting', 11 November 1994.

were common causes for this excess mortality, the situation in the Rwandan refugee camps in Tanzania was somewhat different. For example, epidemics (dysentery, cholera, etc.) did not begin when the camps first opened but after most of the relief operations had already been launched.

In early August, MSF began distributing dry rations to all children under the age of five. These rations of enriched flour were adapted to their specific nutritional needs. Distribution centres were opened in Benaco and Lumasi. In June, a nutrition survey implemented in Benaco had shown fewer than 5 per cent of children under the age of five to be suffering from acute malnutrition.[10] At the end of August, because of the poor state of health of the new arrivals, this had increased to 8.9 per cent in Benaco and Lumasi.[11] By the end of November, it had fallen to 3.7 per cent in Lumasi.[12] At its highest, average mortality in Benaco was just under four deaths per 10,000 refugees per day. In the previous chapter we saw that the average crude mortality rate had been much higher in the internally displaced person camps in Rwanda and in the camps for Burundian refugees.

Rwandan refugees in Zaire

After capturing Kigali on 4 July 1994, the RPF continued its military offensive to the south and west of Rwanda, triggering a massive displacement of Rwandan Hutus towards North and South Kivu in Zaire. Their numbers grew considerably between 14 and 18–19 July, when RPF forces sealed the border crossing near Goma. Sixty-eight international MSF staff were working in the Goma area at the time, and by the end of August, they had increased to 166.

In mid-July, the number of Rwandan refugees arriving in North Kivu was estimated to be somewhere between 800,000 and 1,000,000. MSF, UNHCR and the other humanitarian organisations based themselves on the higher figure, as it was impossible to obtain a more accurate headcount during this surge. MSF noticed among the refugees 'the visible presence of well-armed soldiers (20,000?)', members of the FAR who had been defeated by the RPF.[13] On 24 July, MSF reported that the number of arrivals in South Kivu was also unsure; UNHCR had announced an influx of 200,000 refugees in Bukavu on 20 July, but on 24 July, MSF estimated them to be just 50,000.

During the month of July, the German, New Zealand and Canadian air forces flew in humanitarian aid to Goma airport, which was under French army control. Several military forces took part in the relief operations in east Zaire, not only American (from 24 July until the end of August) but also French, Dutch, Israeli

[10] MSF, UNHCR, AICF, UNICEF, 'Report of a nutrition survey in Benaco', 11 June 1994.
[11] UNHCR, 'Nutrition survey report. Benaco & Lumasi, Rwandan refugee camps Ngara district, Tanzania', 29 August 1994.
[12] MSF, 'Report of nutrition survey in Lumasi', 28 November 1994.
[13] MSF Belgium, 'Rwandan Crisis. Situation report, 18–24 July 94', 28 July 1994.

Map 2.2 Rwandan refugee camps, Goma (Zaire)

and Japanese troops.[14] The presence of these armed forces prompted the refugees to settle as soon as they crossed the border. Although this facilitated the task of the humanitarian organisations working out of Goma (North Kivu) and Bukavu (South Kivu), it also gave the leaders and perpetrators of the genocide the opportunity to establish their authority in camps near the border while profiting from international assistance.[15]

In North Kivu, almost 50,000 refugees died within a month of arrival, with an average daily mortality rate of 25–30 deaths per 10,000 refugees. This high mortality

---

[14] The activities of all the contingents were studied by a team of specialists tasked with evaluating humanitarian operations in Rwanda, Tanzania and Eastern Zaire. See Borton *et al.*, *Humanitarian Aid and Effects*, p. 40 and pp. 58–69.

[15] Terry, *Condemned to Repeat?*, pp. 172–3.

was caused mainly by cholera and dysentery epidemics.[16] A cholera epidemic was confirmed on 19 July and MSF immediately set up five cholera treatment centres (CTC) in three camps (two in Kitale, two in Kibumba and one in Munigi) and another in Goma at the beginning of August. At the start of the epidemic, the situation was catastrophic. Between 22 and 30 July, there were up to 1,000 admissions a day to the treatment centre in Munigi camp, 1,200 to the centres in Kibumba and almost 400 in Katale.

By 28 July, the admission rate had begun to slow down in Kibumba and Katale and UNHCR announced that the situation was no longer critical: 'The cholera epidemic in the Rwandan refugee camps in Goma may be considered over, which does not mean that cholera has disappeared from the camps, said UNHCR spokesman Ray Wilkinson on Thursday. The mortality rate is still falling and there are now 500 deaths per day, compared with almost 2,000 last week.'[17] Yet, at the end of August, there was no end in sight for MSF's medical teams because, although the organisation considered that the cholera epidemic was under control in the camps, meningitis had broken out at the end of July, a dysentery epidemic that had appeared in July was spreading and the global acute malnutrition rate among children aged under five years stood at 21.3 per cent.

During August and September, MSF worked in Mugunga, Kibumba and Katale camps, as well as in Goma itself. On 28 July, MSF took charge of water provision in Kibumba. Throughout August, the cholera treatment centres in the camps were progressively converted into hospitals. The main activities in August and September were measles and meningitis vaccination, refurbishing hospitals and clinics, conducting epidemiological surveys (demography, mortality, morbidity, nutrition, vaccination coverage and medical activities), distributing dry rations to all children under five years, opening nutrition centres in the camps and sanitation. In Goma town, MSF provided nutrition treatment for unaccompanied children suffering from malnutrition. Epicentre's epidemiologists conducted an assessment of the nutrition situation in the orphanages and, finding the situation to be critical, a nutritional rehabilitation centre was opened on 24 August 1994.

MSF launched activities in Bukavu, South Kivu on 22 July. Most of the refugees, around 50,000 people, had settled in the town itself when they first arrived and were still living out in the open, so this is where MSF got down to work. On 23 August, the organisation opened a dispensary in Alphagéry, a college/seminary where about 20,000 people had found refuge, and then set up a cholera and dysentery isolation unit near the general hospital. In August, as the nutrition situation worsened and with no food distributions in the town, MSF and several other NGOs began

---

[16] Goma Epidemiology Group, 'Public health impact of Rwandan refugee crisis: what happened in Goma, Zaire, in July, 1994?', *The Lancet*, 345:8946 (11 February 1995), 339–44. See also L. Roberts and M. J. Toole, 'Cholera deaths in Goma', *The Lancet*, 346:8987 (25 November 1995), 1431.

[17] AFP, 'Cholera outbreak almost over, says UNHCR', Goma, 4 August 1994.

Table 2.2 Mortality: weekly crude mortality rate and child mortality rate (under five) in Katale, North Kivu

Katale, 1994		
25–31 July	50/10,000/day	
14 July–4 August	41.3/10,000/day	<5yrs= 40.4/10,000/day
15–21 August	4.6/10,000/day	<5yrs= 15.5/10,000/day
29 August–4 September	3.70/10,000/day	<5yrs= 10.11/10,000/day
5–11 September	1.2/10,000/day	

Source: MSF epidemiological data, Katale, 1994

distributing porridge to all malnourished children under the age of five years and set up a soupe populaire ['soup kitchen'] for Zairian and refugee children and visibly destitute adults alike.[18] In agreement with WFP, the Zairian authorities had decided not to distribute dry rations in the town to make it easier to move the refugees on.

In August, UNHCR began urging the refugees to move out of Bukavu town and into the camps, but some 15,000 to 20,000 still remained in mid-September and MSF pursued some of its nutrition and sanitation activities.[19] Outside the town, operations were first launched in Chimanga and Kalehe and then Inera, Hongo and Kashusha. Programmes and the duration of operations varied from camp to camp according to the medical, sanitation and nutrition situation but also to the risks posed by the presence of ex-FAR soldiers and the power exerted by Rwandan leaders handling discipline (and indiscipline) among the refugees. The team in Chimanga was thus evacuated on 7 August when around 2,000 ex-FAR soldiers arrived on the site. In Kashusha, despite security incidents and worrying rumours, MSF managed to implement and maintain a broad range of activities for a longer period and took responsibility for health and emergency sanitation.

> In Kashusha, the heads of security and the intelligence service, both accused by other refugees of having a dubious past, reign supreme over the camp. Several members of our staff have been on the receiving end of barely veiled threats or robbed, with total impunity for the guilty – and identified – parties. Rumours are spreading about MSF's supposed role in infiltrating Tutsis and RPF spies into the camp.[20]

MSF later limited its intervention to the emergency phase. The organisation took charge of settling refugees into the new Kamanyola camp (water provision, medical examinations for new arrivals and measles vaccination), and again in Kabira from

---

[18] N. de Torrente, 'L'action de MSF dans la crise rwandaise. Un historique critique. Avril-Décembre 1994', July 1995, MSF, Paris, p. 57 and MSF Holland, 'Regional Report', 26 August 1994.

[19] Torrente, 'L'action de MSF dans la crise rwandaise', p. 58.

[20] MSF Bukavu, 'Bukavu-Zaire mission, Kashusha mission report – Inera 2, 24 July 1994 to 24 October 1994', October 1994.

Map 2.3 Rwandan refugee camps, Bukavu (Zaire)

28 September, providing medical check-ups for people registering in the camp, as well as measles immunisation and dispensary services. However, at the beginning of November, the whole team was evacuated following death threats against a Rwandan nurse and rumours that the MSF hospital was to be looted and that 'the militia were going to "sort out" anyone suspected of being a Tutsi'.[21]

As in Tanzania, former Rwandan dignitaries controlled aid distribution and beneficiary lists, resulting in the same massive diversion of food and the exclusion of certain refugees who thus received only irregular assistance, if any. In Katale in North Kivu, for example, MSF estimated that 24 per cent of refugees were receiving

---

[21] MSF Bukavu, 'Situation à Kabira', 6 November 1994. Following are the population estimates used by MSF at the end of September: 40,000 refugees in Kashusha, 65,000 in Inera 1 and 2, 10,000 in Kalehe and 24,000 in Hongo. See MSF France, 'Activity Report, Bukavu', 30 September 1994. There were 23,000 refugees in Kabira at the end of October.

insufficient food rations (fewer than 2,100 kcal per person per day). To help prevent this diversion of aid, MSF recommended carrying out headcounts to better
assess needs and adjust the amount of food distributed accordingly. But, according
to MSF and other NGOs, refugee numbers were for several months based on dubi-
ous and 'unreliable' estimates. The first estimate was adjusted downwards in August
1994 on the basis of aerial photos and then again at the end of September. UNHCR
had initially adopted the figure of 1.2 million refugees in North Kivu but, by the end
of September, this was reduced to 850,000.[22] So for some time, aid budgets, mostly
allocated to food, were based on overestimates and funded food surpluses that were
a real jackpot for the extremist leaders, helping them to garner and organise the support of their followers.

MSF and other NGOs repeatedly stressed the importance of registering the
refugees. In a communiqué signed by sixteen relief organisations (including three
MSF sections), reliable headcounts were one of the conditions for them to continue to provide assistance: 'Security must be ensured to permit the official and
independent registration of refugees.'[23] On 7 November, the whole MSF movement reiterated the plea: 'Registration should take place as soon as possible in
Goma in order to ensure that all refugees have access to humanitarian relief.'[24] The
view was shared by the UN agencies (especially UNHCR) and other humanitarian organisations. For its part, MSF based its estimates on aerial photos of shelters,
vaccination coverage and surveys. 'In order to describe the camp's population,
estimate the mortality since the arrival of the refugees in Zaire and measure the
nutrition status of children under 5, we conducted a household cluster sample
survey in Katale on August 4th, 1994.'[25] Shortly afterwards, in Katale, where the
refugee population was estimated to be 110,000, the daily mortality rate between
8 August and 11 September was based on the count of bodies who died in the
internal displaced persons camps. 'In Katale few people are thought to be buried
by relatives and a check on the body count suggests it gives a reasonably accurate
estimate of deaths under 5 years and total deaths.' The author of this report recommended that, in Katale, MSF should use the weekly data gathered by the Centers
for Disease Control and Prevention (CDC) on behalf of UNHCR and suggested
that 'the Epicentre report is not necessary as it duplicates information summarised by UNHCR/CDC.'[26]

[22] Borton *et al.*, *Humanitarian Aid and Effects*, pp. 110–112. From the end of August, MSF Holland adopted
the estimate of 850,000 refugees in the Goma region, 400,000 of whom were not living in the camps.

[23] 'Joint declaration by International Organisations working in the Goma refugee camps', 2 November 1994.

[24] MSF USA, 'Appeal to the Security Council. Call for immediate action in Rwandan refugee camps',
7 November 1994.

[25] Epicentre, MSF Belgium, MSF Holland, 'Demography, mortality and nutrition survey, Katale camp, August
4th, 1994, preliminary report', August 1994.

[26] MSF Holland, 'Report on epidemiological data. Katale refugee camp. Short visit to Katale/Goma: 26th
August – 16th September 1994', September 1994.

In 1995, a registration operation implemented at the instigation of UNHCR in nine camps in North Kivu and in Goma town resulted in the figure of 721,000 refugees whereas, before the registration, this had been 850,000.[27] This difference of 129,000 was due partly to refugees returning to Rwanda and partly to an overestimation of the number of refugees.

When UNHCR decided to organise censuses, MSF was on the frontline in some of North Kivu's camps. In February 1995, for example, MSF was tasked with supervising counting operations in Kibumba and met with such violent resistance that the organisation reported to UNHCR: 'On many occasions and on several of the counting sites, the militia have organised very violent attacks on the refugees to prevent them from being included in the UNHCR's census ... Threats have been made against our national staff, putting their safety at considerable risk.'[28] On Wednesday 26 January, the census process was suspended after massive fraud and growing insecurity at census sites. It was resumed with increased surveillance and MSF agreed to participate. In a press release issued in Brussels on 7 February 1995, the organisation reported that its resistance to misappropriations was endangering its team in Kibumba and so was suspending its work in this camp.[29] The press release went on to explain that in other camps in North Kivu the conditions in which the census was carried out were different and MSF would be maintaining its activities in Kahindo, Katale and Kituku.

In South Kivu, a first census organised by UNHCR was carried out between 28 February and 7 March 1995, both in Bukavu and in the camps. Whereas UNHCR had previously estimated there to be 355,000 refugees, the census registered 302,000 spread among twenty-five camps and four centres for unaccompanied minors.[30]

At the end of December 1995, an Agence France Presse journalist related his visit to Kivu. He commented that the camps looked built to last and indeed, as people settled in for long periods, they frequently became a hive of economic activity, with all kinds of businesses growing up. 'Almost a million Rwandan Hutu refugees are still established in Zaire ... there are some 750,000 refugees in Goma and between 200,000 and 300,000 in Bukavu and they have become firmly established in camps which have grown into large villages with food shops, various kinds of stores and even night clubs.'[31] The term large village is bizarre, as several camps had over 100,000 people in them and the paths carved out by bulldozers when the camps were set up were fast becoming 'streets full of shops and small businesses. There were even restaurants and

[27] UNHCR/Goma, 'Sitrep No. 20', 21 March 1995, cited by A. Royer, 'L'instrumentalisation politique des réfugiés du Kivu entre 1994 et 1996', in A. Guichaoua (ed.), Exilés, réfugiés, déplacés en Afrique centrale et orientale (Paris: Karthala, 2004), p. 440.

[28] MSF Belgium to the UNHCR Director for Africa, 'Developments in the situation in Goma, Zaire', Brussels, 6 February 1995.

[29] MSF Belgium, 'Press Release, Violence, threats and frauds during the census of Rwandan refugees: MSF pulls out of Kibumba camp', 7 February 1995.

[30] Royer, 'L'instrumentalisation politique des réfugiés du Kivu entre 1994 et 1996', p. 439 and Borton et al., Humanitarian Aid and Effects.

[31] AFP, 'Près d'un million de réfugiés rwandais toujours établis au Zaïre', Goma, 28 December 1995.

several hotels made out of tarpaulins and bits of junk, as well as some more or less clan-destine bars substituting for Rwanda's cabarets, and cinemas showing videos'.[32] People had small plots, either inside the camps near the shelters or outside. Anthropologist Johan Pottier, who carried out a survey in 1995, observed that in Lumasi (Tanzania) the majority of refugees grew some food around their shelters, whereas in North Kivu they sometimes had access to cultivable land outside the camps.[33]

Insecurity and the power of the leaders

Violence in Benaco was a source of constant concern for aid workers, as confirmed in the field teams' correspondence and the reports and statements produced by desk officers and directors at MSF's head offices.

For example, in a report addressed to Paris on 6 June 1994, MSF's coordinator in Ngara wrote: 'The security situation is getting worse, both in Benaco and on the border. In Benaco, a refugee was lynched last Saturday [4 June]; an investigation is underway … Thefts are becoming more and more frequent and we are not the only victims.'[34] A week later, the report from Ngara was even more alarming: 'In just one week there have been five officially-acknowledged murders (four lynchings and one person hacked to death … A team from MSF Holland witnessed the slaughter of the latter victim. The teams really must start taking security instructions a bit more seri-ously and get out of the camp quickly in the evening.' The author of this report was more than sceptical about the measures adopted by UNHCR: '300 people have been recruited. All they have is a torch and a badge. They can arrest people and turn them over to UNHCR, which deals with handing them over to the Tanzanians. We don't like to use the term "militia", but we have to admit that's what they look like.'[35] This was not an initiative of the Tanzanian authorities but a measure taken by the camp's UNHCR administrators. They had recruited men recommended by the Rwandan leaders, regardless of the role they might have had in the genocide. Indeed, UNHCR had nei-ther the knowledge nor the means to ascertain which refugees had been involved in the mass execution of Tutsis. In June 1994, the Tanzanian authorities decided to set up a security force in the camps, but it would take another four months and considerable pressure from international aid agencies for this force to be deployed.

Nothing changed during the second half of June and MSF's teams, extremely concerned about the violence flaring up in Benaco and the number of murders, remained on high alert.

---

[32] R. Pourtier, 'Les camps du Kivu ou la gestion de l'éphémère', in V. Lassailly-Jacob et al. (eds), Déplacés et réfugiés. La mobilité sous contrainte (Paris: Éditions de l'IRD, 1999), pp. 457–8. The observations of this geographer were collected during a mission in Kivu carried out in February–March 1996.

[33] J. Pottier, 'Why aid agencies need better understanding of the communities they assist: the experience of food aid in Rwandan refugee camps', Disasters, 20:4 (1996), 331–2.

[34] MSF, 'Sitrep Ngara, Tanzania', 6 June 1994.

[35] MSF, 'Sitrep Ngara, Tanzania', 13 June 1994.

In Benaco camp lived a Hutu leader [Jean-Baptiste Gatete] who was the former Chief of Cabinet to the Minister for Family Affairs. He has been widely accused as having been involved in the genocide. On the night of 15 June 1994, the Hutu leader was invited by UNHCR to discuss him leaving the camp. Within minutes a violent crowd of several thousand people, armed with machetes and sticks, surrounded the tent in which the discussions were held. They demanded that he could stay in the camp. The crowd dispersed only after the Tanzanian police shot in the air. Aid workers who had been trapped in the tent were then able to get away. As a result of this incident all foreign staff of the aid agencies was temporarily evacuates. The Hutu leader, however, was able to stay.[36]

On his return to Paris after a field trip to Benaco, MSF's general director described this riot at a press conference held on 17 June: 'Right now, we can't return to the camp. We're on a sort of aid strike.' He denounced the diversion of aid and trafficking orchestrated by the leaders: 'Every night, trucks come into the camp and carry off humanitarian aid intended for the refugees. It's a major trafficking operation designed to further the interests of these leaders ... We have stood by and watched and even helped these executioners to use international humanitarian aid to rehabilitate themselves. It's sickening.'[37] Not all MSF's sections supported these statements and denunciations. On 23 June, MSF Holland, working in Benaco at the time, addressed a letter to MSF France and MSF International expressing its disagreement:

> We all know that on many occasions MSF has been working for refugees and persons who were suspected of serious violations of human rights. For MSF the indiscriminate delivery of humanitarian assistance to people in need is one of the most fundamental principles which flows directly from our Charter. Of course, it is MSF position that these persons should be brought to justice. However, it is not the MSF mandate to establish the guilt of the alleged perpetrators.
>
> However, it is obvious that the fact that the alleged perpetrators of genocide who are reported to have taken control over the situation in Benaco camp has created a serious security risk for all agencies working there.

MSF Holland's letter concluded by calling on MSF to demand that UNHCR 'take all necessary steps to prevent these alleged perpetrators from continuing to be a serious threat to the security and to exert control over the situation in the camp.'[38]

This confrontation reveals the difference in political tone adopted by the two MSF sections: on the one hand, one of vehemence and indignation and, on the

---

[36] MSF Holland, *Breaking the Cycle*, 10 November 1994, p. 10.

[37] AFP, Paris, 'MSF dénonce l'utilisation d'un camp de réfugiés rwandais en Tanzanie, comme "base arrière" des forces hutues', 17 June 1994.

[38] MSF Holland, 'MSF-H position regarding the continuation of our programmes in Benaco Camp', Amsterdam, 23 June 1994.

other, a formally-expressed argument drawing on the 'mandates' of the MSF movement and UNHCR. These conflicting arguments might appear to reflect the canonical distinction between ethics or politics of conviction on one side and ethics or politics of responsibility on the other, but this is not really the case. Although the language is different, the two presentations of the context are consistent and both sections express a similar desire to impugn the criminals, with one referring to them as the 'alleged perpetrators' and the other as 'bourreaux' ['executioners'].

From then on, the MSF sections present in the Tanzanian camps regularly sent their respective headquarters reports on security incidents and the measures taken by UNHCR and the Tanzanian authorities to try to remedy them. MSF Holland's report on the security and protection of Rwandan refugees disseminated within the MSF movement on 30 October 1994 is an example of this.[39] This report followed a field survey carried out between 27 August and 13 December in Ngara and the camps in the district (mainly in Benaco). Beginning with a reminder of the statute of UNHCR and its mandate to protect refugees, the author went on to stress the leaders' well-established power and the relative weakness of UNHCR in dealing with them and their acolytes: 'The leaders are respected by the camp population; most of the leaders participated in the genocide.' After insisting on the climate of hate against Tutsis and RPF, the report listed the incidents witnessed by international staff from the different MSF sections and UNHCR personnel. Thus:

> On 29 August 1994, Z. witnessed the lynching of a man outside UNHCR's registration office in Benaco camp. An angry crowd started to shout and throw stones, accusing the man of being a RPF spy. The Rwandan guards present at the scene did not intervene … It took the Tanzanian police a long time to arrive. The victim was then taken to the German Red Cross hospital where he died an hour later.

In another incident at the end of August, a truck transporting Tutsis refugees back to Rwanda was involved in a road accident and some of the refugees were injured. They were taken to the Red Cross hospital in Benaco. A crowd of men armed with knives and sticks formed outside the hospital and began demonstrating against the injured Tutsis. The situation rapidly became 'explosive and unpredictable' and UNHCR had to evacuate the injured to Rwanda. In six of the eight incidents described in the report, the men acted in groups or even crowds and in public.

The murders, brutality and threats in the camps were directed at Rwandan Tutsis and Rwandan Hutus accused of spying for the RPF. In most cases, these refugees' lives were at risk. MSF Holland's report included data gathered in July and August by UNHCR confirming sixty major protection incidents, including twenty murders in the camps in north-west Tanzania and the area bordering Rwanda. Additional

---

[39] MSF Holland, 'Emergency Team, Report on security and protection of Rwandese refugees in Kagera region, Tanzania, 27 August–13 September 1994', 26 September 1994.

confirmation was provided: on 20 August, the UNHCR manager announced during an inter-agency meeting that nineteen Tutsis had been killed in Benaco camp the previous week. The MSF France coordinator reported that sixteen people had been killed in Lumasi camp that same week.[40]

In August 1994, MSF's international council decided to send an MSF volunteer to Zaire and Tanzania to take charge of the security and protection of the refugees. This decision was taken on the basis of a critical assessment: UNHCR was not guaranteeing the security and protection of the refugees. MSF therefore decided 'to monitor the security situation closely and urge UNHCR to step up its protection activities'. MSF Holland appointed the person tasked with this mission and he, with the help of his colleagues in Goma, defined the responsibilities: maintaining contacts, holding interviews and producing regular reports on incidents and developments, weekly updates and an end-of-mission report that would include recommendations.[41]

We consulted the second weekly report on the Goma area for the period 28 August to 4 September. The author reported on his visit to the three camps (Katale, Kibumba and Mugunga in North Kivu) where MSF was working. His immediate conclusion was that the security situation was still unstable. He also mentioned the effects of rumours in Katale. At the beginning of September, there was a rumour that all the refuges had to leave Zaire before the end of the month and that the NGOs were leaving in three days' time. Refugees then attacked the aid distribution facility belonging to relief organisation CARE. Tensions were calmed thanks to the mediation of Rwandan scouts with the camp's dignitaries. These scouts were young people equipped only with whistles, as they were tasked with controlling traffic inside the camps. UNHCR had suggested them as an acceptable alternative to the militia for certain policing duties.

According to this same report, banditry was the main risk in Kibumba, especially on the road taken by aid workers returning to their accommodation in Goma. This was in stark contrast to Mugunga 'soldiers' camp' (there were many ex-FAR soldiers in Mugunga), where the security situation appeared to be stable. Lastly, the MSF investigator stressed the limitations of his interviews with the handful of refugees he had questioned about the situation in the camps: 'Incidents are reported, but it remains unclear who exactly can be alleged to be the instigator. My position is that it is extremely difficult to obtain reliable information, as refugees and local staff give, maybe out of fear, a very "coloured" view.'[42] At the beginning of November, the MSF coordinator in Bukavu learnt from her staff members, themselves informed by patients, that the militia intended to loot Kabira hospital and sort out two

---

[40] MSF Holland, 'Emergency Team'.

[41] 'Message sent by Amsterdam to MSF-H Goma, Terms of Reference for the security/protection officer', 15 August 1994.

[42] MSF Holland, 'Officer for monitoring protection of the refugees, Preliminary Hand-over Report', 7 September 1994.

employees suspected of being Tutsis. Similar to her colleague investigating the situation in Goma, the author went on to say how difficult it was to get beyond appearances in the camp to grasp what was really going on: 'On the surface, the situation in Kabira looked to be much more under control. But we know nothing about the underground organisation, real or not.'[43] In Tanzania, according to a UNHCR senior field manager, 'A "war of silence" is going on in the camps ... Nobody knows with certainty what is going on in terms of violence.'[44]

It was common knowledge in the dispensaries and on the logistics sites that rumours circulating in the camps could spur violent groups into action at any time, but it was equally plain that most refugees, those who the anthropologist Johan Pottier called 'ordinary citizens', were keeping well out of the way.[45] It was not to these people that the MSF coordinators were referring in the security incident reports they sent to headquarters. They related the circumstances of incidents, who had been targeted and why, which MSF workers had been present and sometimes threatened or attacked and the measures that had been taken to protect the team and patients, preserve the working conditions for the medical and logistics team and notify and mobilise UNHCR's management. We consulted the reports on the incidents related by the MSF coordinator in Bukavu between September and the end of October 1994. We did not find any statistical reports summarising data on security incidents that occurred during this period, but we do know what type of violence was recorded: murders of refugees, riots, attacks on aid workers, thefts, looting and racketeering. Some forms of violence do not appear in these reports, notably rape or attempted rape.[46] At the beginning of October, MSF France's coordinator in Ngara became aware that such incidents were occurring but had no direct knowledge of specific cases: 'Rumours are circulating of women raped at water distribution points and single women being forced into the prostitution industry.'[47] At the time, MSF did not have a programme specifically designed for female rape victims in the camps.

Attempts to maintain order in the camps and repatriate refugees

In July 1994, the United Nations High Commissioner for Refugees, Sadako Ogata, announced that the agency was in favour of the rapid repatriation of refugees to Rwanda, but at the beginning of August, she temporarily gave up encouraging people to return. Nonetheless, between mid-July and mid-September 1994, almost 200,000 Rwandan Hutu refugees had allegedly been willing to be repatriated. Meanwhile, MSF appealed for the deployment (in south-west Rwanda) of an international

[43] MSF Bukavu, 'Situation à Kabira', 6 November 1994. At the beginning of November, there were 23,000 people in Kabira camp, South Kivu.
[44] MSF Holland, 'Emergency Team'.
[45] Pottier, 'Why aid agencies need better understanding of the communities they assist', 326.
[46] C. Newbury, 'Suffering and survival in Central Africa', *African Studies Review*, 48:3 (2005), 126.
[47] MSF-France, Coordinators in N'gara to the Emergency Unit, 'Rwandan crisis', 4 October 1994.

military force to guarantee their return in normal conditions, considering this essential to enable the refugees to overcome their fear (3 August). This message came in anticipation of the planned departure on 22 August of Operation Turquoise soldiers deployed by France on a United Nations mandate in southwest Rwanda since 22 June. On 10 August, a press release issued in Brussels called for 'the recent rumours of "disappearances" on the RPF side to be urgently investigated by specialist organisations'. The same press release and other public statements by MSF claimed 'the massive return of refugees to their home country remains the only solution', but for that to happen 'the refuges needed assurances that they would be treated correctly on their return'. MSF therefore called for the widespread deployment of human rights workers in Rwanda on the grounds 'that the massive presence of observers would foster a greater feeling of security', a recommendation the organisation was to reiterate on numerous occasions.

Also on 10 August, the President of the UNSC declared the rapid return of refugees and displaced persons to their homes to be essential and denounced the former leaders of Rwanda for urging refugees to stay in exile. The UNSC then congratulated the new Rwandan government on its undertakings towards the refugees and confirmed it was willing to ensure their protection and respect for their legal rights. The findings of a survey conducted by UNHCR were then yet to be revealed; at the end of July, UNHCR had appointed a team to carry out an investigation in the refugee camps and in Rwanda to explore possibilities for 'accelerating' the safe return of the refugees. Led by Robert Gersony, the survey took place between 1 August and 5 September 1994. The content of the resulting Gersony report was certainly not what its commissioners and the Rwandan government had hoped for as it provided evidence that, between April and August 1994, the RPF had executed around 30,000 people in the zones under its control in Rwanda.[48] The United Nations immediately prevented the public dissemination of this report, with some UN officials even going so far as to deny its existence. Yet, by September, the international press had begun publishing some of its conclusions. The news soon reached the camps, putting a stop to refugee returns and resulting in another temporary suspension of repatriations by UNHCR.

In a communiqué published on 21 October, UNHCR denounced the threatening presence of soldiers, militia and former civilian authorities in the camps: 'Refugees who said they wanted to be repatriated were terrorised and more than a dozen assassinated.' On 2 November, sixteen NGOs, including three MSF sections, strongly and publicly came out in support of UNHCR's position. Like UNHCR, they

---

[48] Since 1994, only a 14-page summary of the Gersony report has been available. Signed UNHCR Emergency Repatriation Team, this document was entitled: *Summary of UNHCR presentation before Commission of Experts, 10 October 1994. Prospects for early repatriation of Rwandan refugees currently in Burundi, Tanzania and Zaire.* This report is published on the site http://en.wikipedia.org/wiki/Gersony_Report, consulted on 5 April 2001.

condemned the violence against the refugees and the threats that were making them 'hostages'. They were being denied the right to return to their places of origin. This message was repeated in a number of public communications, including in an appeal to the UNSC on 17 November 1994: 'Each refugee has to be free to decide whether to stay or to leave the camps without fear for his or her life.'[49] On 10 November 1994, in a public report on the situation of Rwandan refugees living in camps in Zaire and Tanzania, MSF again warned that the situation was worsening and that the leaders were threatening volunteers for repatriation: 'MSF has witnessed meetings during which refugees are discouraged from returning to Rwanda. Anyone who questions the leaders' authority is seen as an agent of the RPF and subjected to summary justice.'[50]

In their joint press release of 2 November 1994, the sixteen signatory NGOs (including MSF Holland, France and Belgium) had declared their security and working conditions to be unacceptable. They considered that security had deteriorated to such an extent that they would be forced to withdraw their assistance if nothing were done to remedy the situation. This communiqué supported the stance taken by UNHCR published on 21 October denouncing the threats being made against aid workers and the terrorising of refugees wishing to return home. On 7 November, in a statement to the UNSC published in New York, MSF asked for an international security force to be deployed immediately in order to maintain order and security in the camps and protect the refugees. By this time, the main foreign contingents had left Zaire and the armed forces ensuring security in Kivu were made up of Zairian 'red beret' para-commandos, whose behaviour only further increased tensions and insecurity.

On 18 November, the UN Secretary General proposed a number of solutions to the UNSC. One was to deploy a peacekeeping force of between 3,000 and 5,000 men inside the camps in Kivu to be tasked with establishing 'security zones' within the camps. Another was for an intervention by 10,000 to 12,000 men whose mission would be to transfer former political leaders, soldiers and militia to new camps. They would be transferred, 'if possible, voluntarily', but 'we should assume that they will not go of their own accord and are likely to use force to prevent us from evicting them'. This option implied acting under Chapter VII of the UN Charter, which authorises the use of force. In fact, the UNSC did not adopt any of the Secretary General's proposals but asked him to consult countries capable of providing men for a 5,000-strong peacekeeping operation in the camps. On 25 January 1995, the Secretary General informed the UNSC that it would be impossible to assemble the necessary troops, as only one country was willing to participate. So, instead of an international force, the decision was taken to deploy a Zairian Camp Security Contingent (ZCSC) to be paid by UNHCR. Comprising soldiers from the Special Presidential Division (SPD), this contingent

---

[49] MSF USA, 'Call for immediate action in Rwandan refugee camps', New York, 7 November 1994.
[50] MSF Holland, *Breaking the Cycle*.

was despatched to North Kivu (1,000 men) and South Kivu (500 men) in March 1995. Because of the close ties between President Mobutu and high-ranking ex-FAR officers present in Zaire, no action was ever taken against the political and military leaders in the camps. Moreover, these SPD forces engaged in illegal commercial dealings and committed violence against the refugees.[51]

In July 1995, MSF's observations were still pessimistic.[52] Between December 1994 and March 1995, UNHCR had transported 12,775 refugees to Rwanda, but in April repatriation had come to a virtual standstill due to the deteriorating situation within Rwanda. MSF attributed this to the influence of anti-RPF leaders and the climate of fear created by arbitrary arrests and reprisal killings. In April, during the forced closure of the internal displaced persons camps in south-west Rwanda, the Rwandan Patriotic Army (RPA) killed 'more internally displaced than it was possible to count'. It was in these terms that the *Deadlock in the Rwandan Refugee Crisis* report recounted the massacre on 22 April 1995 in Kibeho camp in south-west Rwanda, considering it one of the main barriers to repatriation.[53]

> MSF would like to ensure that it does not place the massacre in Kibeho on the same footing as the 1994 genocide in Rwanda. Apart from the fact that MSF was a witness to the Kibeho massacre, this massacre is mentioned in this report because the events have proven to be one of the main factors seriously inhibiting repatriation.[54]

After the Kibeho massacre, UNHCR suspended its repatriation operations. But in August 1995, the Zairian government announced that the refugees had until 31 December 1995 to leave the country. UNHCR launched an information campaign promoting repatriation, but to little avail.

Stay or leave (October 1994 to August 1995)?

In September and October 1994, MSF's various sections discussed whether to withdraw from the camps. According to the minutes of a meeting held in Kigali on 14 October and attended by all the sections working in the Great Lakes region at the time: 'No-one is planning to pack up and leave tomorrow.' Although opinions differed on whether or not to leave, a consensus was reached on the need to consider – as an ultimate action – the possibility of pulling out of camps.[55] After the meeting,

---

[51] UNHCR/Goma, 'Sitrep n° 28, 6 December 1995', quoted by Royer, 'L'instrumentalisation politique des réfugiés du Kivu', pp. 484–5.

[52] MSF Holland, *Deadlock in the Rwandan Refugee Crisis: Virtual Standstill on Repatriation*, Amsterdam, July 1995.

[53] MSF Holland, *Deadlock in the Rwandan Refugee Crisis*, pp. 32–4.

[54] MSF Holland, *Deadlock in the Rwandan Refugee Crisis*, p. 33.

[55] MSF international and MSF Belgium, 'Report on the visit to the Rwandan refugee camps by the international council', 17 November 1994.

the Dutch section established a list of criteria that would justify its putting a stop to its relief operations:

a) MSF's assistance is not reaching the most vulnerable and those most in need.
b) We are supporting a militarised system and our support has more negative effects than positive.
c) Our advocacy is not effective and we have no other advocacy initiatives to propose.
d) Other.[56]

Before taking any decision to withdraw, operations in progress had to be evaluated and the conditions for continuing them made known. On 27 October, MSF Holland was not planning to pull out – regardless of what MSF France decided to do. It came as no surprise to the sections opposed to withdrawal (MSF Holland, Belgium and Switzerland) when, on 28 October, MSF France's board of directors voted to pull out of all the camps in Tanzania and Zaire. However, it was a real shock when this decision was made public on 7 November, without the President of the French section first informing the rest of the movement.[57] From then on, the disagreement took on a whole new dimension, triggering a crisis within the MSF movement. Mutual accusations abounded.

For MSF Belgium's coordinator in Goma, 'withdrawal is synonymous with silence'. He said he was confident that 'there is room for manoeuvre in the field … I am in favour of a policy of humanitarian resistance in Goma but against simply accepting the situation. This may seem naive, but it's just as naive to think that MSF can change the course of events all on its own by pulling out'.[58] In January 1995, the same manager declared that humanitarian aid was 'without the slightest doubt, feeding a monster … And this monster is arming itself to fight back, using a captive population as a shield. What if working in the camps means becoming the accomplices of the perpetrators of the genocide? Dilemma …'. He responded to his final question by recommending yet again a 'policy of humanitarian resistance', fiercely opposing withdrawal and refuting accusations of 'collaboration'.

> Are we accomplices? Most definitely not … MSF still has, in association with the main NGOs, some room for manoeuvre to influence to a certain extent the situation. We have to use all our operational resources to do so. But if it reaches the stage where we no longer have this room for manoeuvre (too much insecurity, no real impact), the conditions for our presence in Goma will no longer be met and we will have no choice but to withdraw.[59]

---

[56] 'Memo from MSF Holland's department of humanitarian affairs to teams in Kigali, Goma and Benaco', 11 October 1994.

[57] P. Biberson, 'Pourquoi nous quittons le Rwanda', *Ouest-France* (7 November 1994).

[58] MSF Belgium's coordinator in Goma, 'Letter to the Board of Directors. URGENT URGENT', 6 november 1994.

[59] Coordinateur MSF Goma, 'Goma, le monde tourne, le génocide continue', 23 November 1995.

MSF France defended its decision to withdraw by publicly condemning the continuation of humanitarian relief. According to Paris, staying meant giving free reign to the perpetrators of the genocide, affording them legitimacy, becoming their accomplices.[60] This justification for ending relief operations is based on exactly the same observation as that made by the Belgian coordinator in Goma: humanitarian aid is feeding a 'monster'. So the same analysis justified both resistance (MSF Belgium) and withdrawal (MSF France). However, points of view did converge on the very real link between identifiable men's past involvement in the genocide and the nature of these men's behaviour in the camps (misappropriation of aid, propaganda abusing refugees, criminal acts, setting up militias, calls to war, blocking repatriation). MSF France spokespeople emphasised this link in several of their statements: the perpetrators of the genocide had not changed course but were building up their strength in the camps to perhaps resume the genocide in Rwanda. The organisation adopted this same message and issued the same warnings when pulling out of Tanzania, which was announced at a press conference in Nairobi on 20 December 1994. MSF reiterated yet again its call for an international police force. A dispatch from Agence France Presse summarised the section's main argument: 'Is it acceptable to continue supplying aid to a "sanctuary" from which a military force will be able to launch an attack on Rwanda and perhaps finish the genocide started in April?'[61]

From then on, the assertion that continuing to deliver assistance was a form of complicity with the perpetrators of the genocide became a constant feature in MSF France's communication. This is what the desk manager in Paris had to say in a letter dated 24 December 1994 informing the UNHCR desk officer for Tanzania of the closure of the medical programme in Lumasi: 'We consider that it is no longer possible for our organisation to participate in relief operations that afford renewed legitimacy to the perpetrators of the genocide and provide them with the material means to resume it.' Some of the field team in Tanzania were not convinced by the position adopted by the French section's managers. They felt that the demographics of a camp where three-quarters of the population were women and children under the age of fifteen had not been taken into account. Should the majority of refugees be denied aid because their leaders were involved in the genocide of Tutsis in Rwanda?

A few months later, in July–August 1995, MSF Belgium decided that, from a medical and nutritional point of view, MSF's presence was no longer essential and, on 2 August 1995, the Board of MSF in Belgium voted in favour of closing its humanitarian assistance programme. The organisation informed UNHCR, adding that it was planning to 'look into new opportunities and focus on support to repatriation and

---

[60] On the allegations of complicty in the context of the Rwandan refugee camps, see C. Lepora and R.E. Goodin, *On Complicity and Compromise* (Oxford: Oxford University Press, 2013), pp. 135–6. According to Lepora and Goodin, the accusation of complicity is in this instance not appropriate, 'connivence' might seem to be a more fitting description of the behaviour of humanitarian's NGOs. About the negative consequences of humanitarian action, see Terry, *Condemned to Repeat?*, pp. 195–215.

[61] AFP, 'Après le Zaïre, MSF France quitte les camps de réfugiés rwandais en Tanzanie', 20 December 1994.

trans-border dialogue'.[62] As for MSF Holland's Board, on 8 August 1995, it decided to end its medical activities in the Goma area (Katale camp) and the district of Ngara in Tanzania. Two arguments were advanced to justify this decision. The first was medical: the medical emergency is over in Katale and Benaco (but operations continued in the camps around Uvira in South Kivu where 'the medical situation [was] still unstable'). The second was political: 'The people responsible for the genocide in Rwanda still control the refugee population in the camps ... impunity continues to reign and nobody has been arrested as yet', despite MSF's (and other international NGOs') constant condemnation of the situation since the opening of the camps in Tanzania and Zaire. 'The killers are roaming free' and getting ready for 'another attack'. Furthermore, humanitarian aid was having 'a negative impact in that it is consolidating the current situation in the camps: the power structures are providing a breeding ground for genocide [and lastly] advocacy activities have not brought about any visible changes to the situation in months'.[63]

Zaire, Tanzania and Burundi

For a while, deciding whether to stay or leave was a source of conflict between the MSF sections. Yet the French section and the other operational sections did not disagree about everything. Continuing to work with the 93,000 Rwandan refugees in Burundi was never questioned and no accusations of complicity under cover of humanitarian action were ever made.[64] There were two reasons for this moderation. First of all, the refugees were not militarised, nor were they considered a threat, as they were kept under surveillance and confined to the camps by soldiers from the Burundian army, which had close ties to the new Rwandan government. And second, a health catastrophe had to be averted.

But the refugee camps in Zaire did pose a real threat. Soldiers and militia had assembled there and were dangerously close to the Rwandan border. They had weapons, they were training and they made no attempt to hide their criminal and warmongering intentions. They threatened and executed fellow countrymen because they were or looked like Tutsis, were of mixed parenthood, or suspected of being RPF spies. All the MSF sections made similar observations but their political choices and practices continued to differ between October 1994 and July–August 1995. To what extent was it possible to resist the former civilian and military authorities without endangering the medical teams? Could the United Nations be persuaded to carry out an armed international intervention to contain the former soldiers, militia and

---

[62] MSF Belgium, 'Letter to the Director of the UNHCR's Africa Office', 7 August 1995.

[63] MSF Holland, 'Board decision with respect to presence in the camps in Tanzania and Zaire', 8 August 1995 and 'Withdrawal from Rwandese refugee camps, Fax message to all MSF sections', 27 August 1995.

[64] MSF Belgium, 'Report on the situation for Rwanda', 26 August 1994. According to a report by MSF Holland, there were 210,000 Rwandan refugees in Burundi, 150,000 of whom were living in camps (MSF Holland, 'Regional report, Rwanda crisis 4', 26 August 1994).

their leaders by keeping them away from the other refugees? In October 1994, while one section no longer judged this solution to be possible, the others carried on believing in it for several months more.

The camps in Tanzania were a different matter. There was no militarised force threatening Rwanda, the border was effectively controlled by the RPA and the Tanzanian government was not showing the same indulgence towards Rwanda's former leaders as President Mobutu in Zaire. But the health status of the refugees varied from one camp to the next. In some there was no need for emergency doctors, whereas in others the risk of deterioration had yet to be contained. Lastly, several of the sections adopted the same stance towards the camps in Zaire as in Tanzania, even if the situations were different. This meant the decision could be justified either way – withdrawing from everywhere or instead staying everywhere. Finally, in a message addressed to the whole movement on 27 August 1995, MSF Holland made the following observation with regard to a withdrawal from the camps: all the sections 'now share the same position on this issue'.

In October–November 1996, the RPA, helped by Congolese forces opposed to the Mobutu regime, attacked all the Rwandan refugee camps in Zaire, from South to North Kivu. And, at the end of December, the Tanzanian authorities announced the closure of their camps. In mid-December, the refugees were driven back towards Rwanda en masse. Many of them, afraid to return, attempted to flee to Kenya or Malawi. Most were taken back to the camps before being escorted to the border by the Tanzanian army.

3

The new Rwanda

All MSF staff working in Rwanda when President Habyarimana was assassinated on 6 April 1994 had left the country by 24 April 1994. Before deciding to pull out, some teams tried to provide medical care to the wounded. The Butare team, the last to go, left via Burundi after the killing of their patients and some Rwandan staff members. Burundian refugee camps, camps for Rwandan displaced persons in northern Rwanda and humanitarian organisations' facilities (such as health centres, offices, accommodation, warehouses and garages), where most international aid operations were deployed before the resumption of hostilities, had been destroyed by war, massacres and looting.

In the months following the start of the genocide, MSF sent three new teams to Rwanda. The first team, which travelled by road from Bujumbura, arrived in Kigali on 13 April and worked in the ICRC field hospital. The hospital was located in the section of the capital controlled by forces loyal to the interim government, which had taken power after the assassination of the President, Prime Minister and three ministers. The two other teams, which arrived from Uganda, began operating in the part of the country controlled by the RPF and its military arm, the RPA.

One team, which arrived in the north-east in late April, provided support to Byumba hospital and assisted genocide survivors who had sought refuge in the town. The other set up operations in May in King Faisal Hospital situated in the section of Kigali held by the RPA. This was the first time since 1990 and the beginning of the civil war that the RPF had agreed to the presence of international aid workers who were thus witnesses to the rebels' actions on a daily basis. The information they provided was passed on to head office in the form of situation reports, which were then compiled into summary reports.[1] Byumba prefecture's rural Hutu population were forcefully herded into camps where there was virtually nothing.

---

[1] MSF, 'MSF Belgium Coordinator in Rwanda. Summary of incidents with RPF, Byumba', 9 July 1994.

Displaced persons, patients, staff caring for Rwandans and international aid workers recounted stories of massacres, forced disappearances, murders of civilians and kidnappings of hospitalised patients and medical staff. MSF issued press statements condemning the deaths caused by the forced displacement of tens of thousands of people from Gitarama prefecture to Bugesera, the rural part of Kigali prefecture.[2] On many occasions, RPA soldiers threatened to kill Rwandan and international ICRC and MSF personnel. Both organisations attempted to intervene by calling for an end to the violence and reported the attacks during coordination meetings with the rebels.[3]

Winners, losers and survivors

The RPA captured Kigali, Butare, Ruhengeri and Gisenyi on 4, 5, 14 and 17 July, respectively. Since the end of June, the west and south-west prefectures of Kibuye, Gikongoro and Cyangugu had been partially controlled by the French army under a UNSC mandate to deliver humanitarian assistance. Large numbers of soldiers, displaced persons, militiamen and officials from the former regime fleeing the advancing RPF troops had taken refuge in the area. A national unity government, formed according to the principles of the Arusha Accords (August 1993), was announced on 19 July.

Political parties and personalities who had supported the interim government responsible for exterminating Tutsis were, however, excluded from the government. RPF officials were appointed to positions previously reserved for President Habyarimana's party, the MRND. Pastor Bizimungu of the RPF became President, while Faustin Twagiramungu, the new Prime Minister, belonged to the Mouvement Démocratique Républicain (MDR) [Republican Democratic Movement]. It was obvious to everyone that the RPF's Paul Kagame, appointed Vice-President and Defence Minister, was the country's strong man.

The government included personalities known for their commitment to peaceful political process, the rule of law and the instituting of a democratic regime. Interior Minister Seth Sendashonga (RPF) and Justice Minister Alphonse-Marie Nkubito of the Association Rwandaise pour la Défense des Droits de l'Homme (ARDHO) [Rwandan Association for the Defence of Human Rights] were among those who embodied this aspiration.

Travel was once again possible throughout Rwanda. But, even if the war was over, the country was still dangerous, especially along its borders. The population still faced multiple threats, including mined roads, bandits, genocidal militiamen who had infiltrated the country as well as soldiers in the new Rwandan army 'cleaning

---

[2] MSF, 'Rwanda: mass displacement of refugees to Bugesera', Brussels, 1 July 1994.
[3] MSF Belgium Coordinator in Rwanda, 'Summary of incidents with RPF', Byumba, 9 July 1994.

out' a village or a displaced persons camp. In early July, MSF launched further evaluation missions to determine which operations to set up.

The various MSF national sections (Belgium, Spain, France, the Netherlands and Switzerland) shared premises in Kigali to pool some of their logistics and become operational more quickly, ensure greater consistency when negotiating with the authorities on setting up new projects and put together and distribute information on projects as well as on the issues facing all their teams operating in the country.

A stream of visitors greeted the reopening of the offices. Former suppliers, such as car hire firms, asked MSF to pay them and return their property. Employees who had survived came to collect their back pay, request social assistance or return to work. All in all, hundreds of national employees and dozens of private contractors visited the MSF compound. The files had been destroyed or sent out of the country, which made it difficult to weed out the fraud attempts among the many legitimate requests. The value of their personal accounts compensated for a thankless administrative task as they gave the Kigali team a more in-depth understanding of the daily hardships their visitors had suffered as well as their perspectives on the behaviours of the new authorities' low and high ranking civilian and military representatives.

A few scraps of good news surfaced from this flood of information. The staff learned of the survival of two female Tutsi employees, members of the team at the Burundi refugee camps in the south of Kigali prefecture (Bugesera). An international staff member recorded their story and forwarded it to a French nurse who had worked with them a few months earlier.[4] The news provoked a strong emotional reaction, especially since *Messages* (the French association's newsletter) had reported they had probably died in April 1994.

The two women were among the group that had fled the massacres of Tutsis and government opponents. On 8 April, the FAR prevented them from crossing the border to Burundi while allowing their Zairian and European colleagues to cross. They made their way back to MSF's offices and negotiated for their lives by paying off gendarmes when assailants, guided by an MSF employee, attacked the premises. They were able to flee to Butare prefecture where Hutus, relatives of one of the women, hid them until the arrival of RPF soldiers in early July.

While some genocide survivors remained in the hills, many of them sought protection and assistance in urban centres. Thousands of Tutsis, refugees for decades in neighbouring countries, crossed the border to settle in Rwanda. According to the RPF, which had made the return of these refugees a key component of its agenda, hundreds of thousands of Tutsis were considering the possibility of settling in the 'new Rwanda'. MSF's teams were preparing to set up medical programmes for Tutsis returning from Uganda to settle in the north-east of the country.

[4] MSF, 'Untitled document', Kigali, 1994.

In official speeches, Rwandan officials consistently referred to the Batwas as the nation's third largest ethnic group but, in the field, the teams did not discuss the possibility of offering specific aid programmes for this group of people who, in their view, were well-nigh invisible: 'It is difficult to determine with any degree of accuracy how many Batwas died during the massacres and the war. In some villages visited by the UNPO mission, as many as 80% of the Batwa population were killed or were still missing.'[5]

Although based on estimates, the demographic data illustrated the scope of the disaster suffered by the Rwandan population. In a country with some 7.8 million inhabitants, estimates put the death toll at around 1 million, the number of refugees in neighbouring countries at about 2 million and internally displaced persons in Rwanda at approximately 2.5 million.[6]

MSF members who returned to Rwanda noted that judging the state of the country by the exteriors of its infrastructure was deceptive. With just a few exceptions, roads, bridges, warehouses, hospitals, schools, government buildings and places of worship appeared to be intact. But inside lots of these buildings, everything had been looted and many of their usual occupants had been killed or had fled for their lives. There were not enough civil servants to provide the necessary services; moreover, they were unpaid, often lacking accommodation, equipment and work priorities due to most ministries' lack of 'sector-specific programmes'.

Members of the government and parliament usually remained confined to the capital and municipalities had no mayor. In some prefectures, RPA officers acted as prefects. The gendarmerie and police force had almost completely disintegrated and law enforcement was reduced to unpaid RPA soldiers. Some of these rebel soldiers and officers, who had grown up in exile – in Uganda or Burundi, for example – had only come to know Rwanda during the civil war.

Others, such as Tutsis born in Rwanda, learned upon returning home that many relatives, sometimes their entire families, had been killed. RPA soldiers viewed France as an ally of those who had exterminated their families. However, aside from a few insulting comments and some intimidating behaviour, they committed no violence against French nationals working for aid agencies.

By late summer of 1994, Rwanda had become the destination of choice for international relief organisations and more than 120 were already present in the

---

[5] P. Overeem, *Batwa Final Report, Unrepresented Nations and Peoples Organization's (UNPO), Mission with the Association for the Promotion of Batwa (APB) investigating the situation of the Batwa people of Rwanda, 28 September – 15 December 1994* (The Hague, 1995).

[6] United Nations Department of Humanitarian Affairs (DHA), 'Rwanda Civil Disturbance. Sitrep No. 55', Geneva, 25 October 1994, p. 2. Humanitarian Practice Network, *Rwanda/Burundi/Tanzania/Zaire* (London: ODI, September 1994). UNHCR, *The State of World's Refugees: Fifty Years of Humanitarian Action* (Geneva: Oxford University Press, 2000), p. 246.

country.[7] Association Cooperazione Internazionale (COOPI) had returned to Bugesera district and was busy getting hospitals and health centres up and running again. Byumba hosted a growing number of international organisations, which included World Vision, Oxfam, African Medical and Research Foundation (AMREF), Compassion International, Goal, UNICEF, Cooperative for Assistance and Relief Everywhere (CARE), Lutheran World Federation, Samaritan's Purse, ZOA, Medair and World Relief.

Relations with the RPF deteriorated still further after the arrest in late July of some thirty Rwandan ICRC employees and an MSF employee accused of participating in the genocide – but with no evidence to support the accusation. These initial tensions with the country's new masters did not, however, prevent MSF from sending teams all over the country. Its operations focused on several areas deemed priorities: aiding the wounded and displaced persons, helping restore hospitals and health centres to working order and combatting epidemics and malnutrition. By late August 1994, there were as many as 134 international MSF staff members working in the country.

Forty-two of the 134 were based in Kigali. The ICRC field hospital, addressing the needs of some 350 patients and 450 displaced persons, was preparing to close. MSF was continuing to provide support to King Faisal Hospital, which had around 300 patients and 1,200 displaced persons.[8] At Kigali Hospital (CHK), an MSF team was opening a treatment centre for diarrhoeal diseases in response to dysentery and cholera epidemics. Another team was supporting three of the capital's health centres.

Outside the capital, half the personnel were working in the south in the prefectures of Cyangugu (thirteen international staff), Gikongoro (twenty international staff) and Butare (nine international staff), where several teams were restoring a hospital (Kabutare) to working order and providing aid in the displaced persons camps, including water supply, sanitation, vaccination, diarrhoea treatment and nutritional rehabilitation. MSF had also set up several temporary health posts to assist people in transit in the prefectures of Gisenyi (sixteen international staff) and Kibuye (six international staff) in the west. In these two prefectures, as well as in Ruhengeri (thirteen international staff) and Gitarama (five international staff), MSF was also supporting a large number of health centres and three diarrhoeal disease treatment units.

Refugees in neighbouring countries (Burundi, Tanzania and Zaire)

In mid-July, international media attention was focused on the plight of Rwandan refugees in Zaire. Just a few months earlier, there had been few images of the

---

[7] The number amounted to around 250 by the end of 1994. Dr T. Rudasingwa, *Healing a Nation. A Testimony. Waging and Winning a Peaceful Revolution to Unite and Heal a Broken Rwanda* (North Charleston: CreateSpace Independent Publishing Platform, 2013), p. 178.

[8] MSF, 'Rwandan Crisis, Situation report for 4–10 July 1994'.

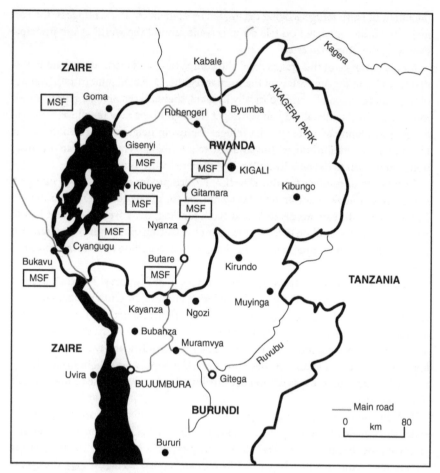

Map 3.1 MSF field teams in the Great Lakes region, August 1994

extermination of Tutsis.[9] During the genocide, journalists had been preoccupied with other major world events, such as Nelson Mandela's election and the war in the former Yugoslavia. But now they were arriving in their droves in Zairian border towns Goma and Bukavu to cover the health disaster unfolding in the refugee camps.

Cholera and dysentery epidemics broke out in mid-July, which led to tens of thousands of deaths among the refugees in just a few weeks. The all too few images of Rwandan Tutsis being massacred were followed by extensive media coverage of

---

[9] J. Siméant, 'Qu'a-t-on vu quand on ne voyait rien?', in M. Le Pape, J. Siméant and Cl. Vidal (eds), *Crises extrêmes. Face aux massacres, aux guerres civiles et aux génocides* (Paris: La Découverte, 2006), pp. 37–56. R. Brauman, *Devant le mal. Rwanda: un génocide en direct* (Paris: Arlea, 1994), pp. 27–8.

the plight of Hutu refugees being decimated by epidemics. These refugees, the vast majority Hutus, appeared on television screens around the world as the principal victims of the 'Rwandan crisis'.

Media coverage of this tragedy and the compassion and international aid it elicited was a boon for supporters of the former regime. Defeated militarily, driven out of their country, morally and politically isolated, they still remained a serious threat to Rwanda. International aid had yet to get through to the new regime as most aid funding was being allocated to the refugee camps in neighbouring countries, the UN military operation and, within Rwanda, to international humanitarian organisations rather than to the new Rwandan government's various ministries.

In 1994, total funding for the UNHCR's Zaire programme was $105 million.[10] UNAMIR's's budget amounted to $453.9 million for the period of October 1994 to January 1996.[11] To gain access to World Bank funding, the government first had to repay part of the $3 million owed by the country.[12] During the Donors Conference in January 1995, the government received pledges of $600 million to meet the country's needs.[13]

Research by historians at the National University of Rwanda shows that, in 1994, the RPF viewed media coverage of the suffering endured by Hutu refugees in Zaire as a new stage in the extermination policy – this time as a denial of the genocide's unique nature: 'This strategy was mainly driven by the will to turn the perpetrators and their accomplices into victims, who took on the only identity now considered appropriate – that of victim. At the same time, the population's flight from advancing RPF troops and the acts of violence attributed to them gave rise to the idea of a double genocide.'[14]

Indeed, this claim that multiple genocides were committed in Rwanda appeared in statements made by French political leaders. French President François Mitterrand endorsed the idea during the French-African summit in November 1994: 'After the Arusha negotiations, which began in July 1992 and ended in August 1993, the events surrounding the death of President Habyarimana and the ensuing civil war and genocides interrupted a peace process that all parties had approved.'[15]

On 10 August, the UNSC declared its support for the return of Rwandan refugees and displaced persons to their home municipalities. While stating that they were

[10] United Nations General Assembly, Executive Committee of the United Nations High Commissioner's Programme (document submitted by the High Commissioner), Executive Committee of the High Commissioner's Programme, Forty-sixth session, *Review of UNHCR programmes financed by voluntary funds in 1994–1995 and of the proposed programmes and budget for 1996, Part 1. Africa, Section 22 – Zaire* (New York: UN, 1995), p. 8.

[11] www.un.org./fr/peacekeeping/missions/past/unamir/facts.shtml.

[12] Rudasingwa, *Healing a Nation*, pp. 178–9.

[13] Déo Byanafashe and Paul Rutayisire, *Histoire du Rwanda. Des origines à la fin du XXème siècle* (Huye: National University of Rwanda, 2011), p. 642.

[14] Byanafashe and Rutayisire, *Histoire du Rwanda*, p. 550.

[15] François Mitterrand, 18th French-African summit, Biarritz, France, 8–9 November 1994.

in favour, as a matter of principle, of the refugees' repatriation, international relief organisations did not encourage a massive return in the short term. They stressed the importance of ending the power the perpetrators of the genocide wielded over the refugees before their return to Rwanda.[16]

Moreover, supporting the repatriation of refugees called for aid agencies such as MSF – who supported a voluntary and safe return on principle – to describe the acts of violence committed by the RPA against non-combatants. The RPF acknowledged that its soldiers sometimes carried out such acts, but denied having ordered them to commit them and promised to punish the perpetrators. The aid community raised the following question: could these acts be characterised as legitimate defence, individual vengeance, the inevitable excesses of purges in the immediate aftermath of a war or a long-term intention to govern by terror?[17]

In August, the UNHCR commissioned a field survey to be conducted in forty-one of Rwanda's 145 municipalities and nine refugee camps in Burundi, Tanzania and Zaire to determine whether the conditions for repatriation were being met.[18] In September, Washington sent to its embassies involved in the 'Rwandan crisis' a summary of the report drawn up by Robert Gersony, a consultant well-known and respected by the US administration for similar work in Uganda, who was tasked by the UNHCR to lead the investigation:

> Pattern/Methods of killings. On the basis of interviews with refugees/individuals, the following pattern emerged and the following categories of individuals were particularly vulnerable; refugees were called for meetings on peace and security. Once gathered, the RPA would move and carry the killings. In addition to group killings, house to house searches were conducted; individual hiding out in the swamps were hunted; returnees as well as the sick, the elderly, the young and males between 18–40 were victims. Methods used were hoes, axes, machete and fire. So many civilians were killed that burial of bodies is a problem in some villages … The Gersony team findings established that systematic killing was taking place and that repatriation could not be promoted by UNHCR under the circumstances.[19]

In the neighbouring countries, the UNHCR and International Organisation for Migration (IOM) took note of the disturbing information in Gersony's report. They were repatriating small numbers of individuals on the express condition that they were returning voluntarily. This policy also suited the RPF, which was in no hurry

[16] United Nations, Security Council, S/1994/1308, 18 November 1994.
[17] L. Binet, *The Violence of the New Rwandan Regime 1994–1995* (Paris: MSF, 2005), p. 26.
[18] UNHCR Emergency repatriation team, 'Summary of UNHCR presentation before commission of experts', Geneva, 10 October 1994.
[19] FM SECSTATE WASHDC TO AMEMBASSY KIGALI, AMEMBASSY KAMPALA, AMEMBASSY NAIROBI, USMISSION USUN NEW YORK, USMISSION GENEVA, AMEMBASSY BUJUMBURA, UNHCR TEAM FINDS EVIDENCE IN RWANDA, UNCLASSIFIED XX2 6, STATE 254232 200312Z, O 200310Z SEP 94. PP: 5–6.

for hundreds of thousands of Hutu refugees under the influence of genocide perpetrators to return home from neighbouring countries.[20]

Displaced persons camps: a place of refuge for some and of danger for others

Between 4 and 10 July 1994, MSF conducted a situation assessment in south-west
Rwanda, where most of the internally displaced were. Entering Rwanda from the
Zairian border town Bukavu, the team was able to move around freely without military escort. The vast majority of displaced persons were in Gikongoro prefecture in
the 'safe humanitarian zone' set up in late June by the French army under the mandate of the UN. The 5,000-troop UNAMIR replaced the French army in late August.

In early July, the displaced population in this prefecture stood at 700,000–
800,000, according to information obtained by MSF from the local authorities and
the French army during an evaluation mission. The team reported that the camps
held some 200,000 displaced persons living without shelter or in *blindés* (wood-
framed huts covered with plants, bits of fabric and even plastic sheeting), no access
to drinking water and little in the way of food supplies.[21] The region's health centres
were overwhelmed, badly organised, short-staffed and lacking essential supplies and
drugs. And, when they did still provide some kind of care, they demanded payment
from patients. In the short term, death was a real threat for thousands of people due
to their extremely precarious living conditions, malnutrition and epidemics such as
cholera, dysentery, measles, meningitis and malaria.

The French army, eager to demonstrate the humanitarian nature of its operation,
exiled members of the former regime determined to prove to the population their
ability to obtain foreign aid and international media correspondents, shocked by the
plight of the displaced, were pushing international relief organisations to take action
as soon as possible. The challenge was to avoid a repetition of the health disaster that
was causing the deaths of tens of thousands of refugees in camps in Zaire – mainly in
Goma and, to a lesser extent, Bukavu.

MSF, already in high demand in Tanzania, Burundi, Zaire, Uganda and other
Rwandan prefectures, was at the limits of its operational capacity. The association
nevertheless managed to send in supplies and an initial fourteen-member team from
Europe to work in displaced persons camps in the south-west.

In reality, none of MSF's national sections showed any enthusiasm at the idea
of working with the authorities and the militias implicated in exterminating Tutsis,
let alone in an area controlled by French armed forces. The French State had been

---

[20] An exception was made for refugees living in Burundi under the control of the Burundian army; because
this army was an ally of the RPA, the authorities were not concerned in the short term about a possible
return.

[21] MSF, 'Debriefing minutes, evaluation mission in Gikongoro, Rwanda', 13 July 1994.

the main political and military ally of Habyarimana's regime, which eroded the French forces' legitimacy and credibility to implement humanitarian operations. The evaluation mission team summarised its position in its report to Paris head office: 'Despite the political problems arising from the presence of the French army and the tight control the militias and civil authorities are exerting over the population, we must provide assistance while taking great care to ensure our independence in terms of funding, equipment and supplies and travel.'[22]

On 12 July, MSF's secretary-general and international board president wrote to UN Secretary-General Boutros Boutros-Ghali about the situation in the displaced persons camps: 'From a health perspective, we think the only way to quickly and effectively help hundreds of thousands of people is to let them return home.'[23]

In the same letter, MSF's directors, distrustful of the so-called 'humanitarian' French military operation, urged the UN to take back command of international military operations in Rwanda.

The last request concerned the issue of justice: 'Impunity must not be granted to those responsible for the genocide, and international efforts, whether political or humanitarian, must take great care not to provide any support or guarantees whatsoever to the perpetrators of this crime against humanity.'

In the autumn of 1994, according to Rwandan historians, the new authorities viewed the displaced persons' return to their home municipalities as an absolute priority:

> Displaced persons camps, where populations were taken hostage to serve as human shields, political pawns and bait for humanitarian organisations, became hideouts for thieves, military training camps for former FAR and *Interahamwe* fighters and a rear base for criminal incursions and efforts to regain power in Rwanda. These camps were a State within a State because they were completely outside the control of the Rwandan authorities.[24]

The authorities also explained that genocide survivors were shocked by the sorry spectacle of the camps. They claimed that those who had killed their relatives and friends and were living with impunity in these camps where they enjoyed protection and international aid. The RPF, the dominant party in the ruling coalition, wanted the IDP (Internally Displaced Persons) camps closed as quickly as possible because it considered them havens for genocide perpetrators who were taking advantage of the 'international community's' indulgence: 'UNAMIR (United Nations Assistance Mission for Rwanda) didn't risk going into the camps and the organisations working in them were not overly concerned about the types of activities being carried out;

---

[22] MSF, 'Debriefing minutes, evaluation mission in Gikongoro, Rwanda'.

[23] MSF, 'Letter sent by MSF's Secretary-General and International Board President to the Secretary-General of the United Nations, Brussels', 12 July 1994.

[24] Byanafashe and Rutayisire, *Histoire du Rwanda*, pp. 596–7.

some of the organisations shared in the same ideology as the forces managing the camps.'[25]

When the new Rwandan government accused the UN of showing indulgence towards the genocide perpetrators, it was all the more embarrassing for the organisation given that several months earlier its peacekeeping forces had not used their weapons to defend Tutsis from massacre. In these circumstances, it was difficult for the UN to publicly announce that it was not appropriate for the IDPs to return to their homes straight away because the only military force that had fought the perpetrators of the genocide was also suspected of having committed systematic and repeated killings, according to the UNHCR-commissioned Gersony report.[26]

Weakened by their inaction during the genocide, the UN and the countries donating aid to Rwanda lacked the political and moral credibility to come out against the new Rwandan regime. Moreover, the Rwandan government had, if needed, the military means to impose its will on the ground.

As a result, the UN worked with the government and army to 'bring home' all the displaced persons by the end of 1994. In August 1994, the UN and the government launched three joint operations: 'Homeward', 'Rondaval' and 'Return'. From this perspective, the conclusions of the UNHCR-commissioned Gersony report (a summary of which was already circulating among the foreign aid community) were unwelcome and the UN decided not to release it.

Shortly after this decision, the two principal international human rights organisations released the findings of their own field surveys. In September, Human Rights Watch (HRW) wrote: 'The RPF massacred groups of unarmed civilians at a number of locations in eastern, central, and southern Rwanda after combat was finished and governmental forces were gone from the area.'[27]

In October, Amnesty International backed this conclusion:

> Although it is not appropriate to make any comparison between the horrendous scale of massacres committed by forces loyal to the former government between April and July 1994 with those committed by the Rwandese Patriotic Army (RPA), Rwanda's new national army which, until July 1994 was the armed wing of the Rwandese Patriotic Front (RPF), hundreds, possibly thousands, of defenceless people have been killed by the RPA and its supporters.[28]

---

[25] Byanafashe and Rutayisire, *Histoire du Rwanda*, pp. 596–7.

[26] See Ian Martin, 'Hard choices after genocide: human rights and political failures in Rwanda', in J. Moore (ed.), *Hard Choices: Moral Dilemmas in Humanitarian Intervention* (Lanham: Rowman & Littlefield, 1998), p. 171. 'It is not hard to focus on any one of these absolute requirements and demonstrate the failure to respect or fulfil it. It is harder to suggest what actions could have led to the least unacceptable compromises of objectives that were simultaneously unachievable or can best reconcile conflicting principles today.'

[27] Human Rights Watch Africa, *The Aftermath of Genocide in Rwanda: Absence of Prosecution. Continued Killings Report* (New York: HRW, September 1994), p. 7.

[28] Amnesty International, *Rwanda Reports of Killings and Abductions by the Rwandese Patriotic Army. April – August 1994* (London: AI, 20 October 1994), p. 1.

Furthermore, field surveys by a number of researchers and journalists showed that the RPA continued its killing spree after the war:

> There have been a disturbing number of 'disappearances', assassinations and even massacres. People are going missing nearly every day; they are arrested by RPA soldiers and taken to unknown destinations.[29]
>
> Does she think it is safe for her sons to come home? She is not sure. Young boys, like the ones who took her cows, said her sons had been members of the Hutu militia; they were not, she said. Such accusations are common, particularly in rural areas, where the person making the charge often has designs on the accused's farm. It is an accusation that results in death or disappearance. No one had been killed in this village since the end of the war, Mrs Icymanizanye said, but she said that 'many' young men had disappeared.[30]

Officially, the UN continued to insist that the return of the IDPs had to be voluntary and safe. To reconcile this official position with information on repeated acts of mass violence committed by the RPA, these acts were often described as the inevitable excesses of an immediate post-war period that the new government would soon bring to an end. One of MSF's European managers expressed his opinion in the press: 'Once again, bodies are floating down rivers in Rwanda. While there is no hard evidence that the new Kigali regime is behind these crimes, it is clear, however, that private reprisals are increasing. Could anything else have been expected after the carnage of these past few months?'[31]

Not everyone was convinced by this optimistic assessment. An inventory of violent acts committed by the new regime and the appropriate definitions used to describe them were the focus of bitter discussions, not only within human rights organisations but also at the UN, ICRC, foreign embassies and NGOs asked by the Rwandan authorities and the UN to conduct campaigns in the camps urging IDPs to return to their home municipalities immediately.

Coming out for or against a return of displaced persons had very practical consequences for the humanitarian organisations. IDPs asked international staff for their opinions, thinking they were privy to information that was largely lacking in the camp population. They wanted to know what the security conditions would be if they returned to their home municipalities and whether they would receive tangible aid. Several hundred Rwandan MSF employees, recruited from among the displaced, discussed these concerns with their colleagues from other countries. Reaching a decision for or against the IDPs' return also had consequences on organising relief

[29] F. Reyntjens, *Sujets d'inquiétude au Rwanda en octobre 1994*. Working Paper (Antwerp: Universiteit Antwerpen College voor de ontwilkkelingslanden, 3 November 1994), p. 3.

[30] R. Bonner, 'Rwandan refugees in Zaire still fear to return', *New York Times* (10 November 1994).

[31] R. Brauman (President of MSF France, 1982–94), 'L'irrésolution des Nations unies au Rwanda', *Libération* (18 October 1994).

and protection for IDPs. Should another hospital be built in the camps or should support to hospitals and health centres be initiated in the various towns and even transit and reception centres set up in the IDPs' home municipalities?

Justice

It was against this backdrop that MSF's legal adviser visited Rwanda for the first time in late August. The work involved in tracking human rights violations was far more complex than simply monitoring the return of displaced persons and refugees. Human rights advocates, humanitarian workers and representatives from the UN and countries determined to provide aid to Rwanda shared the same conviction: there could be no peace without justice: 'Forgive and forget is not a feasible way forward to national reconciliation because those who have taken power represent the genocide victims.'[32]

This opinion, prevalent at the time of the events and still very widespread within international aid circles, is worthy of comment. Unless it is assumed that all Rwandan Tutsi survivors shared the same political opinion, neither the new government nor the RPF represented the genocide victims.

Of course, the RPF enjoyed much legitimacy because it had militarily defeated the interim government responsible for exterminating the Tutsis. But Dr Theogene Rudasingwa, RPF Secretary-General at the time, acknowledged that saving surviving Tutsis was not one of the rebels' priorities when, in May and June 1994, the possibility of an international military intervention was on the table: 'RPF insisted that all Tutsi who were supposed to die had died, and it was unbelievable that the French were coming to save Tutsi. Of course not all Tutsi had died. In retrospect, this was a callous and cynical position that originated from General Kagame.'[33]

In her report, MSF's legal adviser summarised the objectives of her visit to Rwanda:

- On the initiative of MSF B [Belgium]: accompany to Rwanda an exploratory mission of six officials from human rights organisations.[34] MSF made a commitment to accompany and assist them with a programme to deploy non-governmental human rights observers in order to compensate for the UN's shortcomings in this area and address the urgency and seriousness of the situation on the ground.
- Set up a system for monitoring the safety of refugees in the camps and displaced persons within Rwanda.

---

[32] MSF Legal adviser, 'Rwanda Project. 20 August – 5 September 1994', Kigali, 1994, p. 9.
[33] Rudasingwa, *Healing a Nation*, p. 159.
[34] International Federation for Human Rights, Amnesty International Belgium, International Association of Democratic Lawyers and Common Causes.

- Advise the teams on their role to play regarding the general issue of human rights in Rwanda and how to handle acts of violence that they are witness to (local staff and patients) without endangering MSF's programmes.[35]

During this period, in addition to its work providing humanitarian medical care, MSF also saw itself as a 'human rights sentinel'[36] and believed it was logical to provide logistical and financial aid to both national and international human rights organisations. It was clear that it was going be a colossal task to rebuild the country's legal system: 'Only six of Rwanda's judges and ten lawyers still remain. The Ministry of Justice has been completely destroyed. The minister's office is on the third floor of a wrecked building and has no door or windows. Two chairs and the paper have been looted. The law court has been turned into a restaurant and the archives burned to heat the food.'[37]

The UN had pledged to deploy 140 human rights observers throughout the country and appoint twenty investigators to gather the necessary evidence for initiating criminal proceedings. In reality, in August 1994:

> Out of 20 investigators, only one person has been appointed: Karen Kenny. She worked on her own in Kigali for two and a half months without a car, no means of communication or any supplies or equipment ... Nobody seems to be talking anymore about observers, whose mission is very different because they form the bedrock of information-gathering.[38]

Seeking to overcome some of the shortcomings of the State and UN, a group of European human rights organisations decided, with MSF's support, to create a consortium – the Réseau Citoyens [Citizens' Network] (RCN). Its goal was to work towards rebuilding various aspects of the legal system:

Projects:

a) Help create a bar association in Kigali (set up a legal consulting and defence office)
b) Create a centre for lawyers, including a law library, in Kigali
c) Set up a training programme for lawyers and judges
d) Offer an ombudsman service (in Kigali and some municipalities)
e) Provide legal aid to prisoners (draw up a list of prisoners, put prisoners in contact with a Rwandan or foreign lawyer).[39]

---

[35] MSF legal adviser, 'Rwanda Project. 20 August – 5 September 1994', p. 1.
[36] MSF, 'Principes de Chantilly (Chantilly Principles)', 1995. http://association.msf.org/sites/default/files/rst_library_item/Principles%20Chantilly%20FR.pdf MSF, 'MSF et droits de l'Homme au Rwanda, Zarwabuta, No. 1', Paris, 25 August 1994.
[37] MSF legal adviser, 'Rwanda Project. 20 August – 5 September 1994', p. 4.
[38] MSF legal adviser, 'Rwanda Project. 20 August – 5 September 1994', p. 7.
[39] MSF, 'Legal Voluntary Officer', Paris, 1994.

Plans also called for RCN to train judicial police officers to be able to arrest genocide perpetrators in compliance with the code of criminal procedure.

MSF also decided to send three of its own legal officers to Zaire, Tanzania and Rwanda to monitor issues relating to the protection of refugees and displaced persons. In Rwanda, the legal officer was mainly involved in collecting and analysing information on: 'Disappearances and abuse of patients and the wounded, disappearances and abuse of our local employees (medical and non-medical) and serious security incidents involving facilities belonging to MSF and other humanitarian organisations.'[40]

Given the pressures engendered by the return of the IDPs, the legal officer working in Rwanda was reassigned to researching information to establish if they could return home in complete safety. In early November, the UNSC announced the creation of the ICTR (resolution 955 of 8 November 1994), on the model of the tribunal for the former Yugoslavia created in May 1993, and the punishment of mass crimes took a new direction that made the information collected even more significant.

The clearly defined aim was to bring to justice alleged perpetrators of genocide and other serious violations of international human rights law committed in Rwanda or by Rwandan citizens in neighbouring countries between 1 January and 31 December 1994. The ICTR's mandate encompassed both the crime of genocide and any war crimes committed by the RPF.

The end of IDP camps

Scheduled for completion by the end of 1994, closing the camps would in reality take from mid-September 1994 to mid-May 1995.

On 17 September in Rubengera (Mabanza municipality, Kibuye prefecture), the RPA forcibly closed several displaced persons sites by torching shelters. Not one casualty went to the MSF clinic. The team asked the RPA soldiers to respect medical facilities. On 18 September, the team noted during a visit that the same thing had happened in Birambo (Mwendo municipality, Kibuye prefecture). The head of mission in Kigali informed RPA headquarters, UNAMIR and the head of the UNHCR. MSF was particularly concerned by the attitude of the UN peacekeepers during these incidents:

> UNAMIR's acquiescence with RPF's official discourse on the absolute necessity for the internally displaced to return home and its growing passivity toward security incidents (no investigation) and high level of tolerance for RPF methods regarding displacement of civilians (official denial of MSF's allegations regarding forced displacements in Kibuye).[41]

40 MSF, 'Legal Voluntary Officer'.
41 MSF, 'Minutes of regional meeting on the Rwandan crisis attended by heads of mission', 23–24 September 1994.

On 18 October, MSF was working in Ndaba camp (Kivumu municipality, Kibuye prefecture) when the RPA shot and wounded four people. In Ndaba as in other camps, MSF noted that the use of force to close camps came in response to the refusal of the people living in them to return home: 'The main reason cited by the displaced for not returning home is the lack of security (information received from all agencies concurs). The second is the lack of assistance, food and medical care in the areas they are to return to.'[42]

Moreover, how could anyone expect the displaced to be convinced that it was safe enough for them to return? MSF teams were still seeing farmers just a few kilometres away leaving their land to seek protection and assistance in the Gikongoro camps.

On 11 November, the RPA opened fire on people in Musebeya camp (Musebeya municipality, Gikongoro prefecture) in the presence of some of the MSF team. The incident, which occurred during a distribution of jerry cans and soap by NGO Feed the Children, left seven people dead and wounded seventeen – eight seriously and nine less seriously. The soldiers, none of whom were wounded, claimed they were retaliating for the throwing of a hand grenade, even though no one had witnessed such an event. The impassivity of the peacekeepers during the incident shocked the humanitarian workers: 'Troops from UNAMIR who were present at Musebeya, less than 25 meters from the scene of the attack, were unable to provide protection.'[43]

Representatives of Feed the Children, Équilibre, Action Internationale Contre la Faim, Save the Children, Merlin, Oxfam, Trocaire, Goal, MSF and Care et Solidarités decided to suspend their operations in the prefecture for two days in protest and demanded that peacekeepers enforce their mandate to protect the IDPs.

MSF already knew of John Zigira, prefect of Gikongoro and an English-speaking captain in the RPA, when he took up his position in September. In June, an MSF team had heard an eyewitness who said Zigira had ordered the lynching of several civilians in Kinazi IDP camp (Nyamata municipality, Bugesera). During a meeting with him in November shortly after the attacks in Musebeya camp, he summed up his opinion of the displaced people: 'There is only one way to deal with *Interahamwe*.'[44]

In late November, the UN and the government revised the scope of the operation and NGOs, including MSF, were invited to take part in the discussions. At the suggestion of the RPA, the operation was renamed *Taha* – 'return' in Kinyarwanda. Priority was given to closing IDP camps, while envisaging that refugee camps would be shut within two years.[45] Operation *Taha* was based on an action plan (OP TAHA – Concept of Operations) adopted at the highest echelons of the Ministry of Defence, Ministry of Rehabilitation and Social Integration, the UN and several NGOs.

[42] MSF, 'Fax sent by the head of mission to the crisis cell in Paris', Kigali, 7 July 1994.
[43] MSF, 'Fax to the head of mission at Paris head office, Situation in Gikongoro. Statement from NGOs working in Gikongoro prefecture', Kigali, 11 November 1994.
[44] Interview conducted by J.-H. Bradol with the Gikongoro prefect, November 1994.
[45] United Nations, 'OP TAHA – CONCEPT OF OPERATIONS', from TAP Mullarey OIC Op TAHA to SRSG File No. 5000.1(G3 PLANS), Kigali, 21 November 1994, p. 2.

The participants set up a coordinating body, the Integrated Operations Centre, to harmonise the efforts of the various partner institutions. Those promoting Operation *Taha* did not rule out opposition from Interahamwe residing in the camps, but it was agreed that there would be no arrests while people were being moved out. Strict conditions were spelled out for the return of the displaced persons: information, voluntary participation, dignity, security, material assistance, coordination and flexibility by aid workers. One of the core principles, voluntary participation, was accorded special emphasis: '7. No Enforced Camp Closure. Camps will not be forcibly closed. That said, an environment in which the people are motivated to leave voluntarily will be created.'[46]

On 6 December, MSF team members were working in the hospital at Kaduha camp (Nyamagabe municipality, Gikongoro prefecture). Taken up with the job in hand, they realised somewhat belatedly that the RPA, in the space of a few hours, had been emptying the camp of its some 40,000 displaced people: 'The order to evacuate [Kaduha] was given on Tuesday afternoon by a captain who, according to the displaced, threatened to burn down the camp if people did not leave.'[47]

Over the following days, some 20,000 Kaduha residents arrived in nearby Rukondo camp (Rukondo municipality, Gikongoro prefecture) where MSF also worked. These forced population transfers often took place amid health emergencies. In late December, for example, measles and meningitis epidemics were sweeping through Rukongo camp, where daily mortality between September and December exceeded one death per 10,000 residents, a rate considered an emergency threshold.[48] In this tense climate, the MSF teams organised a mass vaccination campaign.

On the evening of 13 December, UNAMIR and the RPA launched an operation they called 'Hope' in Kibeho camp (some 100,000 people, Mubuga municipality, Gikongo prefecture). The peacekeepers had informed neither the UN civil affairs branch, the ICRC nor NGOs. Two thousand peacekeepers searched people's shelters while RPA soldiers formed a cordon around the camp. Each shelter was searched for suspects and arms. By the time Operation Hope ended in the morning of 15 December, the soldiers had arrested dozens of suspects for unspecified crimes.

The peacekeepers confiscated hundreds of machetes, a tool of everyday life, but found no military weapons. The operation went smoothly, except for the sabotage of a large pipe used to supply water. One person who happened to be nearby was killed when the pipe exploded. Meanwhile, work continued as normal at the MSF hospital. MSF's head of mission, aware that the suspects being sought by the soldiers had probably left the camp well before the decision was taken to launch the operation,

[46] United Nations, 'OP TAHA – CONCEPT OF OPERATIONS', p. 2.
[47] MSF, 'Fax sent by the head of mission in Kigali to the Paris office', 9 December 1994.
[48] MSF, 'Médecins Sans Frontières (France) in Rwanda. Gitarama, Kibuye and Gikongoro projects. Activity report, Kigali', October 1994.

commented on the outcome of the thorough search of the camp: 'It's like raiding a bar run by the mafia and confiscating the knives and forks.'[49]

The association of the peacekeepers and RPA in joint military operations meant that, in practice, the status of the displaced persons was changing for the UN, despite its declarations of principle in support of a voluntary and safe return. Sociologist Arnaud Royer, who was working for the UNHCR in the region at the time, wrote: 'As a result, to maintain a modicum of credibility with the authorities, the United Nations had come around to the idea that the displaced persons were more an element of insecurity than a population in need of protection and it was necessary to treat them as such.'[50]

Meanwhile, the MSF legal officer tasked with investigating obstacles in the way of the IDPs' immediate return to their home municipalities was gathering information using the standard data collection forms. The data collected were consistent with those of national and international human rights organisations. In Gitarama prefecture, where large numbers of displaced persons were to return to, priest and long-time human rights activist André Sibomana was drawing up lists of victims of the new regime's political repression.[51] Given who he was, Sibomana was a credible source. Moreover, at the time he was serving as temporary bishop of Kabgayi diocese and therefore had access to an extensive network of contacts throughout the prefecture.[52] He was also a journalist known for his political independence and, under the regime of President Habyarimana, he had been harassed on more than one occasion for his journalistic and human rights activities. The information he collected included lists with the names of several thousand victims.

Some of these lists were shared with MSF head office and representatives of its field team during meetings that took place in October and November 1994. During these meetings, Sibomana specified that the perpetrators of the killings in the prefecture were now demanding more than just simple farmers. Intellectuals, officials from the former local government and individuals viewed as leaders were now their main priority. MSF international personnel were receiving similar reports from their Rwandan colleagues who, either themselves or people they knew, were being confronted with arrests and disappearances.

On 7 January 1995, at the request of the ICRC, a Caritas surgeon and an MSF doctor went to the camp in Busanze (around 4,000 displaced persons, according to the ICRC), a few kilometres from the Burundian border in Nshili municipality in Gikongoro prefecture. The RPA had informed the displaced persons they had

---

[49] MSF, 'Fax sent by an MSF (French section) manager to the programme manager in Paris', 19 December 1994, p. 1.

[50] Royer, De l'exil au pouvoir, p. 342.

[51] In 1992, he became president of the Association for the Defence of Human Rights and Public Liberties (ADL). In 1993, he became the representative for Rwanda of Reporters Without Borders (RWB).

[52] On 5 June 1994, RPA soldiers had executed four Catholic bishops in Gakurazo (Mukingi municipality, Gitarama prefecture); one was Bishop of Kabgayi.

to return home by 31 December. According to the camp's inhabitants, about thirty people with bullet, grenade and machete wounds went to Runoymbi, the closest health centre, after a night attack carried out by men in uniforms and Tutsi civilians. The most seriously wounded, around fifteen, were transferred to Kigali, Butare and Kibeho. In the camp, where the makeshift shelters (*blindés*) had been torched, there were still some 500 displaced persons. A dozen bodies had been pulled out of the latrines: three men, three women and six children.

An examination of the corpses by the MSF doctor indicated that:

1. The bodies have bullet wounds (one to two per person) and machete injuries, but show no sign of beating (no discolouration or contusions) or rape.
2. The bullets were fired from very close range: the bullets have the same entry and exit points. A high-calibre cartridge was found in one of the women's clothing.
3. The victims were not running away. They were not shot in the back.
4. There was an intention to kill. One person was killed by a bullet to the temple. A child with a leg fracture was murdered with a machete. A baby's skull had been shattered with a machete.
5. The fact that machetes were used provides further evidence that not only soldiers were involved in the massacre. Soldiers only rarely use machetes as a weapon. Hutu inhabitants of Busanze questioned afterward confirmed that civilians, identified as Tutsis living in Busanze, accompanied the soldiers during the operation.[53]

Interior Minister Seth Sendashonga, Ministry of Justice official Silas Mumyagishala, RPA intelligence officer Lieutenant-Colonel Emmanuel Karenzi Karake and Major Philbert from the Gikongoro RPA visited the site on 9 January. Major Frank Rusagara, a staff officer with the new Rwandan army, acknowledged during a meeting in Kigali with MSF's head of mission that his soldiers were responsible for the massacre.[54] Promising that the suspects would be brought before a military tribunal, he added that the soldiers were retaliating against a grenade attack, a version of events denied by the UNAMIR officer charged with investigating the incident.[55]

On 6 February, Rukondo camp and small Munini and Kamana camps were partially shut down by the RPA, and 40,000 people moved to Kibeho. On 13 April, Rwamiko camp, also located in Gikongoro prefecture, was forcibly closed and 5,000 of its inhabitants fled to Kibeho.

[53] MSF, 'Fax from MSF France head of mission to the programme manager in Paris', 10 January 1995.
[54] MSF, 'Fax from MSF France head of mission to the programme manager in Paris', 10 January 1995.
[55] UNAMIR, 'Report on provost Marshal's visit to Busanze camp to investigate', To FC / from Force PM/S02 G1 Discipline/Info: DFC, COS, CAO, DCOS ops, DCOS Sp, G2 Mil Info, G3 Ops, CO GHANBATT. File FPM/5, 9 January 1995.

Kibeho

On 14 April, the MSF team reported that the RPA had begun increasing its men in Kibeho camp and the vicinity. On 15 April, the RPA demanded that aid organisations stop distributing food to the camp's inhabitants.

Despite daily meetings between the UN (peacekeepers and human rights monitors) and RPA officers, the Rwandan officers had not yet officially announced the objective of their operation. Was it simply a matter of searching the camp again? Did the RPA want to forcibly close the camp and make arrests, despite agreements between the UN and the Ministry of Defence under Operation *Taha*? The only large camp still open, its location was significant for two reasons. In the 1980s, Kibeho had become a pilgrimage site after religious believers professed to have seen visions of the Virgin Mary and Tutsis who had sought refuge in buildings belonging to Kibeho church were exterminated there in April 1994.

The MSF team had few illusions about the nature of the military operation that was beginning: 'RPA leaders think that if the people have nothing left to eat, they

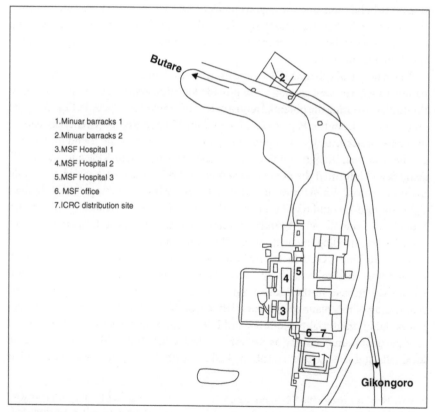

Map 3.2 Kibeho camp

will have to return home and those who refuse will be expelled by force of arms if necessary. The threat is clear.'[56]

The violence that had been seen during the closing of other IDP camps and information received on large-scale disappearances in displaced persons' home villages since September, prompted international organisations to bring in more field staff. UNAMIR had a permanent presence at the site with two military positions inside the camp, while an Australian army medical unit, UNHCR and IOM staff, UNICEF representatives and two field observers from the UN High Commissioner for Human Rights (HCHR) provided support to the Zambian peacekeepers. A number of representatives from humanitarian organisations – Caritas, Oxfam, Save the Children and the ICRC – worked regularly in the camp while some fifteen MSF international staff members helped deliver medical care in the camp hospital near UNAMIR positions and a school where Caritas provided nutritional rehabilitation. All MSF sections had sent doctors, logisticians and paramedics to bolster the team. Several hundred foreigners, including journalists, had been preparing for a possible closing of the camp for weeks. These foreigners worked for international organisations in Kibeho camp and the region's prefectures; they included personnel assigned to organising the logistics prior to the IDPs' departure, providing relief and first aid along the way and offering reception services at transit centres, in hospitals and in IDP home municipalities.

The majority of Kibeho's IDPs came from towns in Butare prefecture where international agencies were gearing up to provide logistics, assistance and protection to the displaced during the potential return of tens of thousands of people. Peacekeepers and monitors from the High Commissioner for Human Rights (twenty-six people in Butare prefecture alone), supported by European Union staff, found themselves on the frontline. They had one or more daily meetings with RPA and UNAMIR soldiers and informed the international organisations so that each could play a role in the operation. When the displaced would begin to leave the camp, the UN human rights monitors would register them as they left and UNAMIR would use vehicles brought in from all over Rwanda to transport them. The peacekeepers were also tasked with patrolling the roads during the return journey.

The ICRC and NGOs, including MSF, were responsible for helping the displaced in temporary medical posts (way stations) set up along roads, in transit centres and, when they arrived, in their home municipalities. The international organisations' monitoring of this planned operation left few of the main details to chance.[57] In the towns, UN human rights monitors and ICRC representatives were able to briefly visit parts of homes serving as makeshift cells for the RPA. Military camps, some local jails and sites where executions had allegedly taken place or bodies hidden

[56] MSF, 'Personal account of the Kibeho massacre, MSF nurse Geneviève Legrand, Kigali', March 1995, p. 3.
[57] United Nations High Commissioner for Human Rights, 'Field Operation in Rwanda, Butare Prefecture, Operation Kibeho, Activity Reports, Butare team, 18 April – 12 May 1995', Butare, 1995.

(Nyungwe forest and Huye military camp, for example), were the only places where international personnel were not allowed to go.[58]

During the night of 17 April, an estimated 2,500 RPA soldiers entered Kibeho camp and small neighbouring camps Ndago, Munini and Kamana. In Kibeho, they forced people out by destroying their shelters. In the panic, nine children and one woman were trampled to death. The displaced population, around 100,000, were assembled around premises occupied by the peacekeepers, Caritas and MSF on the hill in the middle of the camp. The RPA did not allow UNICEF, the ICRC or Oxfam to distribute food. Overall, the crowd stayed remarkably calm. At long last, the RPA announced its intentions in no uncertain terms: cease all relief for the displaced, search them, make arrests, then take them to their home municipalities.

During the first four days of the operation to close the camp, the displaced stayed standing up on the hill in the middle of the camp – in the rain, shivering with cold, without food, water or access to latrines or the hospital. On 19 April, the rain could no longer quench the IDPs' thirst. Some stones were thrown at RPA soldiers who were blocking supplies of water. The same day, the Interior Minister, the RPA commander in Kibeho, representatives from the UNHCR, ICRC and various NGOs and the UN human rights (HCHR) head of mission for Rwanda met in the camp to discuss the operation in progress.

On 20 April, the MSF team found it very difficult to get to the camp and the hospital because of RPA roadblocks. In the hospital, RPA soldiers were preventing staff from providing treatment – to the indifference of the peacekeepers, even though MSF asked them to protect their patients and staff. Late in the afternoon, around fifty RPA soldiers entered the hospital:

> On Thursday 20 April at about 16.30 hrs, just when the MSF-team was leaving the camp to go back to their house, they saw a group of at least 50 RPA military heading towards the hospital. Already during the day many soldiers had been walking in and out the hospital and had hampered the work of the team. At 16.30 hrs. MSF asked UNAMIR if they could put men to guard the hospital for the night. UNAMIR said they would, but did not do so. At 18.00 hrs, the local MSF radio-operator who remained day and night in the hospital radioed the team that there were shots in the hospital square. On Friday morning there were 21 dead laying in a tent nearby the hospital: MSF examined them and concluded that 16 of them were killed by bullets, two by machete, and three by unknown causes – probably suffocation in panic.[59]

Between 18 and 21 April, around 10,000 people were evacuated from the camp. Given that the displaced were returning against their will, on the recommendation of their head offices in Geneva, the UNHCR and International Organization for

[58] United Nations High Commissioner for Human Rights, 'Field Operation in Rwanda, Butare Prefecture, Operation Kibeho, Activity Reports, Butare team, 18 April – 12 May 1995'.
[59] Médecins Sans Frontières, 'Report on events in Kibeho camp, April 1995, Kigali', 16 May 1995, p. 4.

Migration (IOM) initially refused to organise convoys and, for the same reason, the ICRC did not participate in coordinating the IDPs' departures. However, the institution endeavoured to continue providing aid to the displaced every step of the way, including along roads, in hospitals, municipal jails and Butare prison.

As for the UN, its civil affairs arm, the United Nations Rwanda Emergency Office (UNREO), had no high-level official representative in the camp. HCHR monitors decided to fill the administrative gap left by UNREO, UNHCR, IOM and ICRC by working as a civilian partner with the soldiers to organise the IDPs' return, even though it was not part of their mandate. The HCHR were hoping to play a key role in the return operation in order to safeguard to the greatest extent possible the human rights of the displaced. Relations between the MSF staff, the Zambian captain commanding the peacekeepers and the human rights monitor, present around the clock in the camp, were warm and close. Information and documents were exchanged constantly, which gave MSF's staff a more complete picture of the situation since they did not stay in the camp overnight.

In reality, the HCHR monitors were unable to conduct a rigorous registration of IDPs prior to their departure. The RPA wanted to proceed as quickly as possible. It was even a struggle for the monitors to get permission from the Rwandan soldiers to assign the IDPs to vehicles according to their destination. They also intervened to prevent passengers suffocating to death as the soldiers crammed them onto the lorries. On 20 April, again on the recommendation of its European head office, the UNHCR changed its position and decided to assist with the operation. In a hurry to get the evacuation over with as quickly as possible, the Rwandan army decided to allow some of the IDPs to return home on foot. The army thus accepted a request from its international partners that it had rejected only a few days earlier for what it had said were humanitarian reasons.

On 22 April, claiming they were acting in legitimate self-defence after sticks and stones were thrown at them, the RPA opened fire on the crowd they were encircling with assault rifles, machine guns, grenades, anti-tank weapons and a mortar. The attacks took place in three phases: from 7 to 11 a.m., 12.05 to 3.30 p.m. and 3.45 to 6 p.m. In 2011, an Australian soldier recalled the events of the morning of 22 April, before the arrival of the MSF team:

> At about 10 am, some of the displaced persons attempted to break out and we saw them running through the re-entrants. We watched (and could do little more) as these people were hunted down and shot. The RPA soldiers were no marksmen: at times they were within ten meters of their quarry and still missed them. If they managed to wound some hapless escapee, they would save their valuable bullets, instead bayoneting their victim to death. This went on for two hours until all the displaced persons who had run were dead or dying.[60]

---

[60] P. Jordan, 'Witness to genocide, a personal account of the 1995 massacre', www.anzacday.org.au (28 March 2011).

MSF's international team arrived at the camp around noon and witnessed the last two phases of the shooting:

> When we were still dividing the work one of our team members radioed us from outside the UNAMIR compound that he saw a column of RPA soldiers marching down the hill from the church, whistling and singing. Then heavy shooting started just around the hospital, and we all had to lie down. I looked at my watch, it was 12.05 hrs.[61]

An MSF doctor and a logistician managed to briefly enter the hospital with a team of Zambian peacekeepers. The camp hospital had been overrun by RPA soldiers using it as a position to shoot at the displaced, while inside the soldiers were killing patients and looting equipment, especially electricity generators. Only able to evacuate eight hungry, screaming and abandoned newborns, the MSF team left the hospital and took refuge in one of the nearby compounds controlled by the peacekeepers: 'On our way to second UNAMIR compound we had to pass through the crowd, who was standing quietly, terrorized. At a certain point there was no other way for us to get to the compound than to walk over a whole lane of dead and dying bodies, men, women, and children, piled up of 3 deep.'[62]

Early in the afternoon, thousands of IDPs pursued by RPA soldiers shooting at them burst into the Zambian peacekeepers' compound. Others collapsed onto the barbed wire encircling the UN's military position. Dozens of injured people and hundreds of children separated from their families were holed up in the compound occupied by UN forces, who, like the MSF team, were barricaded inside the buildings. When the shooting stopped, the peacekeepers forced any terrorised IDPs who were still able-bodied out of the compound:

> Outside the buildings, the RPA were waiting for them and gave them a brutal beating. We could see through the window the blows raining down on them. An old man accused of entering the UNAMIR buildings with a grenade was slain a little farther away by an RPA soldier.[63]

Mid-afternoon, the soldiers began shooting at the IDPs again:

> This time there was permanent machine-gun fire, combined with heavier weapons. The permanent machine-gun firing was right outside the second UNAMIR compound where we found ourselves. One of the UNAMIR soldiers coming back into the compound commented: 'They are spraying them'. The soldiers were shooting directly into the crowd who fled in panic, inevitably trampling everybody who fell down. After

---

[61] MSF, 'Report on events in Kibeho camp', p. 8.

[62] MSF, 'Report on events in Kibeho camp', p. 9.

[63] MSF, 'Personal account of the Kibeho massacre, MSF nurse, Kigali', April 1995.

one hour nothing was seen any more of the masses that had been standing there pre-
ceding days. The whole area was just covered with thousands of bodies.[64]

The ground surrounding the UN position was strewn with hundreds of corpses.
Some of these scenes were photographed by the human rights monitor based in
Kibeho, Magnum agency photographer Paul Lowe and Mark Cuthbert-Brown,
Provost Marshal of the UN Assistance Mission for Rwanda (UNAMIR).[65] That day,
around ninety wounded patients were transferred to Butare hospital after being given
first aid by peacekeepers, while hundreds of wounded received no medical care at all.
Zambian and Australian peacekeepers present at the scene counted an estimated 4,050
dead. They said that they had still not finished counting all the bodies on the hill by the
end of the day on 22 April. Australian film director, George Gittoes, who had come to
Rwanda to cover the first anniversary of the Tutsi genocide, was the guest of Australian
soldiers based in Kibeho. He recalled twenty years later: 'I filmed the RPA firing mor-
tars and machine-guns into crowds of civilians trying to flee ... I have no doubt there
were many more thousands of people killed than the official number.'[66]

The following day, 23 April, Rwandan soldiers prevented the MSF team from
entering the hospital and the peacekeeper compound. The same day, MSF publicly
condemned the massacre committed by the Rwandan army. In its press releases, the
organisation provided a range for its estimate of the number of deaths (4,000 to
8,000) and protested the RPA's obstruction of medical care and relief.[67] The situation
in Kibeho was covered extensively in the media.[68]

The two hospitals in Butare treated about 600 injured patients between 22 and
27 April, according to information collected by human rights monitors. In the university hospital, nearly all of the injured arrived on foot. Over two-thirds had bullet-
wounds and the others knife-wounds. The situation in the hospital was tense. The
Rwandan staff often refused to treat or speak to the injured patients and the international staff had to do everything themselves. Just as they had done in Kigeme hospital on 23 April, the RPA soldiers regularly came into the hospitals to make arrests
and demand that the displaced immediately return to their home municipalities,
regardless of their state of health. Orphanages in Butare took in 1,726 unaccompanied children from camps in Gikongoro prefecture.

---

[64] MSF, 'Report on events in Kibeho camp', p. 10.
[65] MSF, Photographies Kibeho, April 1994 [Legal adviser archives].
[66] S. Smith, 'Le jour où l'armée rwandaise a tiré sur les réfugiés de Kibeho Paul Lowe, photographe, a été
       témoin du massacre du 22 avril', *Libération* (15 May 1995).
[67] MSF New-York, 'Five to eight thousand victims of massacres in Kibeho camp, and many collapse of exhaus-
       tion among the 80,000 displaced people on a forced march', 23 April 1995.
[68] C. Braeckman, 'Kibeho. La pire manière de crever l'abcès', *Le Soir* (24 April 1995). D. Lorch, 'As many
       as 2,000 are reported dead in Rwanda', *New York Times* (24 April 1995). Author not specified, 'Hutus
       in Rwanda death camp turn down pleas to surrender', *Moscow Times* (28 April 1995).
       F. Fritscher, 'Le gouvernement de Kigali fait évacuer plusieurs camps de réfugiés par la force', *Le Monde* (27
       April 1995).

Their state of health was deplorable and many of them were suffering from dehy-dration, hunger and physical and mental exhaustion.

Under the watchful eye of RPA soldiers, the survivors left Kibeho for the journey home in vehicles or on foot. In Butare prefecture, the plan was for the IDPs to travel via four sites: Runyinya, Niakizu, the stadium and Butare transit centre. At these transit sites, aid organisations such as Concern, Care and Merlin coordinated their efforts with Rwandan soldiers, mayors and local representatives of the Ministry of Rehabilitation. MSF and the ICRC set up way stations along the roads to provide first aid (bandages, analgesics, etc.) and relief (such as water and biscuits) for those returning on foot.

MSF's international teams reported a large number of personal items abandoned between Kibeho and Butare, as if the displaced had been forced to flee hastily while walking to Butare. Judging from the shooting heard and information gathered by HCHR monitors from survivors of the killings, homes along the roads from Kamana (a small IDP camp) to Nyakizu (a local IDP transit centre) served as execution sites. International personnel working for aid organisations were witness to IDPs being attacked by civilians on roads as RPA soldiers looked on. They recognised some of their Rwandan colleagues among the crush of IDPs exposed to the vengeance of civilian crowds:

I saw people being stoned in public on the road between Butare and Runyinya. They were sometimes forced to walk through two lines of people throwing stones at them.[69]

They were barefoot, had nothing with them anymore except the clothes they were wearing and were moving in a numb way ... The team met three of the local staff in the crowds on their way to Butare, who were equally left with nothing ... At the entrance of Butare there was a crowd of civilians who were throwing stones at the displaced who arrived.[70]

The displaced were also met by violence as they arrived at the transit centres, despite the presence of peacekeepers, UNHCHR staff and many aid organisa-tions, which included Concern and Merlin. People identified as genocide survivors pointed out IDPs, who were arrested – when not immediately lynched.

At the entrance to the stadium [in Butare], people held their noses in disgust as the watched the IDPs [internally displaced persons] file by. They were there to identify those who had massacred their relatives or neighbours last year. When they recog-nised someone, the person was violently pulled aside by soldiers and taken away to a makeshift cell in a nearby house. We saw about 10 such arrests and witnessed very violent scenes at the stadium entrance. When we asked civilians and RPA soldiers to stop beating an accused person, they answered: 'Let him die!'[71]

[69] MSF, 'Report on events in Kibeho camp', p. 16.
[70] MSF, 'Report on events in Kibeho camp', p. 15.
[71] United Nations High Commissioner for Human Rights, 'Opération sur le Terrain au Rwanda Préfecture de Butare', p. 42.

Civilian and military staff working for the UN and aid organisations were also present, at least for short visits, in the villages the displaced were taken to. On 23 April, human rights monitors tried to find out what happened to IDPs, once they returned to their home municipalities:

> In the end, the IDPs [internally displaced persons] are left with a strong feeling of anxiety. Today they were all put into one group, relatively well supervised and sometimes protected. But what will happen tomorrow when they go to their neighbourhoods and are separated? Will the hatred so present along the roads today disappear? We asked a civilian why he was hurting children who had nothing to do with the genocide and he answered, 'these children look innocent now but in ten years time nobody will be able to stop them'.[72]

Throughout the morning of 24 April, Australian soldiers in Kibeho carried bodies to a mass grave. The same day, the MSF team was able to provide medical care to the wounded. Sporadic shooting was heard all afternoon. The camp was nearly empty, with only a few hundred displaced persons still holed up in the Caritas buildings while negotiations continued concerning their evacuation. At mid-day on 24 April, Seth Sedashonga and Alphonse-Marie Nkubito, the Interior and Justice ministers, visited the camps with William Clarance, UNHCHR head of mission:

> When the question came up whether or not there had been an exchange of fire between the RPA and displaced, MSF informed them that their team had not heard or seen any exchange of fire on Saturday. They could just report that the crowd had been extremely quiet and disciplined during all the preceding four and a half days, and that MSF staff had never seen any guns neither any sign of aggression.[73]

Late in the afternoon of 24 April, Rwandan President Pasteur Bizimungu also visited the camp and released a statement to the press, foreign diplomats and international aid organisations. It left little doubt as to how Kigali viewed the camp's displaced population and the 'international community's' attitude towards the IDPs:

> The tolerance toward the displaced persons camps within the country has lasted for months in defiance of sovereignty principles, even though these camps have been become hideouts for *Interahamwe*, camps for training militiamen to commit violence and areas for launching attacks against peaceful populations. The Rwandan government can no longer tolerate a situation in which its sons and daughters continue to be massacred by lawless gangs while the international community, more concerned

---

[72] United Nations High Commissioner for Human Rights, 'Opération sur le Terrain au Rwanda Préfecture de Butare', p. 47.

[73] MSF, 'Report on events in Kibeho camp', p. 13.

about feeding the refugees and counting the dead than tackling the real problem and seeking a lasting solution, passively looks on.[74]

MSF's international staff confirmed that in July and August 1994 supporters of the interim government responsible for the genocide were, until the French troops pulled out, active in the area. The Interahamwe militia had become more discreet since the arrival of the RPA in Gikongoro prefecture. The RPA had established intelligence operations in the IDP camps.

During meetings with aid organisation representatives, officers from the new Rwandan army said that they were well aware of what was going on in the camps. Tutsi families living in villages on the hills not far from the camps had been attacked. Generally speaking, the safety of genocide survivors able to testify against the perpetrators could not be taken for granted in this region. Chantal Umuruza, a genocide survivor who lived in Nshili municipality (Gikongoro) and worked for Feed the Children helping the displaced, described the unremitting threat: 'We don't know our rescuers [French soldiers] and hadn't received any news from them, but the Hutus militias sent us an anonymous letter from Zaire saying it wasn't over for us. They would be back.'[75]

But while the threat persisted, supporters of the former regime did not undertake any large-scale military action. The thorough search of Kibeho camp in early December in the joint operation run by the peacekeepers and the RPA had unearthed no military weapons and very few people on the RPA's list of suspects had been found (three-quarters of the camp population were women and children under the age of fifteen).

During the President's visit to the site, a dispute broke out with Captain Francis Sikaongo, the Zambian officer in charge of the peacekeepers. He had contacted his superiors in Kigali several times during the massacre; they had ordered him to observe without intervening.[76] The peacekeepers' officer accused the President of providing false information, particularly concerning the number of dead. A few hours later, the UNAMIR commander in Kigali revised that number downward.[77]

The UN was now officially declaring 2,000 deaths while the peacekeepers present during the shootings had counted at least 4,050.[78] The Zambian captain kept saying to Rwandan officials that you do not shoot women and children with an antitank weapon. RPA soldiers rewarded his comments with thinly veiled death threats

[74] Pasteur Bizimungu, President of Rwanda, Declaration by the Rwandan government concerning the decision to close the displaced persons camps in Gikongoro, Kigali, 24 May 1995.

[75] C. Umuraza, *Une jeunesse rwandaise* (Paris: Karthala, 2008), p. 75.

[76] 'Interview with MSF Field coordinator. Gikongoro Rwanda. November 1994 to May 1995', in Binet, *The Violence of the New Rwandan Regime*, p. 83.

[77] AFP Kigali, 24 April 1995.

[78] AFP Sydney, 24 April 1994.

uttered in front of the authorities visiting the camp.[79] He left Rwanda precipitously a few weeks later.

On 25 April, RPA soldiers refused to let the MSF team enter the camp, while authorising access for journalists and the ICRC. On 26 April, the team did gain access to the camp, only to be denied entry to the hospital by RPA soldiers. On 27 April, President Bizimungu and Vice-President Kagame visited the Kibeho site accompanied by UN Secretary-General Special Representative Shaharyar M. Khan, a group of ambassadors, journalists and representatives of various UN agencies, international organisations and NGOs.

As a sign of protest, the MSF team kept a conspicuous distance from the group. Several mass graves were opened and 338 corpses discovered. This number became the government's official figure. A communications manager, the only MSF employee present nearby the officials, was ordered by Kagame in front of the entire delegation to refute MSF's press statement that the RPA had killed several thousand people. She replied that her organisation stood by its statements. During the visit, President Bizimungu announced the creation of an international commission of inquiry to shed light on what had come to be known as the 'events in Kibeho'. Meanwhile, the RPA began removing bodies from the camp. The MSF received confirmation of this from UNAMIR soldiers, even though the organisation officially denied it.[80]

Twenty years later, tongues are loosening and archives opening, but publications on these events are still all too few.[81] The RPF split into factions and some of its officers fled to other countries. Embassies and international organisations are either making available internal documents from the time or arranging information leaks, which is how, for example, journalist Judi Rever says she tracked down the account of a Directorate of Military Intelligence officer in UN documents. This officer describes the fate that, according to him, awaited the Kibeho IDPs held in Huye military camp (Butare prefecture) after the camp closed: 'For three days, for 24 hours straight, we killed Kibeho survivors with ropes, hammers, and plastic bags.'[82]

The camps were now empty. During conversations between the MSF team and UN human rights monitors, the key issue had become IDPs who had been arrested upon their return home after the closure of the camps. Men made up the vast majority of those held in local jails. They were imprisoned either after being denounced or simply because they were adult Hutu men who had left their municipalities before the victors arrived.

[79] D. Lorch, 'As many as 2,000 are reported dead in Rwanda', *New York Times* (24 April 1995).

[80] AFP, Annie Thomas, 'L'armée rwandaise accusée de déterrer et dissimuler les corps des victimes de Kibeho, Rwanda', 1 May 1995.

[81] Cl. Vidal, 'Les humanitaires, témoins pour l'histoire', *Les Temps Modernes*, 627 (April/May/June 2004), 92–107.

[82] J. Rever, 'Kibeho: a story of blood and flesh', *Foreign Policy* (27 April 2015).

On 26 April, an UNHCHR official, accompanied by an RPA major, discovered twenty-eight bodies in Rusatira municipal jail (Butare prefecture). These people had suffocated to death in the overcrowded prison. About one hundred inmates were released when an RPA officer opened the doors and, the following day, Médecins du Monde and the ICRC managed to treat the survivors. During a visit to the jail, the UN human rights monitor reported:

> In a second room, a group of seventy prisoners were also very weak. Outside, another group of nineteen prisoners were lying on the ground hovering between life and death. Moaning and trembling, they were obviously terrified of the soldiers. Signs of abuse could be clearly seen on their bodies, including multiple scratches, scars and bruises; one had a bullet wound on his lower lip, while another had a machete gash on his forehead.[83]

The authorities moved swiftly to give legal form to the arrests. Judicial gendarmerie police officers and Ministry of Justice police inspectors – with logistics and legal advice provided by HCHR – began putting together case files for arrested people. This task had the support of the Interior and Justice ministers, who had no desire to cover up illegal arrests, ill-treatment and executions. Begun in early May 1995, it would lead to the release of 842 prisoners out of the 2,194 IDPs incarcerated and registered by HCHR monitors.[84]

At the end of May, municipalities in Butare prefecture had recorded 68,052 returns and the UNHCR 16,000 Rwandans arriving in Burundi from the displaced persons camps in Gikongoro prefecture. Compared to the total estimated number of IDPs in the Gikongoro camps originally from Butare prefecture, around 20,000 people were missing, according to an HCHR estimate.[85] Were they dead or had they simply fallen between the cracks?

The international commission of inquiry announced by the President was established on 3 May and met for the first time on 8 May. It presented its report to the President on 18 May. The commission comprised ten members: a French prosecutor, Canadian diplomat, Belgian international law professor, German diplomat, UN diplomat, British forensic pathologist, American lawyer, OAU military expert, Dutch prosecutor and a lawyer representing Rwanda (Christine Umutoni, chief of staff at the Ministry of Rehabilitation). The commission of inquiry operated by consensus. A few days before presenting its conclusions, it had yet to contact MSF personnel who had witnessed the 'events in Kibeho'. At the last minute, the head of mission

---

[83] United Nations High Commissioner for Human Rights, 'Opération sur le Terrain au Rwanda Préfecture de Butare', p. 73.

[84] United Nations High Commissioner for Human Rights, 'Opération sur le Terrain au Rwanda Préfecture de Butare', p. 163.

[85] United Nations High Commissioner for Human Rights, 'Opération sur le Terrain au Rwanda Préfecture de Butare', p. 152.

was able to give three of the commission members a report on the events. The few questions that the members asked the head of mission all focused on the presence of genocidal militiamen in the IDP camps. In its final report, however, the commission did acknowledge the RPA's responsibility: 'At this stage, the RPA soldiers' reactions were disproportionate and thus in violation of international law. RPA members shot [at IDPs] without distinguishing between hostile and non-hostile elements and RPA soldiers opened fire indiscriminately.'[86]

According to the commission's report, the RPA soldiers had underestimated the influence of a 'hard-core' group among the displaced, which had, according to them, attacked the RPA. Did this hard-core really exist? The commission acknowledged that it did not have concrete evidence to back up this allegation: 'The commission was unable to obtain any detailed information on the organisation and the structure of this "hard-core" group.'[87]

Otherwise, the report accepted on behalf of the commission all of the claims made by the country's authorities. It highlighted the RPA's lack of means of communication and the fact that its soldiers were neither trained nor equipped to maintain order. It did not mention the total number of deaths. Responsibility for the persistence of this mysterious 'hard-core' in this camp under international protection was attributed to the inadequacies of the peacekeepers. The report reproached the NGOs for not having persuaded the IDPs to return home.

The report stressed that the 'events in Kibeho' were not caused by an operation carried out by the Rwandan army alone but by a joint operation with the peacekeepers. The commission of inquiry praised the manner in which the operation had been planned and coordinated between national and international forces, with particular recognition of the work of the Integrated Operations Center (IOC).[88]

In its conclusions, the commission made a recommendation about the attitude the 'international community' should adopt moving forward towards the Rwandan authorities. The commission recommended that the international community continue to encourage and help the Republic of Rwanda in its efforts to establish justice, reconciliation and national reconstruction.

Donor countries like the Netherlands and Belgium had announced the suspension of aid following the 'events in Kibeho'. Now that they had the endorsement of an 'independent' commission of inquiry, they could resume providing financial support to the new regime.

---

[86] 'Report of the independent international commission of inquiry on the events in Kibeho, April 1995', Kigali, 18 May 1995, p. 10.

[87] 'Report of the independent international commission of inquiry on the events in Kibeho, April 1995', p. 12.

[88] Fourteen years later, Patrick Nyamuvumba, the officer who commanded the RPA at Kibeho, was appointed Force Commander of the peacekeeping operation in Darfur by UN Secretary-General Ban Ki-moon (Sudan, 2009–13). Meanwhile, Kofi Annan, head of peacekeeping operations at UN head office (1993–96) in New York during the 'events in Kibeho', had completed two terms as UN Secretary-General (1997–2006).

Prisons

MSF teams' disquiet about the prisons began in early autumn 1994. The disastrous conditions of health and hygiene had been noticed during a visit by European human rights organisations and had resulted in the RCN, a coalition supported by MSF. After visits to the prisons in Kigali, Gitarama and Butare, MSF considered that the medical care provided to prisoners by Ministry of Health personnel – assisted by members of the ICRC – was inadequate.

In this situation of armed conflict, for historic, legal and organisational reasons, it was the ICRC that was able to offer the best care and protection to prisoners. While certain detention centres remained off-limits, 112 ICRC representatives were nevertheless able to visit more than 120, including thirteen prisons.[89]

During MSF's international meetings, the organisation's Belgian section had been announcing its intention to provide targeted support for medical care in prisons since October 1994.[90] For its part, the ICRC did not deny the deplorable health conditions prevailing in prisons but did not view the shortage of health workers to be the main problem. In their opinion, which was shared by the French section and MSF's legal adviser in Europe, the health disaster was due to the lack of inmates' living space (less than one square metre per person).

It was the government's responsibility to rectify this situation. The ICRC was worried about increasing the number of foreign organisations in the prisons,[91] fearing that the authorities would pit the various humanitarian agencies against each other and choose those least likely to oppose their detention policy. In reality, the government was divided. The Interior and Justice ministers were aware that many of the detainees were probably innocent because most of them had no criminal record. The Minister of Justice sent police inspectors into the prisons to release these inmates. With this aim, a committee had been set up in Kigali to establish the validity of remand prisoners' cases: 'Out of 20,000 prisoners counted, we estimate that 20% are innocent and were incarcerated on the strength of highly questionable denunciations.'[92]

At the same time, repression by the RPA was filling all the prefectures' detention facilities at a brisk pace, with more than 1,000 new incarcerations a week in March 1995, according to information passed to MSF by RCN.[93] During another field visit, MSF's legal adviser saw for herself that RPA officers wielded much more

[89] MSF, 'Minutes of meeting in Brussels between MSF B – F [Belgium and France) and ICRC on the prison problem in Rwanda', 27 March 1995, p. 1.
[90] MSF Belgium, 'Medical Assistance Project for Rwanda's Civilian Prisons. Project Proposal Addressed to the Ministry of Justice, Kigali', 26 May 1995.
[91] MSF, 'Minutes of meeting of MSF Belgium and MSF France teams in Rwanda on the issue of prisons, Kigali', 5 March 1995.
[92] Alphonse-Marie Nkubito, Minister of Justice, quoted by A. Frilet, 'La justice rwandaise en panne', Libération (2 March 1995).
[93] 'Fax from the operations manager in Brussels to teams working for all MSF sections in Kigali. Summary of conversation with Daniel Debeer, RCN Kigali', March 1995.

power in these centres than judges and prison directors.[94] With their dominant role in the repressive system, RPA officers often blocked efforts to increase the number of prisoners eligible for release and generally opposed any improvement in prison conditions.

MSF shared the ICRC's opinion that the main problem – extreme overcrowding – was the responsibility of the authorities. UNAMIR suggested that the government save time and money in the short term by opening detention centres ringed by barbed wire instead of an outer wall. RPA officers responded that this solution would be intolerable for genocide survivors as they would be able to see their torturers through the wire. From this standpoint, new prisons surrounded by walls were required, but building them would take months or even years.

Meanwhile, the number of prisoners and deaths of inmates continued to climb. Not counting the prisoners in facilities off-limits to monitoring by the ICRC and other UN organisations, the estimated number of inmates was 25,000 in March 1995, according to a report written by MSF's legal adviser.[95] MSF Belgium was unsuccessful in its attempts to work inside the prisons for several reasons: the unavailability of MSF staff specifically trained for this type of work, opposition from the ICRC and the difficulty with obtaining the necessary authorisations. MSF focused on treating the most seriously ill prisoners in the hospitals they were transferred to.

Between early September 1994 and late February 1995, the MSF team working in Kabgayi Hospital treated 218 sick or wounded prisoners transferred from Gitarama prison. The 4,500 square metre prison had been built to house 400 inmates. In late August 1994, the prefecture's prison had eighty inmates, a number that rose to 5,150 by the end of February 1995, and included 105 women and sixty-six minors.[96] Forty-five prisoners had been released since August 1994.

Due to the extreme overcrowding, injuries were the main issue, according to the observations of MSF's doctors. All the prisoners had foot wounds and gangrene was common. To reach food distribution and sources of drinking water, inmates would rub their neighbours' ears roughly to force them to move out of the way. The epidemic of bruising to the ear this caused, sometimes leading to infection and the destruction of the outer ear, was entirely new to the medical staff. In some cases, wounds were also due to human bites. Along with these injuries, there was dysentery, malaria, pneumonia, septicaemia, malnutrition and dehydration. In such an environment, the care provided inside the prison by Ministry of Health employees and in Kabgayi Hospital by the Caritas surgeon and the MSF team was not enough to reduce mortality.

By the end of February, 154 out of the 218 patients admitted had left Kabgayi Hospital. Sixty-eight of them (44 per cent) went straight to the cemetery. A total of

[94] MSF legal adviser, 'Rwanda Mission report, 30 January – 7 February 1995', Paris, February 1995.
[95] MSF, 'Situation assessment. Prisoners' health: case of Gitarama. Médecins Sans Frontières in Rwanda', March 1995.
[96] MSF, 'Situation assessment. Prisoners' health: case of Gitarama. Médecins Sans Frontières in Rwanda', p. 1.

244 Gitarama inmates died between the beginning of November 1994 and the end of January 1995. Over a three-month period, this number of deaths corresponded to a crude mortality rate of 9.6 deaths per 10,000 people per day. At the time, it was the highest mortality rate of any segment of the Rwandan population and close to five times higher than the threshold considered to be a health disaster, i.e. two deaths per 10,000 people per day.

In March, MSF sent a preliminary report describing the situation in Gitarama prison to the authorities and embassies. The report was not released to the press because it was hoped that it would foster dialogue with the authorities. Jacques Bihozagara, Minister of Rehabilitation and Social Integration, wrote a letter to MSF in reply. Bihozagara did not deny the gravity of the situation but warned MSF:

> We cannot, however, tolerate anyone taking advantage of this situation to interfere in affairs that are the responsibility of the government. In particular, we insist that MSF France strictly confine itself to its humanitarian and medical work and refrain from any political considerations in its assessments and in its public and official statements.[97]

In April and May, some refurbishment was undertaken to improve conditions at Gitarama prison. At the same time, the inmate population kept growing, reaching 6,957 and 902 deaths (between the beginning of August 1994 and the end of May 1995). The transfer of 2,500 prisoners had been announced, but was reduced to less than one hundred. Under these conditions, the planned expansion of the prison would not change the fact that each inmate had to try to survive in less than one square metre.

In early July, MSF decided to make public in a second report its findings on the health situation in Gitarama prison. The only aspect of the report that yielded any result in Gitarama and in the other prisons concerned incarceration of minors, with organisations such as UNICEF and RCN allowed to pay a fine for the release of certain minors. MSF also helped with the construction of washroom facilities at a new juvenile detention centre (Gitagata).

A new Rwanda was being established, but that did not mean mass crimes had disappeared. The fact that they persisted, however, ended up causing a political schism within the government and, at the end of August 1995, the Prime Minister and several ministers – Interior, Justice, Finance, Transport and Communication – stepped down.

Expulsion

In the everyday provision of medical care, relations between the authorities and MSF were not as bad as the events of the first half of 1995 would suggest. Whenever discussions broached matters other than the displaced or prisoners, working relationships

---

[97] MSF, 'Letter from Minister of Rehabilitation and Social Integration to MSF France's head of mission', 17 May 1995.

with Ministry of Health personnel were constructive. MSF had provided material and financial support to Ministry of Health administrative staff in several prefectures and there were real and wide-ranging opportunities for cooperation to improve the health status of certain population groups. Ministry of Health workers coordinated all the ministry's partners, including the Red Cross, ICRC, WHO, UNICEF and non-governmental organisations.

In addition to restoring hospitals to working order – an area MSF had moved its focus to since late 1994 in Ruhengeri, Gyseni, Gitarama, Butare, Kibuye and Gikongoro prefectures – there were many urgent tasks.[98] The principal causes of mortality were malaria, respiratory infections and dysentery and treatments used for malaria and dysentery had become ineffective, due to the development of resistance. Breaking the impasse required conducting more epidemiological surveys, improving their quality and instituting new treatment protocols. MSF offered the services of its Epicentre to combat diarrhoeal diseases and provided physical and psychological treatment for war casualties, particularly female victims of rape.[99] Despite the recent tensions with the authorities, MSF France was the first NGO to be officially registered by the Ministry of Rehabilitation.

But, on 6 December 1995, the government announced the expulsion of thirty-nine NGOs, which included two of MSF's sections – France and Switzerland. This decision did not come as a complete surprise to the French section, due to its nationality and the tensions with the authorities over the closing of Kibeho and the health situation in Gitarama prison. Meanwhile, relations between the Swiss section and the Ministry of Rehabilitation regarding MSF's medical activities had deteriorated with the arrival in Byumba of hundreds of thousands of Tutsis from Uganda. More geared towards emergency services, MSF's medical expertise was ill-adapted to the needs of these people who had not lived through the war. This led to criticism by the Ministry of Rehabilitation, which viewed the former Tutsi refugees returning to Rwanda as a priority. For its part, MSF staff was concerned about helping to develop medical services exclusively for one group, the Tutsis.

On 11 December, the Ministry of Rehabilitation gave representatives of the expelled NGOs seven days to leave the country. On 12 December, their telephone lines were disconnected and their bank accounts frozen. Furthermore, the Minister demanded that these international aid organisations turn over all their property. This last measure came as little surprise to MSF as late 1995 had seen an increase in night thefts of vehicles and money kept in aid agency offices.[100] Uniformed men, whose precise identity was officially mysterious, carried out these thefts. In reality,

---

[98] MSF, 'Activities of Médecins Sans Frontières in Rwanda', 7 December 1994.
[99] C. Paquet, 'Appui au programme rwandais de lutte contre les maladies diarrhéiques Proposition de création d'une unité de surveillance et de recherche opérationnelle sur les dysenteries et le choléra à l'hôpital universitaire de Butare, Epicentre', Paris, March 1995.
[100] MSF, 'Fax from Kigali to European head office', 17 July 1995.

only Rwandan army soldiers in this new Rwanda could engage in such nocturnal activities without running into trouble with law enforcement officers.

A year and a half after the RPF came to power, the choice the authorities were proposing to the aid organisations became all too clear: either speak out about the crimes committed by the new power and suffer its wrath (administrative obstacles, thinly-veiled physical threats, expulsion), or remain silent and give credence to the idea that the crimes committed by the victors did not warrant attention. According to the advocates of remaining silent, this at least had the advantage of ensuring that operations would be allowed to continue. But for those in favour of speaking out, it meant no complicity. It is a fact that the perpetrators of the mass crimes had become accustomed to obtaining the silence of the humanitarian organisation – if not their active participation in joint operations which, as seen during the closure of Kibeho camp, could culminate in thousands of deaths. So, for or against? After the closure of the IDP camps in Rwanda, the shutting down of refugee camps in Zaire would shed new light on this quandary.

4

Refugees on the run in war-torn Zaire, 1996–97

In 1995, the leaders of the Tutsi genocide had free reign in Zaire and set about mar-
shalling their partisans in the refugee camps. Embarking on a combat strategy, they
launched increasingly frequent and murderous incursions into Rwanda where they
targeted civilians. In October and November 1996, the RPA, with the help of Zairian
rebels, destroyed all the camps set up in North and South Kivu in east Zaire.[1] These
rebels included many Banyamulenge – Congolese Tutsis originally from Rwanda –
who had been living in South Kivu for generations.[2] In mid-November, these forces
attacked and took control of Mugunga camp near Goma in North Kivu where large
numbers of refugees had assembled after escaping from areas already in the hands of
the rebel movement and the RPA. This attack on 15 November set in motion a massive return to Rwanda. From Mugunga, the refugees were channelled towards Goma
before crossing over the border to Gisenyi.

Fearing further attacks by the rebels, and more especially by the RPA, large numbers of refugees fled towards the interior of Zaire. Meanwhile, no longer content
with ensuring a protective buffer zone on Rwanda's borders, the RPA and the ADFL
(Alliance of the Democratic Forces for the Liberation of Congo/Zaire)[3] began

---

[1] Numerous books and articles have been published on Rwanda's political, economic and military intervention in Zaire in 1996–97. See notably T. Turner, *The Congo Wars: Conflict, Myth & Reality* (London
and New York: Zed Books, 2007); F. Reyntjens, *The Great African War: Congo and Regional Geopolitics,
1996–2006* (Cambridge: Cambridge University Press, 2010), T. Longman, 'The complex reasons for
Rwanda's engagement in Congo', in J.F. Clark (ed.), *The African Stakes of the Congo War* (New York: Palgrave
Macmillan, 2002).

[2] K. Vlassenroot, 'Citizenship, identity formation & conflict in South Kivu: the case of the Banyamulenge',
Review of African Political Economy, 93–94 (2002), 499–516; J.-C. Willame, *Banyarwanda et Banyamulenge.
Violences ethniques et gestion de l'identitaire au Kivu* (Brussels and Paris: Cahiers Africains, Institut Africain,
L'Harmattan, 1997).

[3] The ADFL was created on 18 October 1996 by a handful of Zairian political personalities, including several
Banyamulenge leaders. Laurent Désiré Kabila was appointed as the movement's spokesperson. The agreement protocol establishing the Alliance was signed in Lemera, Zaire, in the region where the Banyamulenge
had carried out their first attacks at the beginning of October 1996; Lemera hospital had been one of the
first targets. See G. de Villers and J.-C. Willame, *République démocratique du Congo. Chronique politique d'un*

advancing on several fronts. After overpowering the Zairian army, they marched triumphantly into Kinshasa on 17 May 1997. By this time, president Mobutu had already left the capital, relinquishing the power he had seized back in 1965.

It is at this point that our study examines another period: the first international war in Zaire, from 1996 to 1997. During this war, Angola, Uganda and Rwanda fought alongside the ADFL, while Burundi, Zambia, Zimbabwe and the United States were the principal providers of political and logistical support.[4]

During this war, what became of the refugees living in camps in east Zaire who refused to return to their home country when the conflict started? They fled. There are many accounts of their flight across Zaire. The academic François Lagarde undertook a methodical compilation of these accounts and published, in French, a total of thirteen between 1994 and 2013 (the authors were adults at the time of their flight).[5] These testimonies provide us with insight into how people managed to survive and escape from their pursuers (the ADFL and RPA forces) and describe the aid delivered by international NGOs. They also reveal the physical and moral state refugees were reduced to before being assisted by humanitarian aid workers.

Here is an example. Marie Béatrice Umutesi fled the town of Bukavu in east Zaire on 28 October 1996. She walked 2,000 kilometres from Bukavu in South Kivu to Mbandaka in Equateur province before reaching Kinshasa on November 1997 and finally leaving the DRC.[6] Her account is painstakingly detailed. She gives the names of all the places she passed through (villages, towns and rivers), the chronology and the time spent travelling between safe resting places and temporary camps; she explains how she obtained food, water, medical care, assistance and refuge; she describes the natural environments she encountered: dense forests, wide rivers, tropical rainfall and dangerous animals; she relates the living conditions in the villages she went through and in the camps where she broke her journey and stopped off with her family. It was in these camps where refugees had assembled that she once again came into contact with the international assistance.[7] Her and some of the

entre-deux-guerres, octobre 1996-juillet 1998 (Tervuren and Paris: Cahiers africains, Institut Africain-CEDAF, L'Harmattan, 1998).

[4] On prevailing perceptions of the conflict in the United States, see J. Pottier, *Re-Imagining Rwanda: Conflict, Survival and Disinformation in the Late Twentieth Century* (Cambridge: Cambridge University Press, 2002), pp. 53–108.

[5] F. Lagarde, *Mémorialistes et témoins rwandais (1994–2013)* (Paris: L'Harmattan, 2013), pp. 165–221. See also B. Jewsiewicki, *La première guerre du Congo-Zaïre (1996–1997). Récits de soldats ADFL et FAR* (Paris: L'Harmattan, 2012).

[6] On 17 May 1997, Laurent-Désiré Kabila, spokesperson of the ADFL, proclaimed himself President and changed the name of the country from Zaire to the Democratic Republic of the Congo (DRC).

[7] M.B. Umutesi, *Surviving the Slaughter: The Ordeal of a Rwndan Refugee in Zaire* (Madison: The University of Wisconsin Press, 2004). Originally published in France as *Fuir ou mourir au Zaïre* (Paris: L'Harmattan, 2000). On the subject of M.B. Umutesi, see the articles by A. Mari Tripp, R. Lemarchand, A. Habimana, A. Songolo, C. Newbury, D. de Lame in *African Studies Review*, 48:3 (December 2005), 89–141. J.K. Stearns analyses this account of her flight and sets it in the context of the war. See J.K. Stearns, *Dancing in the Glory of Monsters: The Collapse of the Congo and the Great African War of Africa* (New York: PublicAffairs, 2011), pp. 33–8, 127–31, 134–5.

other accounts relate memories of the dangers they faced and the behaviours they adopted to overcome them. They describe the material conditions of their flight at different times, in different situations and when exposed to different risks. We will make frequent reference to these first-hand experiences.

This chapter is divided into five periods. We begin by looking at the start of the war, with the attacks on refugee camps in east Zaire between September and November 1996. We then examine the flight of some of the refugees towards the interior of Zaire and relate what happened to them at a site (Tingi-Tingi) where they stayed until February 1997. We go on to look at a further episode of flight, temporary settlement and massacre between March and July 1997 while the fourth episode discusses the conditions in which refugees in Zaire and Tanzania were repatriated to Rwanda. The fifth and final episode will look at those who refused to return and walked on to Mbandaka before finally crossing over into Congo-Brazzaville.

The end of the camps in Zaire (September to November 1996)

How much did MSF know about the politico-military context in North and South Kivu in September–October 1996? A report appended to the sitrep (situation report) dated 24 October and drafted by MSF Holland's 'Context Unit' in Amsterdam (a unit tasked with data collection and situation analysis) concluded that there was very little prospect of a diplomatic resolution to the clashes between the various political and military groups. In terms of humanitarian objectives, 'the major concern [was] the reaction of (Hutu) refugees in Zaïre'.[8] What direction would they take in fleeing the combat zones? Was there a risk of them becoming trapped if the fighting spread? How and where to reach out to them?

Two days after MSF Holland's sitrep, an IRIN news bulletin on the ADFL was much more emphatic about its military capacity.[9] Its analysis was accurate, as the town of Uvira fell into rebel hands during the night of 24 October and their forces rapidly took control of almost the entire area between Uvira and Bukavu in South Kivu and the border with Rwanda.[10] Refugees who had fled from camps around Uvira began to arrive in the Bukavu region. UN humanitarian agencies planned to supply them with water and high-protein biscuits along the road. But, it is to be noted that these armed forces were at the time being portrayed by observers and those in the field as defending the cause of the Banyamulenge, who had been oppressed by the

[8] MSF, 'Sitrep Kivu Explo 003', 24 October 1996.
[9] The United Nations Department of Humanitarian Affairs published a regional news bulletin on 26 October 1996, which became a daily bulletin on 31 October. It was first called IRIN *Emergency Update on Eastern Zaïre* and then, with issue 54 of 11 December 1996, it became IRIN *Emergency Update on the Great Lakes*. We use these bulletins as one of our sources, referring to them as IRIN (Integrated Regional Information Network) with the publication date.
[10] On the weakness of the Zairian armed forces and the political conflicts within Kivu, see R. Lemarchand, *The Dynamics of Violence in Central Africa* (Philadelphia: University of Pennsylvania Press, 2009), pp. 226–30.

Zairian government and threatened with genocide by armed Hutu militia groups formed in the camps.[11] An MSF sitrep on 23 October suggested, however, that the conflict could well involve forces other than the Banyamulenge and mentioned the existence of 'unidentified combatants' who might be Rwandan.[12]

Once Uvira fell to the rebels on 24–25 October, the armed conflict spread rapidly to the whole of Kivu. All the camps (five in the Goma region, twenty-two in the Bukavu region and thirteen nearby Uvira.) were attacked and destroyed, forcing hundreds of thousands of refugees to take flight. For example, Kibumba camp to the north of Goma, which hosted some 200,000 refugees, was emptied in the space of only a few hours on 26 October after being hit by shells fired from Rwanda. The same day, all the international agencies were evacuated from Bukavu, with the exception of three International Committee of the Red Cross (ICRC) staff and members of religious orders. Logistics equipment left behind by NGOs and the ICRC was looted. According to a UNHCR spokesperson, after the destruction of these camps, almost half a million refugees were on the move. Those fleeing from Kibumba headed for Mugunga camp, thirteen kilometres west of Goma.[13] A UNHCR spokesperson reported that, on 28 October, 420,000 refugees were crowded into this camp. He also confirmed that UNHCR had lost direct access to all but two camps, Lac Vert and Mugunga.[14] Working in Mugunga to cope with the influx of refugees from other camps, MSF participated in setting up emergency clinics and sanitation facilities.

On 30 October, the rebels announced they had taken control of Bukavu and were fighting to take Goma. On 31 October, MSF accused Western nations of non-assistance to populations in danger and called for 'the creation of a safe space where civilians could access aid'. According to this press release, more than two million people were suffering from malnutrition and epidemics in the Great Lakes region and massacres were being perpetrated in Kivu. On 2 November, forced to evacuate because of the ferocity of the fighting, six of MSF's international staff left Goma for Kigali. They had witnessed the murder of refugees and Zairian civilians, but at this stage MSF did not communicate what they had seen to the media. On 4 November, ADFL spokesperson Laurent Désiré Kabila announced an immediate unilateral three-week ceasefire and claimed to have taken control of Uvira, Bukavu and Goma. He gave the refugees three weeks to return to Rwanda. At this time, several journalists were reporting that RPA forces had participated in the battle to take Goma.

So, during the period described above, the rebels seized the three main towns in North and South Kivu, huge numbers of refugees were on the move and only two camps remained around Goma. Summarising the available information on

---

[11] On 7 October 1996, the vice-governor of South Kivu made an announcement, giving the Banyamulenge one week to leave Zaire.

[12] MSF, 'Sitrep Kivu Explo 001', 23 October 1996.

[13] Stephen Powell, 'Human tide of refugees on the move in Zaire', Reuters (27 October 1996).

[14] Reuters, 'Zaire rebels advance, refugees report many dead', 28 October 1996.

the situation and on current and planned operations, a sitrep on 5 November concluded: 'The doomsday scenario continues.'[15]

On 7 November, while aid workers were being denied access to Mugunga camp, journalists reported that military preparations were underway to attack the camp and, on 8 November, a Voice of America (VOA) dispatch announced that there had been fighting in the camp overnight.[16]

On 11 November, the Rwandan authorities authorised, for one day only, an aid convoy and seventy international journalists to travel from Gisenyi to Goma. An MSF communiqué drafted that same evening described the day's events: crossing the border had taken three hours and the whole convoy had been sent to the stadium. But the MSF teams left their vehicles outside so they could get around the town. They headed straight for ASRAMES (Regional Association for the Supply of Essential Medicines), where the warehouses had been completely looted, and then to the Baptist Community Hospital where they dropped off medicines and foodstuffs. The team went back to the stadium at about 6 p.m. to find the other NGOs still waiting for the outcome of a meeting with the authorities. MSF decided not to wait and headed straight back to Gisenyi. In their debriefing, they described the town as more or less deserted. Many houses had been destroyed and the teams were told by acquaintances that the population had been trapped there.

On 14 November, the shelling of Mugunga ended and thousands of refugees fled towards Goma.[17] The same day, MSF's team in Gisenyi reported that 12,000 refugees were crossing the border into Rwanda each hour. By 11 p.m. on 16 November, 12,000 an hour continued to cross over. The refugees were extremely hungry, but organising a distribution of biscuits was impossible because of the risk of the crowd becoming uncontrollable. One MSF health centre was still functioning. On 18 November, a cholera treatment unit was set up in a transit camp on the Rwandan side of the border, and within a day, MSF and Medical Emergency Relief International (Merlin) each treated fifty cases. A number of way stations had been set up along the road between Gisenyi and Ruhengeri – a distance of eighty kilometres – and all were equipped to treat cholera. But, on 20 November, the Rwandan government, which had been refusing to allow camps to form in Gisenyi and along the roads back, demanded that the refugees return to their municipalities without delay and ordered all these way stations to be dismantled. In one station near Gisenyi, soldiers literally strong-armed patients onto trucks to get them to leave, prompting MSF to protest to UNHCR and the Rwandan authorities. The flow of refugees crossing the border began to slow down. But, according to an UNHCR estimate published on 18 November, 500,000 refugees had crossed into Rwanda in just three days.[18] As pointed out by a number

[15] MSF, 'Sitrep Kivu Explo 011', 4–5 November 1996.
[16] Voice of America (VOA), 'Outsiders have been turned away from Mugunga Camp', 8 November 1996.
[17] Reuters, 'Mass of Hutu refugees head for Rwanda border', 15 November 1996.
[18] UNHCR, 'Zaire crisis at a glance', 18 November 1996.

of organisations and journalists, this also meant that at least 500,000 refugees were now unaccounted for.

Prior to this massive return, the war in Kivu had already created grave fears for the fate of the refugees and international NGOs and governments had begun to consider the need for military action. As mentioned earlier, MSF had on 31 October called for the creation of a safe space for the refugees. On 4 November, the organisation held a press conference in Rwanda, calling for 'an international military intervention to set up safe areas'. As things stood, the priority was to provide assistance and security to the refugees and not set up a corridor that could be used to force them to return. This was the second time in its history that MSF had campaigned in favour of such an intervention.

On 9 November 1996, the UNSC affirmed in resolution 1078 its support for the creation of a multinational force to be set up for humanitarian purposes in eastern Zaire. Resolution 1080, adopted on 15 November, specified that this force would be temporary and that its mandate would end on 31 March 1997. Its mission would be 'to facilitate the immediate return of humanitarian organizations [and] the voluntary, orderly repatriation of refugees by the United Nations High Commissioner for Refugees'.

On 22 November, Oxfam was one of several organisations to criticise the major powers meeting in Stuttgart for their indecisiveness, despite reliable information from missionaries and aerial photos showing the location of 700,000 refugees.[19] As for the new Rwandan authorities and the ADFL, they were campaigning against the planned military operation in Zaire. Finally, on 14 December, the United Nations ordered the withdrawal of the first units of the multinational force already positioned in Rwanda and Uganda, a decision that effectively put an end to the project for a military engagement in Zaire. The main public argument for deciding against this engagement was based on the claim that the satellite pictures known to US political and military authorities did not show any significant concentrations of refugees heading towards the interior of Zaire.[20]

From the flight of the refugees to the storming of Tingi-Tingi camp, end of February, 1997

Most of the refugees fled west towards Kisangani (the capital of Orientale province), although some headed for Angola and Zambia. We will begin, however, with what was actually known by UN agencies and NGOs about refugee movements towards the interior of Zaire. Aid workers could only deliver assistance if

[19] United States Information Agency, 'Transcript: Canadian general briefs press on Zaire crisis after Stuttgart', 23 November 1996.
[20] For a history of the planned military intervention in Zaire, see P. Dupont, 'La communauté internationale face à la question de l'intervention humanitaire lors de la rébellion au Kivu (octobre-décembre 1996)', *L'Afrique des Grands Lacs, Annuaire 1996–1997* (Paris: L'Harmattan, 1997), pp. 205–20.

Map 4.1 Movements of Rwandan refugees in Zaire, 1996–97

they could localise the refugees, calculate or make an intelligent guess at their number and anticipate as accurately as possible the positions of the ADFL and Rwandan armed forces. In this respect, the end of 1996 was a period of uncertainty that sparked much controversy on the motives of the various political stakeholders engaged in Zaire.

Since 6–7 November 1996, several UN agencies, including UNHCR, had been insistently but unsuccessfully requesting access to satellite pictures, especially those produced by the United States. But, on 8 November, Action by Churches Together (ACT) managed to take aerial photos showing a large concentration of people in a forest towards Walikale. By 20 November, according to UNHCR, 475,000 refugees had returned to Rwanda while 700,000 were still in Zaire and the agency said it had aerial reconnaissance to localise them.[21] The same day, Paul Kagame, Vice-President of Rwanda, accused aid agencies of overestimating the number of refugees still in Zaire. Also on 20 November, the ICRC published an account by one of its Zairian employees. Like thousands of others, he had fled Bukavu on 30 October and, after walking 355 kilometres, arrived in Kisangani on 16 November.[22]

The American administration was itself torn on how many Rwandan refugees were still in Zaire. While the US Ambassador to Rwanda claimed that most of the fugitives in Zaire were Burundians or internally displaced Zairians and that the number of Rwandan refugees in Zaire was being grossly exaggerated by aid agencies, the US Agency for International Development (USAID) confirmed UNHCR's estimate of 700,000 Rwandan refugees still in Zaire and claimed to have aerial reconnaissance to localise them.

On 10 December, MSF's coordinator in Kisangani reported that an aerial observation had picked up 50,000 refugees heading for Kisangani.[23] Five days later, the UN Department of Humanitarian Affairs (UNDHA) reported that Zairian forces had stopped 100,000 Rwandan refugees at Tingi-Tingi, 240 kilometres from Orientale province capital Kisangani. The UNICEF official in Tingi-Tingi estimated that almost 121,000 refugees in deplorable condition were already assembled there.[24] He also reported that access to the site was difficult, but that a runway was being built for small planes.

For its part, MSF had sent a doctor and a coordinator to Kisangani on 9 November to deliver an immediate programme of assistance to internally displaced Zairians. Anticipating an influx of displaced persons and refugees, MSF was planning to set up a base in Kisangani, but as opportunities for action were limited, the coordinator opted for a small team of three people – a team manager, a logistician-cum-administrator and a doctor.[25]

At the end of December, the team estimated the number of refugees in Tingi-Tingi at over 70,000, with more arriving every day. There is a notable difference between this estimate and that previously made by UNICEF. Indeed, fluctuations in the assessments of refugee numbers were a permanent feature throughout this period, as each international organisation had its own methods and agenda when it came to head counts. MSF had set up seven health posts and a central medical unit in Tingi-Tingi, as well as a therapeutic feeding centre and two supplementary feeding centres. MSF doctors were also working at the hospital in Lubutu, a town where the team lived seven kilometres away. According to this team, the population of Tingi-Tingi could be divided into three categories: strong people (young

[21] USAID, 'Rwandan returnee numbers and flows', 22 November 1996.
[22] ICRC, 'News 46, Displaced: a Zairian's first-hand account', 20 November 1996.
[23] Reuters, 'Red Cross finds refugees in bad state in Zaire', 10 December 1996.
[24] UNICEF, 'Great Lakes Region Update', 18 December 1996.
[25] MSF, 'Kisangani mission report (9–30 November 1996)', 3 December 1996.

men), average and vulnerable people (women on their own with children).[26] Meanwhile, the team had received back-up: five people in Kisangani and seven in Lubutu/Tingi-Tingi.

At the end of December, there were growing fears of a doomsday scenario. The frontline was drawing closer to Kisangani and tension was mounting in the town. More looting was predicted and possibilities for evacuation were getting slimmer. The decision was taken to cut back to three the team in Lubutu. By this time, UNICEF had already withdrawn from Tingi-Tingi and MSF was the only aid organisation still present. The managers of the MSF team in Kisangani affirmed the need to prepare to evacuate the Lubutu/Tingi-Tingi team, but also to set the conditions for its return: MSF should no longer be the only operator in this war zone assisting 'a refugee population that no-one else cares about'.[27]

On 30 December, the three members of the team who had stayed behind in Lubutu sent a long fax describing the situation in Tingi-Tingi camp.[28] Lubutu's administrative and military authorities were still in favour of MSF staying there. Many of the refugees had come from camps in Bukavu and Uvira. The biggest problem was lack of food and, with what remained of WFP, MSF and UNICEF stocks, rations had to be reduced until a convoy of ten ten-tonne trucks could get through. Dry food rations distributed to MSF's employees in exchange for their work (food for work) were reduced by thirty per cent.

Run by the refugees themselves, the camp's inhabitants were divided up according to their home prefectures. A representative structure was put in place with a president, a management committee and 'neighbourhood' representatives. During a meeting with the MSF team, these representatives brought up the subject of a Radio France Internationale broadcast during which a journalist interviewing an MSF manager in Paris mentioned the presence of militia in the camps. The representatives criticised the interview, but the discussion remained 'courteous'. The MSF coordinator concluded by saying that the health situation was deteriorating and would worsen still further if food didn't get through within the next week. The future of the relief programme was in the balance and everything could change in a matter of hours. The team decided to stay put, but was ready to evacuate at a moment's notice.

In the end, international humanitarian aid was in fact stepped up, due notably to the efforts of WFP. By the beginning of January 1997, UNHCR, Doctors of the World, Action Against Hunger, UNICEF and Caritas International had arrived in Kisangani and all were working in the Kisangani-Lubutu region. On 14 January 1997, there were more than seventy-five foreign aid workers from various organisations in Kisangani and Lubutu. But WFP was still not getting sufficient food through to

---

[26] MSF, 'Record of a telephone conversation with Kisangani', 21 December 1996.
[27] MSF, 'Kisangani coordination, situation in Lubutu/Tingi-Tingi', 27 December 1996.
[28] MSF, 'Fax from Lubutu', 30 December 1996.

meet needs in Tingi-Tingi[29] and the MSF coordinator in Kisangani reported that sometimes the team had been forced to stop work and leave the camp precipitously because of the growing tension: 'It's quite staggering to see thousands of people converging and starting to protest because they are hungry.'

Philippe Mpayimana arrived in Tingi-Tingi in December 1996. In his account, he describes how the camp leaders and their employees diverted food aid for profit: 'In collusion with the camp managers, the guards in charge of the stores were selling biscuits intended for under-nourished children.' In the camp, 'the statistics were largely arbitrary. The rough inventories drawn up by the first to arrive and managed by a small committee of dignitaries were riddled with injustices and falsifications'. WFP's reaction was to make its own estimates and halve all the existing figures. After this measure was introduced,

> distributions became a real trial of strength, with displays of primal brutality by some and evidence of extreme vulnerability in others … Thus some individuals managed to get five times the quantity meant for one person whereas others, too weak or too honest, went home with nothing or with just a tenth of the weekly ration … I observed this brawl, which I participated in – albeit reluctantly – and was forced to admit that there was still a long road ahead.[30]

In February, an MSF report on the nutrition situation in Tingi-Tingi revealed a mortality rate higher than the alert threshold and rising: between 18 December and 7 February, the crude mortality rate went up from 0.88/10,000 deaths a day to 2.44/10,000 per day and the under-five mortality rate from 1.82/10,000 per day to 9.17/10,000 per day. The main causes of mortality were malnutrition and malaria. The food rations were 330 Kcal/person/day, far below the minimum ration generally considered essential which, according to usual standards, should be 2,200 Kcal/day. This report, dated 20 February, reviewed activities between December 1996 and February 1997 and explained that feeding the 80,000 refuges in Tingi-Tingi necessitated 40 metric tonnes of foodstuffs, which would only require two truckloads a day.[31]

The MSF team in Tingi-Tingi regularly mentioned the presence of Interahamwe and ex-FAR soldiers.[32] The latter, especially the leaders, organised and controlled

---

[29] At the start of February 1997, Howard W. French accompanied Sadako Ogata (United Nations High Commissioner for Refugees) on a visit to Tingi-Tingi. He relates his interviews with several refugees. See H.W. French, *A Continent for the Taking: The Tragedy and Hope of Africa* (New York: Alfred A. Knopf, 2004), pp. 144–9.

[30] P. Mpayimana, *Réfugiés rwandais entre marteau et enclume. Récit du calvaire au Zaïre (1996–1997)* (Paris: L'Harmattan, 2004), pp. 57–63.

[31] MSF, 'Health and nutritional situation of Rwandan and Burundese refugees in Tingi-Tingi, Eastern Zaire, between December 1996 and February 1997', 20 February 1997.

[32] These were soldiers who had belonged to the Rwandan Armed Forces (FAR) before the Rwandan Patriotic Front (RPF) seized power.

the camp in association with literate refugees – with disastrous consequences for the fair distribution of food rations, as the most vulnerable rapidly became the most undernourished. MSF workers in Tingi-Tingi and Kisangani reported that many refugees wanted to be repatriated to Rwanda, but would only admit to this in secret for fear of the camp leaders who were opposed to the return, as had been the case in 1994–95. Yet some members of the field team criticised MSF's insistence on communicating on the presence of armed groups implicated in the genocide.[33] In their opinion, foreign governments were exploiting this insistence to justify their non-intervention while the mortality rate among the vulnerable, especially children, continued to rise.

Rwandan witnesses have all mentioned the presence and actions of ex-FAR in the camps. After fleeing from Tingi-Tingi, the refugees had to cross a bridge. The road was so congested that there was a very long wait to get to the bridge. Benoît Rugumaho describes what happened as he made his way towards it: 'The ex-FAR were letting the refugees over in small groups and in order, choosing only their own people, family members of people they knew and the families of Rwanda's former leaders.'[34] In a similar situation, Philippe Mpayimana recounts:

> Young people, believing they were the ones the enemy was after, wouldn't tolerate women or children going ahead of them … 'Make way for the lieutenant and his family, clear the middle of the road, the colonel is coming through!' shouted two young men, grabbing my mother's garment, though it was obvious from their appearance that they were just new recruits … So, those who were not part of the armed elite got off the road, grumbling that officers were no longer of any use.[35]

ADFL troops were moving closer to Tingi-Tingi. By 9 February, they were already in control of Amisi camp. As Tingi-Tingi was only sixty kilometres away, all the refugees who could walk fled in that direction.[36] In mid-February, the international aid workers who had decamped to Kisangani for several days left in a convoy of eighty trucks that reached Tingi-Tingi in twenty-four hours, a record time. On 16 February, they were able to organise the distribution of 430 tonnes of food, enough for several days. On that day, UNHCR estimated the refugee population on the site to be 160,000, including the additional 30,000 who had arrived after fleeing the advancing front line. Soon after, more trucks delivered another 410 tonnes of food to the camp. On 24 February, despite very difficult transport conditions due to the rainy season,

[33] Administrator MSF in Kisangani, 'After three months in Kisangani, strong feelings and several questions', 20 February 1997.

[34] B. Rugumaho, *L'Hécatombe des réfugiés rwandais dans l'ex-Zaïre. Témoignage d'un survivant* (Paris: L'Harmattan, 2004), p. 83.

[35] Mpayimana, *Réfugiés rwandais*, p. 81.

[36] AFP, Pierre Briand, 'Les rebelles zaïrois se rapprochent de Tingi-Tingi, dernier camp de réfugiés', 9 February 1997.

WFP managed the biggest food distribution so far: seven days' worth of rations, containing corn, beans, corn-soya blend and oil.[37]

Confronted with a distribution that she judged unfair, Marie Béatrice Umutesi created a Women's Committee:

> The first to arrive at Tingi-Tingi camp had been the young men and they took the initiative in organising the camp into districts and sub-districts and, of course, giving themselves the top jobs. When food was distributed, they got the most while households with more people got less ... It was mainly to find a solution to this problem that the women decided to get organised and play a more important role in distributing food aid.

The Women's Committee also assigned itself the task of identifying isolated individuals, especially 'people on their own or with small children who lived alone and who could not eat or take care of themselves when they fell ill ... to help them as soon as possible. Unfortunately, this organisation was never actually able to do anything because we had just set it up when we had to leave the camp very suddenly'.[38]

On 28 February, an ADFL representative announced that their troops were just six kilometres from Tingi-Tingi.[39] Twenty-two international staff were airlifted from the camp on the orders of the Zairian army and ex-FAR. The ADFL forces captured Lubutu and Tingi-Tingi camp on 1 and 2 March, respectively.

From Tingi-Tingi to Kisangani: war and massacres, 1 March to 4 September 1997

On 28 February, hearing that the frontline was getting closer, the refugees left Tingi-Tingi and started to walk to Kisangani. But the Zairian army diverted them from their route towards the town of Ubundu, linked by a single 125-kilometre railway line to Kisangani. On 6 March, WFP carried out an aerial reconnaissance flight over Ubundu and two days later sent in sixty-five tonnes of food by train.

To reach Ubundu, the refugees had to cross the Congo River (then the Zaire River). They were then sent towards Obilo, eighty-two kilometres from Kisangani, a site alongside the railway line where the Zairian Red Cross had set up a base. On 13 March, while attempting to cross the Congo, thirty people drowned in a violent storm. Marie Béatrice Umutesi tells of the risks taken by some of her compatriots to cross the river:

> Sick of waiting, some people made improvised rafts from bamboo and sheeting. Fifty were made and entire families got on them. Few of the rafts, which were difficult to steer, reached their destination. Some, driven by the violent wind that came up in the

[37] WFP, 'More food reaches Zairian refugee camps amid new constraints', 25 February 1997.

[38] Umutesi, *Surviving the Slaughter*, pp. 146–8.

[39] Reuters, 'Zaire rebels stay near camp, took part of town', 28 February 1997.

late afternoon, capsized and their passengers drowned. Around thirty people were lost in this tragedy.

After three days, a Red Cross boat arrived and M.B. Umutesi boarded it with her friends and relatives.[40] All the authors of testimonies describe getting to the banks of rivers and the ordeal they faced each time they had to cross.

On 15 March, Kisangani fell into the hands of the ADFL authorities – with whom MSF would have to negotiate from then on. On 17 March, according to UNHCR, 150,000 refugees were massed opposite the town of Ubundu across the Congo River. The crossing was dangerous, there were too many people on the pirogues and the boatmen demanded payment. The biggest group of Rwandan refugees in Zaire was to be found on the banks of the Congo. UNHCR estimated that a further 260,000 refugees were unaccounted for.[41]

During the last week of March, MSF started operations in Kisangani. Several sites had been set up where refugees had assembled along the railway line. There were some 25,000 in Lula camp seven kilometres south of Kisangani, 30 to 40,000 had settled twenty-five kilometres and twenty-nine kilometres south of Kisangani in Kasese 1 and Kasese II camps, 20 to 30,000 forty kilometres south in Biaro, whereas only the very sick remained (250) in Obilo, eighty-two kilometres away. A clinic was set up in Lula and, on 29 March, foodstuffs were delivered to groups of refugees between Lula and Biaro, but no further as the ADFL soldiers refused to advance from there and escort the convoy to Ubundu. On 30 March, these soldiers ordered the refugees who had settled in Lula to turn back and go to a site nineteen kilometres south of Kisangani, where nothing had been prepared for them. Two MSF volunteers in Lula managed to assemble 700 people too exhausted to walk, rehydrate and feed them and provide them with medical care. But they received the order to leave the next morning, which, according to the medical team, was as good as a death sentence for many of them. The team thought about trying to negotiate at least another forty-eight hours. They were worried about this new manoeuvre on the part of the ADFL, which was now making the refugees turn back when it had previously forced them to stay put in Lula camp and wait to be repatriated. MSF wondered whether the soldiers weren't deliberately sending refugees into the forest where no aid could reach them. If this is true, then it was a premeditated massacre as the refugees had a white flag to show they would rather return to Rwanda than die in the forest. The same day, 31 March, MSF decided to alert public opinion to the dramatic situation of the refugees along the railway line and demand direct access to all the refugees. MSF's team in Kisangani was increased from six international volunteers to twenty-two.[42]

[40] Umutesi, *Surviving the Slaughter*, pp. 169–71.
[41] UNHCR, 'Great Lakes at a glance', 19 March 1997.
[42] MSF, Press release, Zaire, 'Epuisés et sous alimentés: la situation des réfugiés rwandais est dramatique. MSF envoie des renforts à Kisangani', 31 March 1997.

In a report sent from Kisangani in mid-April, MSF guesstimated the number of refugees along the railway line to be somewhere between 65,900 and 80,900. This estimate included the five main sites and indicated the population of each camp.[43] It was, however, lower than UNHCR's estimate, which believed there to be a total of 93,800 Rwandan refugees between Ubundu and Kisangani. As in Zaire and Tanzania in 1994, the official figures were based on lists drawn up by the camp leaders, via the heads of prefecture via the cell leaders, and again produced higher figures than MSF, which finally adopted a global working figure of 80,000.[44] The report went on to review the activities deployed in each camp.

During the second half of April, a series of events confirmed that the ADFL's military wing and the RPA were implementing a murderous plan. On Friday 18 April, following rumours that refugees had killed seven villagers, relief operations were suspended. The next day an MSF lorry was attacked and the teams had to be escorted back to base by the army. On Sunday evening, a train carrying food supplies was stopped seven kilometres south of Kisangani and, later that night, some villagers congregated around it. As it was moving off, several people attacked one of the carriages, stayed on board and looted the rest of the carriages when it reached Kasese. This apparently led to fighting among the villagers. On Monday and Tuesday, the military authorities announced their intention to investigate these incidents and refused aid workers access to the refugees, without telling them how long this ban would last. These events seriously undermined the team's morale, as the coordinator explained in his correspondence: 'A really difficult time, with lots of painful decisions and feelings of frustration, depression, manipulation and shame, as well as a context of insecurity that is hard to gauge and an accumulation of physical and mental fatigue.'[45] On 23 April, the team sent some terrible news to the Brussels operational centre. An MSF driver and a transporter had been heading for Kasese. As the transporter approached Kasese I, all he saw was women and children. He heard shooting and didn't go any further. As for the driver who was supposed to pick up a lorry from Kasese II, he saw no refugees at all in the four kilometres between the two camps, 'only dead bodies, at least 500 of them'. Armed men, who he identified as Rwandan, ordered him to go and kill refugees with the villagers. He refused. They then forced him to help bulldoze the bodies into mass graves. This was the first time that RPA soldiers had asked a member of MSF's staff to take part in the execution of refugees. MSF decided to evacuate part of its Kisangani team.[46]

A Rwandan refugee, Maurice Niwese, has written an account of the three days of massacres that he witnessed in Kasese from 22 to 24 April:

[43] MSF Coordination, Kisangani, 15 April 1997.
[44] The cell is Rwanda's smallest administrative unit, made up of an average of fifty households.
[45] MSF, Coordination Kisangani, 'Sitrep 12', 22 April 1997.
[46] MSF, Operations Division, Paris, 23 April 1997 and MSF, Operations, Brussels, 23 April 1997.

It was 22 April, 1997, at about 6.15 in the morning ... We could hear machine guns, heavy and individual weapons firing ... The camp was completely surrounded. The soldiers led us to the railway line. Anyone who hesitated was shot on the spot. Dead, of course ... At about two in the afternoon, we had started to get settled along the railway line and look for something to eat ... These soldiers who had herded us there with their machine guns and crates of shells set up opposite us. They turned their guns on us ... Showing no pity, they opened fire. People were killed in their hundreds ... All of a sudden, everyone, injured or not, started running towards the forest. I went with the flow and plunged into the forest.[47]

These events that took place between 18 and 22 April sparked international protests. On 24 April, a UN mission and a group of journalists saw for themselves that Kasese camp was empty. A villager told them he had heard shooting throughout the morning of 22 April. In a long internal memo, the Kisangani team expressed their feelings of powerlessness.[48] They had been refused access to the refugees for five days, with the ADFL denying all their requests to enter the camps. While the UN mission confirmed that Kasese was indeed empty, it provided no useful information as to the fate of the refugees. The MSF coordinator's tone became accusatory and he criticised the UNHCR for its 'impotence' and suspected it of 'complicity' with the new authorities. He upheld that these events were proof of a 'hidden military agenda' being implemented with deadly effect. He concluded by spelling out the dilemma faced by field teams in this type of situation: 'either we stay put and try to bear witness, or we withdraw massively from the Great Lakes region as a political protest'.

In March-April 1997, Hubert Sauper filmed a documentary along the railway line between Kisangani and Ubundu. He took a train transporting aid. As it went through the forest, it was surrounded and then almost engulfed by vegetation. He filmed huge throngs of refugees along the track: a crowd waiting for the train, the arrival of aid organisations and the distribution of food. The film hints at a massacre with pictures of a devastated camp, dead bodies on the side of a path, abandoned and emaciated children and relief workers searching for survivors. There were several shots showing members of the Red Cross, MSF and UN agencies.[49]

Another reconnaissance flight took place on 25 April, with UN, ADFL and Rwandan representatives on board, as well as several journalists. Biaro camp, forty-one kilometres south of Kisangani, was seen to be empty. The massacre perpetrated here was discovered later. CNN filmed decomposing bodies and people dying in a hospital tent. The refugees who had managed to hide said that the camp had been

---

[47] M. Niwese, *Le peuple rwandais un pied dans la tombe. Récit d'un réfugié étudiant* (Paris: L'Harmattan, 2001), pp. 159–62.

[48] MSF, Kisangani, 'Sitrep 13', 25 April 1997.

[49] H. Sauper, *Kisangani Diary*, 45.35 minutes, 1998.

attacked by army groups. On 28 April, MSF and WFP regained access to Biaro, but were unable to obtain any information about the refugees who had fled.

At the end of March 1997, the ADFL had authorised an exploratory mission to South Kivu. Its objective was to establish where to set up transit camps for the repatriation process of Rwandan refugees. The mission lasted from 26 March to 3 April 1997. A member of the ADFL was part of the group that included MSF, Care and UNHCR personnel. In Shabunda, the military commander responsible for the operations against the refugees was Rwandan, as were his men. He announced that: 'All those in the forest are considered to be the enemy.' According to a number of accounts, these soldiers were executing refugees who, reassured by the presence of the international organisations, were coming out from the dense forest. The MSF coordinator affirmed in his mission report that this commander had been tasked with eliminating the refugees and intimidating locals to stop them from helping the Rwandans: 'we heard from both the local population and refugees alike that the military was following us. When we passed, refugees heard that we were in the area, felt safe and emerged from the forest. The soldiers who were following us then eliminated the refugees who had emerged from the forest.'[50] This document was made into a report initially kept confidential.[51] However, on 24 April, a summary was given to journalists on the condition that they did not quote MSF as the source – a condition they respected. The information that the RPA was using aid workers as bait to help them find and execute refugees sent shockwaves throughout the whole MSF movement. Being used by killers as facilitators would, from that point on, have to be considered an abiding risk for humanitarian workers.

Repatriations to Rwanda

On 27 April 1997, the first UNHCR repatriation flight left Kisangani for Kigali with thirty-three people on board. On 30 April, a second flight took 236 people back to Kigali and, on 1 May, a further 1,113 were taken to Kigali and 400 to Cyangugu.

The refugees along the railway line were transported by train and truck to Kisangani. On 4 May, the train was so packed that ninety-one refugees were crushed to death. MSF published a press release condemning the systematic brutality endured by refugees during the repatriation process. MSF was working in a transit camp seven kilometres from Kisangani, attending the refugees as they arrived. A medical triage was carried out to separate those fit enough to be repatriated from those unlikely to survive the journey. As the political staff and armed wing of the Zairian rebellion were carefully monitoring all MSF's activities, the coordinator insisted that contacts with these new authorities be stepped up to improve the conditions in which relief was delivered. A sitrep on 18 May began by describing the

---

[50] MSF Holland, 'Exploratory mission report-Kigalube-Catchungu-Shabunda', April 1997.
[51] MSF Holland, *Summary. Reconstruction Report: Bukavu-Shabunda (South Kivu, Zaire)*, 16 April 1997.

work in the transit camp (now called Lula camp) and then related the personal experience of an MSF international staff member who had taken the train to Biaro on 6 May and seen 'lots of dead bodies along the railway line'.[52] It also revealed that the intent of the armed forces and UNHCR to repatriate all the refugees as fast as possible was resulting in extreme brutality at every stage of their journey, including as they were boarding planes chartered by UNHCR.

As soon as the repatriation flights began, MSF set up a health post at Kigali airport and organised a preliminary medical check-up and triage of the returnees: medical screening was based on physical signs of severe anaemia and obvious malnutrition and spontaneous complaints of illness. Serious cases were transferred to Kigali Central Hospital or twenty kilometres away to the field hospital in Runda camp where MSF also worked. MSF treated undernourished children on a site close to the transit camp. MSF teams also conducted a medical triage of returning refugees at Gisenyi and Cyangugu airports (at Cyangugu this activity was later taken over by the ICRC) and worked in the field hospital and therapeutic feeding centre in the Butare transit camp. Following negotiations at the beginning of May, permission was obtained to open a field hospital in the compound at the Central Hospital in Kigali and an MSF medical team started work there in mid-May.

From the very beginning of the repatriation process, the Rwandan authorities considered it of paramount importance to do everything in their power to prevent the creation of camps – hence the policy of transferring returnees to their municipalities as rapidly as possible. The civilian, medical and military authorities constantly berated the medical teams about the duration of inpatient care and treatment for severely anaemic children. It was one long negotiation for MSF's medical and coordination staff who did meet with some success as they managed to obtain some improvements to relief provision and logistics services.

In his sitrep of 22 May, MSF's coordinator noted that, once the refugees returned to their municipalities, he did not know what happened them: 'Communes: this is of course the black hole as nobody can say what happens there.' In fact, on several occasions since the beginning of May, the coordinator had reported ambushes, murders, attacks and fighting, especially in west Rwanda. It was considered far too dangerous for international staff to access most of the municipalities.[53] On 17 June, the UN agencies announced that they could not guarantee the safety of returnees in the west of Rwanda.

The security situation in the north-west had been an issue since January 1997, and a number of aid workers had already lost their lives there. Three Spanish members of Doctors of the World were murdered in Ruhengeri in the night of 18–19 January.[54]

[52] MSF, Kisangani, 'Sitrep Fabien', 18 May 1997.

[53] MSF, coordinator Kigali, 'Sitrep', 22 May 1997.

[54] MSF, 'Some information about the murder of three Spanish members of Doctors of the World', 22 January 1997.

That same night, MSF's compound and then Save the Children's were attacked by armed assailants, but neither attack caused any victims. From January to June, in order to continue their work and ensure the security of their teams, NGOs and UN agencies sought all available information on the murderous operations of the ex-FAR and the massacres being perpetrated in the west by the RPA.

In July, UNHCR continued repatriating refugees from the DRC before rapidly sending them on to their home municipalities. By 23 July, 58,000 refugees had been flown back to Rwanda, 42,000 of them from Kisangani and 9,000 from Mbandaka. Another 24,000 refugees had been localised in the DRC and UNHCR teams were trying to get to them. However, in mid-July, an UNHCR spokesperson announced that around 200,000 Rwandans were unaccounted for in the DRC.[55]

At the beginning of July, medical activities were still being provided in Lula transit camp in Kisangani. The author of a sitrep dated 7 July confirmed what other MSF workers had already said: some refugees did not want to go back to Rwanda and so would be in danger once the repatriation process was over. With this date fast approaching, which activities should MSF deploy? The author also felt that UNHCR's protection mission was ineffective with the refugees in Lula camp afraid as soldiers were able to enter at will. On 10 July, the authorities gave the transit camp three days to close. On 14 July, they confirmed that the camp should be emptied of all refugees, including the sick and those under UNHCR protection. MSF's coordinator, supported by UNHCR, requested an extension of two or three weeks for the most seriously ill. The reply was: 'That's much too long; you can put them on a drip on the plane.'[56] Some 379 patients and 190 UNHCR protection cases remained in the camp and would be particularly at risk if the camp closed as, at this point, UNHCR had no other solution to offer them. On 19 July, the medical evacuations started up again. On 25 July, MSF dismissed its Congolese staff and ceased its medical activities in the transit camp and, on 30 July, the international staff in charge of these activities left Kisangani.

On 4 September 1997, UNHCR confirmed that 488 Rwandans were still present in the transit camp in Kisangani; some had applied for refugee status. That night, soldiers entered the camp and forcibly transported everyone to the airport where they were put on a plane to Rwanda.[57] UNHCR immediately condemned what it called a blatant breach of international refugee treaties. On 5 September, MSF published a press release in support of UNHCR's protest, denouncing forced repatriations and expressing its concern that this expulsion could create a dangerous precedent for other Rwandans still in the DRC.

Meanwhile, during the last few months of 1996, some 535,000 Rwandan refugees were still in Tanzania (according to UNHCR estimates), many of them from

[55] IRIN, 'Emergency Update No. 211 on the Great Lakes', 15 July 1997.
[56] MSF, Kisangani, 'Sitrep 37', 14 July 1997.
[57] UNHCR, 'Great Lakes Briefing Notes', 5 September 1997.

Kibungo prefecture on the border with Tanzanian district Ngara. On 6 December, the Tanzanian authorities announced in the camps that the repatriation of refugees was about to begin and started making preparations. On the other side of the border in Rwanda, the authorities put a repatriation system in place. Only the Rwandan Red Cross and the International Federation of the Red Cross (IFRC) were authorised to provide returning refugees with assistance during their journey.

On 22 December, the message from an MSF mission in Ngara district (Tanzania) noted that a crowd was heading for the border, numerous supply stations had been set up along the road between Benaco and Rusumo (on the border), everything was well-organised and there was no evidence of violence. The authors of the message did add, however, that this operation was 'against the most basic principles of refugee law (as it is a forced repatriation)'.[58] The number of Rwandan refugees in Tanzania was estimated at 540,000 and, according to UNHCR figures, 470,000 of them had been repatriated in December 1996. Earlier that year, in July–August 1996, Rwandan refugees in Burundi had been forcibly repatriated by the Burundian authorities.

Where are the 'unaccounted for'? The flight to Mbandaka and neighbouring countries

In the middle of March 1997, refugees on the road between Ubundu and Biaro realised that the rebel advance would cut off their access to the Central African Republic. They were left with the choice of being sent back to Rwanda or heading west to Congo-Brazzaville. This moment of choice was dramatically described in a communiqué from the UNHCR: 'The refugees have been through a harrowing experience and they are at the end of their strength. Their odyssey has to stop now. If they move further west they will end up in complete wilderness west of Ubundu, in a terrain even more difficult and less accessible that the one they have crossed to date.'[59]

Those who chose Congo-Brazzaville all related in their accounts the moment when they had to make up their minds. Their perceptions and apprehensions differed from UNHCR's discourse, and more particularly on one specific point: as far as they were concerned, it wasn't the forest that terrified them the most, but the Congolese rebels and their Rwandan allies. So they made the perilous decision to go through a dense forest and walk a further 1,500 kilometres, a distance estimated by those with hand-drawn maps.

> Most people were very afraid of the forest. According to the maps, there were no paths through it, not the slightest trace of a man-made habitat or anything growing that could be eaten. It was a jungle in the truest sense … I made the sign of the cross as I headed towards the forest.[60]

[58] MSF, Explo Ngara, 'Sitrep 01', 22 December 1996.
[59] Sadako Ogata, United Nations High Commissioner for Refugees, 14 March 1997.
[60] Mpayimana, *Réfugiés rwandais*, pp. 97–8.

A few people had hand-drawn maps of Zaire ... The only remaining way out was through Mbandaka, more than fifteen hundred kilometres to the west on the border with Congo Brazzaville, and to get there you had to get through one hundred kilometres of untraveled forest. The locals we consulted about this adventure tried to dissuade us. For them, going into this forest with no paths and no water was suicide ... Was it necessary to risk everything and go through the equatorial forest to go as far as Mbandaka? ... I decided to go into the forest.[61]

On 9 May, MSF reported that there were around 13,000 Rwandans in Wendji, not far from Mbandaka, and on 13 May, the town was captured by the ADFL. Two massacres immediately ensued, one in Wendji and the other in the port of Mbandaka where a crowd was waiting to cross the Congo River on a barge.[62] On 15 May, radio contact impossible the previous day was re-established between Kinshasa and MSF's team in Mbandaka. The team asked for back-up. On 19 May, they reported that a camp with around 2,000 people was forming near the airport: 'Those 2,000 are refugees left over from a group of 15,000 who were attacked near Wenje [Wendji]. Discussions with them confirmed this. After the attack most of them had hidden in the bush: little by little people are now coming out to join the rest of the group near the airport.'[63] A number of eyewitness reports taken later in Congo-Brazzaville confirmed the massacres committed by the ADFL and its Rwandan allies.

In the middle of May, MSF's Dutch section completed a report on the massacres perpetrated by the ADFL between December 1996 and April 1997.[64] It was agreed that this report would be given to a handful of journalists selected by MSF. In France, Stephen Smith from the newspaper *Libération* was one of those chosen. On 20 May, *Libération*'s headline was '190 000 réfugiés hutus disparus au Zaïre. MSF accuse' ['190,000 refugees disappear in Zaire. MSF accuses']. Although the directors of the different MSF sections operating in Zaire had reached prior agreement on this strategy, the publication of this article deeply angered some field team members working for MSF Holland and Belgium who considered it endangered their safety and they criticised the 'irresponsibility' of MSF France.[65] The ensuing controversy between the sections was extremely heated and resulted in sitreps sent by the field team members to headquarters in Holland and Belgium no longer being communicated to MSF France. But the

---

[61] Umutesi, *Surviving the Slaughter*, pp. 172–3.

[62] The refugees had settled in a camp near Wendji, about twenty kilometres from Mbandaka. The massacres at Mbandaka and Wendji, on 13 May 1997, have been described many times. See A. Maykuth, 'Rebels murder hundreds of refugees in Congo. The news emerged as horrified townsfolk told what they had seen. The victims had trekked 750 miles', *Philadelphia Inquirer* (5 June 1997),http://articles.philly.com/1997-06-05/news/25526458_1_rwandan-hutu-refugees-rebels-laurent-kabila.

[63] MSF, Kisangani, 'Sitrep 5', 19 May 1997.

[64] MSF Holland, *Forced Flight: A Brutal Strategy of Elimination in Eastern Zaire*, 16 May 1997.

[65] MSF Holland, Zaire team, 'Field response from MSF-H Zaire/Congo to report leaked by MSF-F to French press on 19 May 97', 21 May 1997.

fact remains that sitreps never mentioned whether the article had actually harmful or lasting consequences.[66]

UNHCR, WFP, UNICEF and the ICRC were also working in Mbandaka. On 22 May, repatriation flights began from Mbandaka to Kigali. On 27 May, for example, three flights took off with a total of 900 people on board. In a transit camp near the airport, MSF teams provided ambulatory medical care, handled water supply and set up latrines. They also carried out medical triage before repatriation. When the first flight arrived in Rwanda, MSF's coordinator noted that the returnees were all immediately photographed in the airport and that most of them were men in relatively good physical condition.

At the end of June, UNHCR was still searching for refugees. MSF's coordinator in Mbandaka described it as 'a complicated (and delicate vis-à-vis authorities) operation of treasure hunting for refugees', because UNHCR had decided to pay any Congolese taking part in the search for refugees and trying to persuade them to come out of the forest: they were paid per day and not per refugee found.[67] UNHCR then announced that it would only be continuing its repatriation operations until the end of July. Yet the protection of the pockets of refugees assisted by MSF was dependent on UNHCR. Without its protection, what would become of the refugees? Indeed, as MSF had discovered in Shabunda in March 1997, if they were not given protection while waiting to be repatriated, tempting the refugees out of hiding with offers of assistance could endanger them by literally placing them in the firing line. The author concluded in capital letters: THIS SUBJECT IS RATHER TRICKY.[68]

Not everyone's flight ended in Mbandaka. A message dated 6 May 1997 announced the arrival of refugees in Congo-Brazzaville. Initially it was just a small group of fifty or so people, but their number increased rapidly. On 23 May, MSF estimated there to be about 10,000 Rwandan refugees, with around 1,000 in Lukolela.[69] In the north of Congo, 400 kilometres from Brazzaville, they were assembled mainly on two sites, Lukolela and Njoundou. Lukolela is situated on the right bank of the Congo River in Congo-Brazzaville, opposite the DRC. Reaching it from inside Congo-Brazzaville meant crossing swamps, and Congo River crossings were being controlled by the armed forces of the DRC's new government.

> ADFL troops are still potentially dangerous. There have been a number of incidents during which our presence alongside the refugees has been violently criticised. Tensions are still running high and it's obvious that the Alliance leaders have been charged with strict surveillance and controlling movements on the river, and that

[66] On the controversy caused by *Libération*'s front page article, see L. Binet, *The Hunting and Killing of Rwandan Refugees in Zaire-Congo: 1996–1997* (Paris: MSF, 2004), pp. 184–98.

[67] MSF, Kisangani, 'Sitrep 8', 26 May 1997.

[68] MSF, Kisangani, 'Sitrep 22 for 30 May to 1 June', 2 June 1997.

[69] MSF, 'Project of assistance to refugee populations in Congo', May 1997.

they'll stop at nothing to complete this task. This means that referrals to the sisters [a reference to a hospital in Zaire run by nuns] are still impossible and, as river travel is under close surveillance, we have to be careful to avoid any future incidents.[70]

On 5 June, fighting broke out on the streets of Brazzaville, creating concern that aid work in the camps at Lukolela, Njoundou and Liranga would be disrupted because of difficulties in getting supplies of food and drugs out of the town. Repatriation flights from Lukolela to Kigali organised by UNHCR began on 5 July. In August and September 1997, MSF's team estimated there were 4,800 people in Lukolela camp. MSF's activities in the camp included providing medical assistance in a clinic and working in a Ministry of Health hospital; treating children in a therapeutic feeding centre; running a supplementary feeding centre for children and adults; managing food distributions (partly supplied by WFP); and logistics, which included sanitation and water supply and construction work. Refugees, who included many ex-FAR soldiers and some former officers, were recruited as logistics workers and were given food in exchange for their work. This involvement of former soldiers led to heated debates on the appropriateness of providing relief to men who may have had a hand in the Tutsi genocide.

In July 1997, an Epicentre epidemiologist compiled medical data and conducted a retrospective mortality survey in Njoundou to obtain objective data on a group of Rwandans who fled the camps in Kivu between September and June 1997. At the time, the population of Njoundou stood at 3,370. During the survey, 266 people were interviewed to determine how many members their families had before fleeing from Kivu; this came to a total of 3,121. Out of these 3,121, only 530 made it to Njoundou. The questionnaire also established what had happened to those who were missing: 19 per cent had been killed by firearms and 59 per cent were 'unaccounted for'.[71] The purpose of the exercise was to estimate the number of victims among the refugees since they had left the camps in Kivu. The author was thus able to establish a crude mortality rate of 15.5/10,000/day (for the period from 1 October 1996 to 31 May 1997). He believes that mortality due to firearms was underestimated as the 'unaccounted for' category included both returnees and deaths caused by firearms. This attempt to quantify the effects of war on a refugee population was new to MSF.

On 20 February 1998, MSF informed the High Commissioner for Refugees of its decision to leave the Rwandan refugee camps in northern Congo Brazzaville on 31 March, as 'the emergency phase is now over'.[72]

[70] MSF, Emergency Coordinator, 'End of mission report. Congo Brazzaville – North Region – From 2/09 to 1/11/97', 9 November 1997.

[71] Médecins Sans Frontières, Epicentre, *Epidemiological Survey of Rwandan Refugees in Ndjoundou Camp, Congo July 1997*, Paris, September 1997; P. Nabeth, A. Croisier, M. Pedari, J.-H. Bradol, 'Acts of violence against Rwandan refugees', *The Lancet*, 350 (29 November 1997), 1635.

[72] MSF, 'Letter to Mrs. Ogata, Lukolela, Njoundu and Liranga refugee camps', 20 February 1998.

Dealing with the uncertainty

In this chapter we have covered a period of international war. The swift advance of the ADFL, supported by the RPA, destabilised Zaire in the space of a few months and caught international stakeholders by surprise.[73] But seizing power was not the sole objective of the military campaign. The Rwandan authorities were also seeking the return of the refugees while considering all those who had not immediately given themselves up and had not returned to Rwanda as enemies to be destroyed. After each defeat, the Zairian armed forces fled towards the interior of Zaire, whereas the ADFL and the RPA, after each territorial gain, tracked down Rwandan Hutus, the vast majority of whom never received protection from the United Nations, or even – with a handful of exceptions – from UNHCR. Around 500,000 Rwandan refugees headed west, as well as thousands of Zairians trying to escape the fighting.

We have described some of the significant episodes of the war, notably the capture of towns and camps. We have examined these situations and sought to determine their consequences for the refugees during the period extending from November 1996 to September 1997. At the same time, we have tried to show how all the international relief operators, NGOs and UN agencies, were forced to submit to the diktats of the victors at every step of the way. We have described the indicators used by MSF's field teams to determine their actions, for example, compiling of epidemiological data and political developments, such as the power struggles between authorities and behaviours of the new leaders.

We have seen that the authors of sitreps and reports sometimes eschewed standard language to express their opinions, emotions, doubts – especially when writing about the forced nature of the repatriations to Rwanda, UNHCR policies, maintaining impartiality when confronted with participants in the genocide, tensions with the new authorities and criticism of decisions taken at the different headquarters. Lastly, we have also seen that, in this context of uncertainty, communication between headquarters and the field intensified, becoming daily during critical periods as each endeavoured to collect and select reliable data – when the political and logistical conditions allowed. On occasions, information from the field was very rapidly turned into a press release alerting public opinion to the extreme violence being perpetrated against the refugees. International NGOs, UN agencies, journalists and religious leaders tried to decipher situations, power plays, refugee movements and military engagements as evidenced in the numerous reports and communiqués, periodic and regular bulletins and sitreps interpreting contexts and defining programmes of action. This information was particularly crucial for appeals for funding, as vast amounts of money were required for assistance and repatriation purposes, whether for transporting food and material by WFP, the airlift between Kisangani

---

[73] About the effects of war on congolese society, most notably in east DRC, see S. Autesserre, *The Trouble with the Congo: Local Violence and the Failure of International Peacebuilding* (New York: Cambridge University Press, 2010).

and Rwanda or for logistical operations. Because of the scale of its operations and its experience with providing medical assistance in refugee camps, MSF played a specific role in the public debates, especially when its stances were based on analyses provided by aid workers, their eyewitness reports and their face-to-face contact with refugees.

Epilogue: the effectiveness of aid in the face of repeated mass atrocities

MSF's teams had been operating in the African Great Lakes region for more than ten years before the genocide of the Rwandan Tutsis. The organisation's first operation was delivering assistance to victims of famine in north-west Uganda in 1980. It subsequently maintained its presence in Uganda and neighbouring countries Burundi, Rwanda, Tanzania and Zaire ensuring emergency responses to disasters such as epidemics, food shortages, famine, sudden influxes of casualties and mass arrivals of displaced people or war refugees and, at the request of UNHCR, providing over a period of several years medical care to refugees and displaced people living in camps. During the 1980s, MSF also ran technical assistance programmes to support public health administrations, sending in qualified personnel, administering health districts and provinces, providing medical supplies to healthcare networks and combatting major endemics. Some of the foreign doctors sent out by MSF were appointed by national administrations to key positions, such as head of public health for an entire Burundian province.

From 1982 onwards, MSF conducted exploratory missions and implemented activities in response to virtually all the health crises occurring in Rwanda and its four neighbouring countries. Our reviews have focused primarily on activities implemented between 1990 and 1997, a period during which political violence was the main cause of mortality among Rwandan people.

From April 1994, MSF's teams were not only confronted with the indirect consequences of the war, such as food shortages and epidemics triggered by massive and sudden population displacements, but they also regularly witnessed murders and massacres. As for the organisation's Rwandan staff, they were victims or sometimes accomplices or co-authors of these crimes. Accounts found in MSF's archives relate an extreme and oft-repeated experience, unprecedented in the organisation's history: the presence of humanitarian aid workers as people were sorted into those who would die and those to be spared.[1] At best, these aid workers were being enjoined

---

[1] An MSF team was present in Sbrenica in July 1995 when several thousand men were massacred by the soldiers of Ratko Mladić, commander-in-chief of the army of the Serbian Republic of Bosnia. Several patients and members of MSF's local staff were executed.

or forced under threat to facilitate the enterprise of murderers, and at worst, to participate actively in executions. During the genocide, the militia ordered MSF's Hutu staff to denounce and sometimes even kill their Tutsi colleagues.

The repetition of mass atrocities in the presence of teams of humanitarian workers sparked two non-mutually exclusive reactions within MSF. The first was to try and maintain operations as political violence sent needs through the roof and the capacity of aid workers to take action was reduced. The second was to try and resist attempts by the perpetrators of political violence to instrumentalise humanitarian aid at the risk of being treated as undesirables by the authorities (legal and rebel), prevented from working, expelled or even executed. And the threats against aid workers were not empty ones: on 18 January 1997, three members of Médecins du Monde [Doctors of the World] (MdM) Spain's international staff were murdered in Ruhengeri in north-west Rwanda.[2] 'It was an execution: the members of MdM were made to kneel on the ground and were then shot in the head. The American [member of the MdM team] was hit in the legs by machine-gun fire. He was later amputated.'[3] Earlier that same night, armed men had fired shots outside MSF Holland's compound but had not forced their way into the building itself where five members of international staff and one Rwandan had taken refuge.[4]

Humanitarian relief under strain in the face of extreme violence

When the Rwandan conflict began in 1990, MSF had already undergone its first wave of 'professionalization'. With the expertise it had acquired in the refugee camps of South-East Asia, Central America and Africa during the 1980s, the organisation felt confident in its ability to maintain control over the health situation of large groups of displaced people or refugees. The practical knowledge considered necessary to meet this objective was detailed in articles and guidelines and, in 1997, was about to be compiled in a handbook.[5] The European sections' headquarters had set up technical departments (operational, medical, logistics, finance, recruitment and communications) and satellite associations run by MSF (Liberté Sans Frontières for critical reflection on international aid, Epicentre for field epidemiology and MSF Logistique and Transfer for developing and delivering intervention kits to the field). Training courses had been designed to pass on to new volunteers this knowledge

---

[2] On 6 February 2008, Judge Fernando Andreu Merelles of Spain's National Court issued arrest warrants against 40 senior RPA officers for crimes committed in Rwanda and DRC between 1 October 1990 and 2002. He accused four high-ranking RPA officers of having taken the decision to eliminate the three MdM staff because they had witnessed massacres perpetrated against the civilian Hutu population in the region of Ruhengeri. So far, no-one has been tried. According to an article published in *El Mundo* and reproduced in full in Rwandan daily newspaper *The New Times* (23 November 2015), an investigation is still underway. See www.newtimes.co.rw/section/article/2015-11-23/194647.

[3] MSF France, 'Murder of three members of MdM Spain', 20 January 1997.

[4] MSF Kigali, 'Report on the attack on MSF Holland's compound', 20 January 1997.

[5] MSF, *Refugee Health, an Approach to Emergency Situations* (Oxford: Macmillan, 1997).

acquired in the field and explain the workings of the logistics and other such special-ist technical support available at headquarters.

So it was with a certain degree of confidence in their skills and technical capacities that MSF's teams arrived in the camps in the Great Lakes region, only to find a rude awakening awaiting them. Violence had become the main cause of mortality among civilians and huge population movements were being triggered by large-scale mas-sacres, leaving more people dead than were injured.[6] Refugee camps were opened, but were just as quickly closed or destroyed. After months of efforts, as soon as a situation began to improve, the political violence would start up again, bringing with it the destruction of humanitarian infrastructure and yet more population displace-ments. As a result, it was usually impossible to control the health situation during the months after sites were set up in places where displaced people and refugees had assembled, with dire demographic consequences: 10,000 deaths for 260,000 people (around 3.8 per cent) in the first three months after the arrival of the Burundian refugees in Rwanda at the end of 1993 and 50,000 deaths (about 6 per cent) during the first few weeks after the arrival of 850,000 Rwandan refugees in Goma, Zaire.[7]

Observed and discussed by the humanitarian aid teams, this inability to contain health crises was a source of great concern for field practitioners. They reported the inadequate care and assistance to their hierarchy and forwarded comments and requests to the coordination teams in capital Kigali and in Europe who documented these situations for themselves during visits to the sites. These attempts to improve care and assistance were facilitated by the professional mobility of operational man-agers between aid agencies. For example, from MSF's point of view, the UNICEF doctor who chaired the medical coordination meeting of all the agencies working in the Burundian refugee camps in Rwanda (1993) was an 'old boy' as he had worked for MSF France in Ethiopia in the mid-1980s. The person in charge of food aid in Rwanda for the European Union and the ICRC medical coordinator had worked for the same MSF section in Thailand a few years earlier. UNHCR's medical coordina-tor in Goma in 1995 was one of the co-founders of MSF Belgium while the person in charge of medical techniques at UNHCR headquarters in Geneva had also worked for MSF.

Despite the efforts made by aid agencies to better coordinate and improve their ser-vices, the gap between the needs of 'vulnerable populations' and the performance of the 'aid system' was too big to be closed simply by changing the internal dynamics of the agencies already working in the field. In September 1994, as tens of thousands of Rwandan refugees were losing their lives in Goma, it was Denmark – as an aid donor

---

[6] M.J. Toole and R.J. Waldman, 'The public health aspects of complex emergencies', *Annual Review of Public Health*, 18 (1997).

[7] These estimations are sometimes found in summary reports or were made by MSF on the basis of weekly mortality counts carried out in difficult conditions in the camps. They are not the result of careful calcula-tions based on reliable data gathered in the field but are approximations and extrapolations based on frail and partial data giving an idea of the demographic consequences of the conflict.

country – that first took the initiative of organising an evaluation of the international response. The first Joint Evaluation of Emergency Assistance to Rwanda (JEEAR) meeting was held in November 1994 in Copenhagen and attended by the main aid donor countries, UN agencies, the Red Cross and a handful of NGOs. The evaluation was divided into four studies: Rwanda's history; early warning and conflict management; humanitarian aid and effects; and rebuilding post-genocide Rwanda. The first field visit by the JEEAR team took place in the spring of 1995, thus coinciding with the Kibeho massacre. The evaluation's overall findings were published in March 1996, a few months before the attack by the RPA and its Zairian allies on the refugee camps in Zaire. The exercise mobilised fifty or so researchers and was supported by around forty institutions. Its cost, US$1.7 million (communications costs included), represented just over 0.01 per cent of total spending on international aid, i.e. US$1.4 billion between April and December 1994.[8] The third study, focused on humanitarian aid and its effects, underlined the fact that humanitarian aid could not make up for the absence of appropriate political and military responses on the part of governments: 'A key lesson, then, is that humanitarian action cannot serve as a substitute for political, diplomatic and, where necessary, military action.'[9] The JEEAR recommended the setting up by the UNSC of a humanitarian affairs sub-committee. Its authors also made the following recommendations:

- Donor countries should be prepared to provide advance funding for emergencies.
- Aid agencies should strengthen their coordination.
- The possibility of using logistics and military engineering should be explored.
- NGOs should improve their performance.
- Aid agencies should improve the way they account for their operations, including towards the beneficiaries of international aid.
- Camp security should be improved.
- Quality of supplies, logistics and food aid distribution should be improved.
- Organisations should learn to better manage the media as a means of improving relief efforts.
- The negative impact of refugees on host communities should be offset by specific actions.[10]

A few months after the Joint Evaluation had been submitted, and against the backdrop in November 1996 of the attack on refugee camps in Zaire, the forced repatriation of several hundreds of thousands of refugees in just a few days and the exodus

---

[8] John Borton, 'The Joint Evaluation of Emergency Assistance to Rwanda', *Humanitarian Exchange Magazine* (26 March 2004). See also the special issue on the Joint Evaluation published by *Disasters*, 20:4 (1996).

[9] The Joint Evaluation of Emergency Assistance to Rwanda, *Synthesis Report, Study III Principal Findings and Recommendations* (London: ODI, June 1996).

[10] The Joint Evaluation of Emergency Assistance to Rwanda, *Synthesis Report, Study III Principal Findings and Recommendations*.

of hundreds of thousands more towards the interior of Zaire, medical review *The Lancet* published in an editorial entitled 'Emergency medical aid is not for amateurs' a severe judgement of the performance of medical aid organisations:

> There will also be medical-aid teams organised by national and international chari-
> ties. But do those who give so generously get their money's worth? Too often, they
> do not. In the flurry to arrange emergency aid, charities may send equipment that is
> inadequate or inappropriate, organisers who may be ignorant of the languages and
> culture of the area, and doctors who often lack the requisite skills to intervene and the
> expertise to know what interventions are likely to be effective (some charities have
> included medical students in emergency aid teams).[11]

The remedy proposed by the British medical review called for the setting up of a new international agency specialised in medical emergency interventions to be run by a board of experts. In their response, two directors of MSF expressed a different opinion on the origin of the new medical emergency emerging within the Rwandan refugee population in Zaire.

> Indeed, we agree with you that this kind of work cannot be for amateurs. However,
> we strongly contest the suggestion that a new international body should be created
> to cope with medical emergency aid. It would result in a UN-like organization, wher-
> ever it is located ... Better coordination is needed but you hardly pay attention to
> the central role the Rwandan government had in this repatriation process ... If the
> International community has any lesson to draw from the massive, yet hardly spon-
> taneous, return of the Rwandese, it is that a more genuine, more morally courageous
> and more effective international commitment to the weakest and the poorest on this
> planet is needed. It might not only address the consequences but also the roots of the
> problem.[12]

As can be seen in this letter, MSF's management was largely reluctant to address the issue of potential improvements to the international humanitarian response to armed conflicts on the basis of technical or managerial proposals alone (def-inition of technical standards to be reached and strengthening of coordination mechanisms). To begin with, it feared that these technical standards would be of a lesser quality than those already adopted by MSF, but its main objection was that this approach masked the principal issue: 'the inaction of governments'. Indeed, in this post-Cold War period so productive of utopian thinking, MSF hoped that the 'new international order' might enable states gathered together in an 'interna-tional community' to reach an understanding on the urgent need to contain the violence being committed against non-combatants in civil wars such as those in

---

[11] Editorial, 'Emergency medical aid is not for amateurs', *The Lancet*, 348:9039 (23 November 1996), 1393.
[12] M. Boelaert and M. Henkens, 'Letter', *The Lancet*, 349:9046 (18 January 1997), 213. Boelaert and Henkens were respectively the president and medical director of MSF-Belgium.

former Yugoslavia, Somalia, Sudan, Angola, Chechnya, Liberia and Sierra Leone. According to this interpretation of befitting international relations, governments had the possibility to take action but evidently did not have the desire to do so, and were shirking their responsibility by responding with humanitarian initiatives to situations that called for forceful diplomatic action, or even military intervention to protect civilian lives.[13]

MSF, along with other charitable agencies, made it clear that it refused to be the 'humanitarian alibi' for this 'inaction on the part of the international community', a political stance confirmed in June 1994 when the organisation campaigned for an international intervention against the authors of the genocide, proclaiming 'You can't stop genocide with doctors'.

For MSF to be making political and military recommendations to governments was also evidence of the porosity between the world of politics and that of humanitarian action. In human terms, the phenomenon was already noticeable at the end of the 1980s as some of MSF's former leaders had already accepted government or parliamentary posts and others were on the verge of doing so, helped by events in Rwanda. In France, several former MSF presidents were given government jobs: Claude Malhuret, Secretary of State for Human Rights (1986–88), Bernard Kouchner, Minister for Health and Humanitarian Action (1992–93) and Xavier Emmanuelli, Secretary of State for Emergency Humanitarian Action (1995–97). In Belgium, Alain Destexhe, International Secretary of the MSF international movement in 1994, was elected senator in 1995 and, after calling for its creation, in 1997 became secretary of the Belgian Senate's parliamentary commission of inquiry into the events of 1994 in Rwanda. Reginald Moreels, President of MSF Belgium in 1994, was Secretary of State for Development Cooperation from 1995 to 1999, Georges Dallemagne, Operations Director for MSF-Belgium, became a senator in 1999 and then federal deputy. In Holland, Jacques de Milliano, President of MSF's Dutch section in 1994, entered parliament in 1998.

While the debate on the political and military role that the 'international community' should be taking continued, broad consensus had already formed concerning the inability of humanitarian aid agencies to respond effectively to the numerous crises of the 1990s. A multitude of objectives were formulated by NGOs, international organisations and governments: the creation of technical standards in areas such as food, water, sanitation, shelters and health; the adoption of principles to improve the guidance of humanitarian action; the standardisation of requirements concerning the professional qualifications of aid personnel; improvements to the coordination process and aid agencies' obligation of accountability regarding implementation of operations, particularly towards their beneficiaries. In 1994, the Steering Committee for Humanitarian Response (SCHR) adopted the Code of Conduct for International Red Cross and Red Crescent and NGOs in Disaster

---

[13] R. Brauman, 'Introduction', in F. Jean (ed.), *Populations en danger* (Paris: Hachette, 1992), p. 15.

Relief setting out ten key principles.[14] The same year, four British-based aid agencies submitted a project proposal to the UK's Overseas Development Administration (ODA) to establish minimum standards for the recruitment of humanitarian aid workers. In the United States, the coordination platform for Private Voluntary Organizations (PVO) – Interaction – submitted a proposal in 1995 to the Office of US Foreign Disaster Assistance (OFDA) for the development of training for PVOs in 'complex humanitarian emergencies', specifically to improve their response capabilities. Also in 1995, Oxfam prepared a position paper drawing on the JEEAR to support the adoption of the Code of Conduct for IFRC and NGOs in association with a set of technical standards for material assistance.

Also drawing on the final report of the Joint Evaluation, SCHR and Interaction engineered the most complete proposal: the Sphere project.[15] In 1997, they proposed complementing the Red Cross and NGO Code of Conduct for Disaster Response with a Humanitarian Charter and a set of minimum standards for four key sectors of emergency assistance: water and sanitation, food, shelter and health. This Humanitarian Charter was a reformulation of the humanitarian action principles enshrined in international humanitarian law, underlining the rights of beneficiaries and the obligation of aid agencies to be accountable to them.[16] MSF took part in the drafting process of the technical standards and the 'trial' version of the Sphere handbook was finished in 1998.[17]

Besides the need to disseminate humanitarian action principles and technical standards, another major cause of concern for observers and evaluators was the lack of appropriate coordination mechanisms. Indeed, neither the aid recipient and donor countries, nor the UN agencies (DHA, HCR, WFP, UNICEF and WHO), nor the Red Cross movement, nor the NGOs had succeeded in setting up coordination platforms with the necessary authority to apply their decisions. Donors and aid agencies alike singled out the performance of the United Nation's Department of Humanitarian Affairs (UNDHA) for its inadequate handling of aid coordination tasks, which resulted in the creation by the United Nations of the Office for the Coordination of Humanitarian Affairs (OCHA) in 1998.

Back at MSF, after the French section pulled out of the Rwandan refugee camps (end of 1994) and fleeing refugees were attacked in Zaire (April to June 1997), the intensity of the dissent among the different national sections, had convinced most

---

[14] Oxfam, the League of Red Cross Societies, the World Council of Churches, the Lutheran World Federation and Catholic Relief Services set up the SCHR in 1972 to improve cooperation between the main humanitarian aid organisations. Save the Children joined in 1983, MSF in 1997 and ICRC in 1999.

[15] M. Buchanan-Smith, *How the Sphere Project Came into Being: A Case Study of Policy-Making in the Humanitarian Aid Sector and the Relative Influence of Research*, Working Paper 215 (London: ODI, July 2003).

[16] www.spherehandbook.org/fr/la-charte-humanitaire/ (link checked in October 2015).

[17] J. Orbinski, 'On the meaning of Sphere standards on States and humanitarian actors', Lecture delivered in London on 3 December 1998, www.msf.fr/sites/www.msf.fr/files/1998-12-03-Orbinski.pdf (link checked in October 2015).

of the organisation's leaders of the need for better coordination at the international level within their own movement. In 1997, a text was adopted setting out the social mission and forms of organisation of MSF's international movement.[18] In addition to this programmatic reaction, there was also a more pragmatic one that reflected the decisions taken at the end of the 1980s and the assessments of operations conducted in the early 1990s in other intervention contexts contemporary with the Rwandan conflict (Somalia, Liberia, Iraq, Former Yugoslavia, etc.). The aim was for MSF to learn to do – in its opinion – what nobody else seemed capable of doing. The organisation therefore began recruiting staff from new professional sectors to broaden its skills base, and soon new functions such as press, legal, security and food supply officers began to appear in organisational charts, both in the field and at headquarters.

Integrating these new professions so as to allow them to play a full part in MSF's workings – without being restrained by the corporations and powers already ensconced within the organisation – sometimes involved creating satellite institutions and entities. Thus, in 1997, an emergencies and food supply unit (UDA) was created to focus on food shortages and, after a conference was held in Paris on the response to major epidemics and endemics, a unit was set up in 1996 to try and identify the mechanisms responsible for the shortage of drugs effective against infections encountered during interventions in the 1990s, notably in Rwanda. In 1999, this initiative went on to become the Campaign for Access to Essential Medicines, still active today.

Recognising mass atrocities and reacting to them

The chapters in this book show the extent to which the relationship between humanitarian aid workers and criminal politicians gradually evolved in places where people under threat sought refuge and assistance (refugee and IDP camps, hospitals, churches, orphanages, schools, etc.). The criminals concerned usually held government authority, or de facto authority as a result of the rebellion. Consequently, to be able to work, collaboration was more a necessity than a choice. In Rwanda, this collaboration first took the form of development aid under the regime of President Habyarimana. And for the donors and numerous providers of this aid, the persecution of Tutsis was rarely a source of contention with the Rwandan authorities.[19] Then, at the start of the armed conflict in 1990 and as the pogroms against the Tutsis intensified, food aid intended for the internally displaced began to be diverted to extremist leaders linked to the presidency.[20] This was when discussions were engaged within aid agencies about the existence of food aid diversion for political purposes

---

[18] MSF, 'Principes de référence du mouvement Médecins Sans Frontières', Brussels, 1997.
[19] P. Uvin, *Aiding Violence: The Development Enterprise in Rwanda* (West Hartford: Kumarian Press, 1998).
[20] The Joint Evaluation, p. 31.

and personal enrichment. As for the relationship between humanitarian workers and the rebels, this dated back to before the foundation of the RPF in 1987. In fact, it began in 1984 in the Rwandan refugee camps in Uganda, which served first as cradle and then as sanctuary for the armed rebellion.

After multi-party government was restored in 1992, many Rwandans became engaged in a public life now characterised not only by the diversity of its political parties but also its associations active in a variety of sectors, which included human rights. In this context of emerging democracy, although aid agencies came under intense pressure from the perpetrators of political violence, they also received considerable support from within Rwandan society. Many 'ordinary Rwandans' came forward to assist their fellow citizens and Burundian refugees, thereby rejecting the politics of extremism intended to foster radical opposition between Hutus and Tutsis. Present at all the tragic events witnessed by MSF's teams, it would not have been possible for international aid agencies to deploy their activities without the support of these 'moderates'. Rwandan nutritionists (Tutsis) joined forces with MSF, for example in Bugesera, to provide nutritional rehabilitation for Burundian children (Hutus) who were dying of hunger and dysentery in the refugee camps – in the full knowledge that they were risking their lives by working in such places. The same was true of the FAR liaison officer (Hutu) who worked with the ICRC and whose actions on several occasions during the genocide protected aid workers from militia whose objective was to eliminate Tutsis and anyone they considered opponents. The vast majority of MSF's Rwandan employees – in the several thousands – belonged to this category of 'ordinary Rwandans' who stood by their compatriots. Yet distinguishing the killers from those willing to engage in acts of solidarity at the risk of their lives would not have been easy for MSF's international staff without the help of their Rwandan colleagues.

However, these endeavours were complicated by the asymmetric relationship between national and international staff. International staff members of MSF not only had voting rights at its annual general assemblies but also held most of the decision-making power in the field, whereas the Rwandans and Zairians, of whom there were many on the teams, only occasionally attended the internal coordination meetings held in capital Kigali or in the field. They were considered 'just' as employees, to whom their bosses, usually Europeans, but in any event foreigners, gave instructions.[21] Furthermore, these foreigners spent only a relatively short time – a few weeks or months – in the field. The divide created by the internal hierarchy and the brevity of the foreigners' stay created a barrier between people of similar age and occupation brought together to provide concrete assistance and very often sharing the same motivations.

[21] One innovation introduced during the operation was to send members of MSF's national staff in Madagascar to Rwanda to work as international staff. Some of them held coordination positions, such as the post of medical coordinator for the whole country.

This distance between staff members was all the more regrettable as gathering and analysing information about shifts in political, military and criminal dynamics were vital, everyday tasks. In the camps in Goma, Bukavu and Ngara, MSF witnessed or was told about the lynching of refugees. The teams attempted to reconstitute the circumstances of these murders, not in an attempt to substitute for the police, but rather to understand what they said about the reality of the camps and act accordingly. To do this meant obtaining information from Rwandan contacts.

As far as most of these contacts were concerned, the simple fact of being Tutsi was enough to explain the executions. Spying for the RPF was another accusation with a potentially fatal outcome. Some reports from the field described investigations into the circumstances of such murders, explaining how information or even rumours were channelled: patients talked to MSF's Rwandan staff who in turn spoke to the international staff who then informed the coordinator who sent a report to the relevant headquarters. Information thus adhered to an ordered process, predefined by the institution.

> Kabira situation: 5/11 Threats to loot MSF's hospital. These threats are not direct, but several people coming for medical visits have told members of staff that because we are employing Tutsis (this concerns 2 people; their noses are probably too thin or they're too tall), the militia are planning to loot the hospital and take out the supposed Tutsis. We have also been told that some patients left without their treatment after catching sight of the pharmacist, and rumour has it that some people are refusing to come to the hospital for treatment because we employ Tutsis.[22]

Most aid workers only learnt about what was happening in the Great Lakes region once they got to the field,[23] discovering the situation on the job and through talking to volunteers who had been there longer and Rwandans and other aid workers. As for the field coordinators, their knowledge of the context came from negotiating with the authorities (on whom MSF's continuing presence depended), coordination meetings with other NGOs, discussions with international institutions and organisations (ICRC, HCR, WFP, UNICEF, NGOs) and local aid NGOs, and their contacts with journalists.

The climate of persistent menacing uncertainty in which aid workers operated worried and distressed them, but it also angered them. Some of the messages they wrote testify to this, especially when referring to the Tutsi genocide and the fate

---

[22] MSF Bukavu, 6 November 1994.

[23] They were not the only ones. Reporter for the *New York Times*, Howard French, wrote that at the beginning of the war at the end of 1996, 'the Western Press understood precious little'. He added: 'How normal it was for reporters to operate in nearly perfect ignorance of their surroundings on this continent. Africa remained terra incognita for most within my profession.' With regard to the American diplomats, he considered that 'they were playing sides in the conflict and doing all they could to avoid owning up to it'. H.W. French, *A Continent for the Taking* (New York: Alfred A. Knopf, 2004), p. 128. Howard French covered Central Africa for the *New York Times* during the war from 1996–97.

of the refugees. Remember this observation made by MSF's manager in Bukavu in November 1994: 'On the surface, the situation in Kabira [camp] looks to be much more under control. But we know nothing about the underground organisation, real or otherwise.'[24]

Disagreements arose between MSF sections about the legitimacy of public denouncements. The level of validity of evidence needed to justify such denouncements was raised for argument's sake.[25] Thus, when on 26 April 1997 MSF France published a press release denouncing 'the policy of total liquidation of Rwandan refugees in the Kivu',[26] later that day, the directors of operations in Brussels and Amsterdam expressed their disagreement. In their opinion, the Paris press release failed to reflect the uncertainty surrounding the situation. They objected to the claim that the 'total elimination' of refugees was underway in the following terms: 'We are not witnessing this directly and therefore we can only say that it is strange to see that there is no protection or assistance tolerated ... We don't even know if and how many people have been killed by the military forces.'[27] To which the director of operations in Paris replied: 'We don't want to keep quiet about what we have seen.'[28] She referred to the accounts of three members of MSF France's international staff just back from Kisangani. They reported a recent massacre of refugees in the camps where they had been working, which a driver employed by MSF had witnessed directly. Soldiers, who he identified from their language as Rwandan, ordered him to take part in the executions (he refused) and then to help bury the bodies (he complied). Yet, despite these eyewitness accounts by MSF staff, two operational sections persisted in saying: 'We are not witnessing this directly.'

In other cases, obstructions to humanitarian aid really did prevent international staff from being direct witnesses. And there were many, notably the temporary bans on access to certain sites in Rwanda and Zaire – camps, towns, rural communes, regions and forests. Under such conditions, aid workers could provide neither assistance nor evidence of what was happening in places to which they were denied access.

But, in light of the sheer gravity of the situation in Rwanda, relations between sections were not always contentious. Thus all the MSF sections agreed that the systematic massacre of the Tutsis constituted genocide, campaigned together for it to

---

[24] MSF Bukavu, 6 November 1994.

[25] J.-H. Bradol and Cl. Vidal, 'Les attitudes humanitaires dans la région des Grands Lacs', *Politique Africaine*, 68 (1997), 69–77.

[26] MSF, 'Three proposals for putting an end to the policy of exterminating Rwandan refugees in Zaire', Paris, 26 April 1997.

[27] Director of Operations, MSF, Belgian section; Operational Director and Head of Emergency Desk, MSF Amsterdam, 'Comments on today's press communiqué from Paris on refugees', 26 April 1997.

[28] Director of Operations Paris to all operations: Brussels, Paris, 1 May 1997. She concluded as follows: 'Without wishing to be a revisionist, without comparing it to the genocide of '94, what has been happening since November in Kivu and Rwanda (and in Burundi for three years) is out of the ordinary and we cannot continue to see just those victims to be assisted. MSF-ly yours.'

be recognised as such and concurred in their critique of the French government's responsibility. They also concurred on the concrete measures needed to provide assistance to Rwandan refugees in Zaire, then in Congo-Brazzaville, and ceaselessly denounced the hold of extremist leaders and militia over the population and their diversions of food aid. In other words, there was considerable consensus on most advocacy issues and urgent operational adjustments. Finally, MSF adopted a position that was unprecedented for the organisation, making three appeals for international military intervention during the period 1994–97. The first came in the spring of 1994: 'Genocide calls for a radical, immediate response. You can't stop genocide with doctors.'[29] Then, at the beginning of November 1994, the whole MSF movement appealed to the UNSC for the immediate establishment of an international security force to protect the Rwandan refugees from the violence and threats in the camps orchestrated by the authors of the genocide and their militia.[30] This force was never deployed in Zaire. As for the third appeal made in November 1996, MSF France and MSF Holland called for the urgent deployment in eastern Zaire of 'an armed intervention force to set up safe areas and ensure access to assistance for civilians'.[31] This armed intervention never took place.

An historic and practical contribution

Long shrouded in controversy, the events in Rwanda have been the object of the kind of indictment with which we are now only too familiar. Since 1994, these have involved academics, former politicians and aid workers, journalists, activists and the Rwandan authorities. There is thus no doubt in our minds that we will also be subjected to criticism, and even to accusations – which has prompted us to a rigorous analysis of our sources.

Indeed, we have exploited the documents produced by members of MSF as if they had been conserved to serve as sources for historians. When, despite the pressure of an emergency, aid workers take the time to record what they see, what they hear and their interpretation of events, their intention is to combat the uncertainty, identify the perpetrators of violence and possibilities for intervention. They don't see their writings as a 'source' for future historians. In fact, given the passion that characterises their investment in moments of extreme violence – a sentiment that can sometimes compromise the objective tone of a report – they are more likely to find intolerable the notion of producing documents for posterity. And yet, years later, when such

[29] Appeal by MSF France to the President of the Republic, published in *Le Monde*, 18 June 1994. The President of the Republic and the French government launched Operation Turquoise in June under a UN mandate. See United Nations, Resolution 929, adopted by the Security Council on 22 June 1994. This resolution authorised a 'multi-national operation' with 'humanitarian objectives'.

[30] MSF, New York, 'Appeal for immediate action in the Rwandan refugee camps', 7 November 1994.

[31] MSF France and MSF Holland, 'Call for Immediate Dispatch of an Armed Intervention Force to Protect Civilians', 15 November 1996.

events start to be revised and negated, when they become the object of mystifying propaganda, 'humanitarian' sources produced by eyewitnesses become crucial for historians working to constitute accurate knowledge of them.

MSF had never been confronted with genocide and repeated mass atrocities such as those seen in Rwanda. The exceptional character of the situation was reason enough for a study: in the face of such events, what could a humanitarian aid organisation do? What did it do? Our objective was to produce historical knowledge while providing professional information for aid practitioners, and so we focused on the practical and political difficulties they encountered and the consequences of their actions. Although the violence of the situation was exceptional, we have highlighted issues common to all humanitarian relief operations during armed conflict: their relative ineffectiveness when faced with the needs of human beings subjected to particularly serious attacks, war criminals employing the discourse of victims to mask their crimes, diversion of aid and heavy losses among humanitarian workers.

Select bibliography

Books and articles

Amselle, J.-L. and E. M'Bokolo (eds), *Au cœur de l'ethnie. Ethnies, tribalisme et état en Afrique* (Paris: La Découverte, 1985).

Autesserre, S., *The Trouble with the Congo: Local Violence and the Failure of International Peacebuilding* (New York: Cambridge University Press, 2010).

Barrère, B., J. Schoemaker, M. Barrère, H. Tite, K. Athanasie and N. Mathias, *Demographic and Health Survey of Rwanda, 1992* (Kigali and Calverton: National Office of Population (Rwanda) and Macro International Inc, 1994).

Binet, L., *Genocide of Rwandan Tutsis* (Paris: MSF, 2003). http://speakingout.msf.org/en/genocide-of-rwandan-tutsi.

Binet, L., *Rwandan Refugee Camps in Zaire and Tanzania 1994–1995* (Paris: MSF, 2004). http://speakingout.msf.org/en/rwandan-refugee-camps-in-zaire-and-tanzania.

Binet, L., *The Violence of the New Rwandan Regime 1994–1995* (Paris: MSF, 2004). http://speakingout.msf.org/en/the-violence-of-the-new-rwandan-regime.

Binet, L., *The Hunting and Killing of Rwandan Refugees in Zaire-Congo: 1996–1997* (Paris: MSF, 2004). http://speakingout.msf.org/en/the-hunting-and-killing-of-rwandan-refugees-in-zaire-congo.

Boelaert, M. and M. Henkens, 'Letter', *The Lancet*, 349:9046 (1997), 213.

Borton, J., 'An account of co-ordination mechanisms for humanitarian assistance during the international response to the 1994 crisis in Rwanda', *Disasters*, 20:4 (1996), 305–23.

Borton, J., 'Doing Study 3 of the Joint Evaluation of Emergency Assistance to Rwanda: the team leader's perspective', in A. Wood, R. Apthorpe and J. Borton (eds), *Evaluating International Humanitarian Action: Reflections from Practitioners* (New York and London: Zed Books, ALNAP, 2001).

Borton, J., 'The Joint Evaluation of Emergency Assistance to Rwanda', *Humanitarian Exchange Magazine*, 26 (April 2004). http://odihpn.org/magazine/the-joint-evaluation-of-emergency-assistance-to-rwanda/.

Borton, J., E. Brusset and A. Hallam, *Humanitarian Aid and Effects, Study III of The International Response to Conflict and Genocide: Lessons from the Rwanda Experience. Joint Evaluation of Emergency Assistance to Rwanda* (Copenhagen and London: Danida, ODI, 1996).

Bradol, J.-H., 'Rwanda, avril-mai 1994, limites et ambiguïtés de l'action humanitaire', *Les Temps Modernes*, 583 (July–August 1995), 126–48.

Bradol, J.-H. and A. Guibert, 'Le temps des assassins et l'espace humanitaire, Rwanda, Kivu, 1994–1997', *Hérodote*, 86/87 (1997), 116–49.

Bradol, J.-H. and Cl. Vidal, 'Les attitudes humanitaires dans la région des Grands Lacs', *Politique Africaine*, 68 (1997), 69–77.

Bradol, J.-H. and Cl. Vidal (eds), *Medical Innovations in Humanitarian Situations. The work of Médecins Sans Frontières* (New York: Médecins Sans Frontières, 2011).

Brauman, R., 'Introduction', in F. Jean (ed.), *Populations en danger* (Paris: Hachette, 1992).

Brauman, R., *Devant le mal. Rwanda: un génocide en direct* (Paris: Arlea, 1994).

Buchanan-Smith, M., *How the Sphere Project Came into Being: A Case Study of Policy-Making in the Humanitarian Aid Sector and the Relative Influence of Research*, Working Paper 215 (London: ODI, 2003).

Byanafashe, D. and P. Rutayisire (eds), *Histoire du Rwanda des origines à la fin du XXème siècle* (Huye: Université Nationale du Rwanda, 2011).

Caravielhe, R., *Ou tout, ou rien. Journal d'un logisticien* (Lunel: Presses de Lunel, 2002).

Chrétien, J.-P., *Rwanda, les médias du génocide* (Paris: Karthala, 2000).

CICR, *Activités du CICR au Zaire/RDC 1994–3 février 1999* (Genève: CICR, 1999).

De Villers, G. and J.-C. Willame, *République démocratique du Congo. Chronique politique d'un entre-deux-guerres, octobre 1996-juillet 1998* (Tervuren and Paris: Cahiers africains, Institut Africain-CEDAF, L'Harmattan, 1998).

Dupont, P., 'La communauté internationale face à la question de l'intervention humanitaire lors de la rébellion au Kivu (octobre-décembre 1996)', *L'Afrique des Grands Lacs, Annuaire 1996–1997* (1997), 205–20.

Engel, P., 'Faut-il croire ce qu'on nous dit?', *Philosophie*, 88 (2005), 58–71.

Eriksson, J., *Synthesis Report. The International Response to Conflict and Genocide: Lessons from the Rwanda Experience. Joint Evaluation of Emergency Assistance to Rwanda* (Copenhagen and London: Danida, ODI, 1996).

French, H.W., *A Continent for the Taking: The Tragedy and Hope of Africa* (New York: Alfred A. Knopf, 2004).

Gaillard, P., 'Rwanda 1994: La vraie vie est absente (Arthur Rimbaud)', lecture by the head of the ICRC delegation to Rwanda from 1993 to 1994, International Red Cross and Red Crescent Museum (Geneva, 18 October 1994).

Ginzburg, C., 'Microhistory: two or three things that I know about it', *Critical Inquiry*, 20:1 (1993), 10–35. www.jstor.org/stable/1343946.

Goma Epidemiology Group, 'Public health impact of Rwandan refugee crisis: what happened in Goma, Zaire, in July, 1994?', *The Lancet*, 345:8946 (1995), 339–44.

Guichaoua, A. (ed.), *Exilés, réfugiés, déplacés en Afrique centrale et orientale* (Paris: Karthala, 2004).

Guichaoua, A., *Rwanda 1994. Les politiques du génocide à Butare* (Paris: Karthala, 2005).

Guichaoua, A., *From War to Genocide: Criminal Politics in Rwanda, 1990–1994* (Madison: University of Wisconsin Press, 2015).

Jewsiewicki, B., *La première guerre du Congo-Zaïre (1996–1997). Récits de soldats AFDL et FAR* (Paris: L'Harmattan, 2012).

Lagarde, F., *Mémorialistes et témoins rwandais (1994–2013)* (Paris: L'Harmattan, 2013).

Legros, D., C. Paquet and P. Nabeth, 'The evolution of mortality among Rwandan refugees in Zaire between 1994 and 1997', in H.E. Reed and C.B. Keely (eds), *Forced Migration & Mortality* (Washington, DC: National Academy Press, 2001).

Lemarchand, R., *The Dynamics of Violence in Central Africa* (Philadelphia: University of Pennsylvania Press, 2009).

Lepora, C. and R.E. Goodin, *On Complicity and Compromise* (Oxford: Oxford University Press, 2013).

Longman, T., 'Genocide and socio-political change: massacres in two Rwandan villages', *Issue. A Journal of Opinion*, 23:2 (1995), 18–21.

Longman, T., 'The complex reasons for Rwanda's engagement in Congo', in J.F. Clark (ed.), *The African Stakes of the Congo War* (New York: Palgrave Macmillan, 2002).

Martin, I., 'Hard choices after genocide: human rights and political failures in Rwanda', in J. Moore (ed.), *Hard Choices: Moral Dilemmas in Humanitarian Intervention* (Lanham: Rowman & Littlefield Publishers, 1998).

Médecins Sans Frontières, *Refugee Health: An Approach to Emergency Situations* (Oxford: Macmillan, 1997).

Mpayimana, P., *Réfugiés rwandais entre marteau et enclume. Récit du calvaire au Zaïre (1996–1997)* (Paris: L'Harmattan, 2004).

Myfanwy, J., *The Refugees of Eastern Zaire: The Forgotten Chapter of the Great Lakes Conflict* (Final year undergraduate dissertation, University of Bristol, 2015).

Nabeth, P., A. Croisier, M. Pedari and J.-H. Bradol, 'Acts of violence against Rwandan refugees', *The Lancet*, 350:9091 (1997), 1635.

Newbury, C., 'Suffering and survival in Central Africa', *African Studies Review*, 48:3 (2005), 121–32.

Niwese, M., *Le peuple rwandais un pied dans la tombe. Récit d'un réfugié étudiant* (Paris: L'Harmattan, 2001).

Office of the United Nations High Commissioner for Human Rights, *Report of the Mapping Exercise documenting the most serious violations of human rights and international humanitarian law committed within the territory of the Democratic Republic of the Congo between March 1993 and June 2003*, Geneva, OHCHR, 2010. http://www.ohchr.org/Documents/Countries/ CD/DRC_MAPPING_REPORT_FINAL_EN.pdf.

Orbinski, J., 'On the meaning of Sphere standards to states and humanitarian actors' (Lecture delivered in London, 3 December 1998). www.msf.fr/sites/www.msf.fr/files/1998-12-03-Orbinski.pdf.

Paquet, C., P. Leborgne, A. Sasse and F. Varaine, 'Une épidémie de dysenterie à *Shigella Dysenteriae* type 1 dans un camp de réfugiés au Rwanda', *Cahier Santé*, 5:3 (1995), 181–4.

Pons, F., S. Rigal, Ch. Dupeyron and J. de Saint-Julien, 'Activité chirurgicale d'une antenne du service de santé des Armées dans le cadre de l'opération Turquoise au Rwanda de juin à août 1994', *Chirurgie*, 121:1 (1996), 19–27.

Pottier, J., 'Relief and repatriation: views by Rwandan refugees; lessons for humanitarian aid workers', *African Affairs*, 95:380 (1996), 403–29.

Pottier, J., 'Why aid agencies need better understanding of the communities they assist: the experience of food aid in Rwandan refugee camps', *Disasters*, 20:4 (1996), 324–37.

Pottier, J., *Re-Imagining Rwanda: Conflict, Survival and Disinformation in the Late Twentieth Century* (Cambridge: Cambridge University Press, 2002).

Pourtier, R., 'Les camps du Kivu ou la gestion de l'éphémère', in V. Lassailly-Jacob, J.-Y. Marchal and A. Quesnel (eds), *Déplacés et réfugiés. La mobilité sous contrainte* (Paris: Éditions de l'IRD, 1999).

Prunier, G., *The Rwanda Crisis 1959–1994: History of a Genocide* (London: Hurst & Company, 1995).

Reyntjens, F., *The Great African War: Congo and Regional Geopolitics, 1996–2006* (Cambridge: Cambridge University Press, 2010).

Roberts, L. and M.J. Toole, 'Cholera deaths in Goma', *The Lancet*, 346:8987 (1995), 1431.

Royer, A., 'L'instrumentalisation politique des réfugiés du Kivu entre 1994 et 1996', in A. Guichaoua (ed.), *Exilés, réfugiés, déplacés en Afrique centrale et orientale* (Paris: Karthala, 2004).

Royer, A., 'De l'exil au pouvoir, le destin croisé des réfugiés burundais et rwandais dans la région des Grands Lacs africains' (Sociology thesis, Paris I University, 2006).

Rudasingwa, Dr. T., *Healing a Nation: A Testimony. Waging and Winning a Peaceful Revolution to Unite and Heal a Broken Rwanda* (North Charleston: CreateSpace Independent Publishing Platform, 2013).

Rugumaho, B., *L'Hécatombe des réfugiés rwandais dans l'ex-Zaïre. Témoignage d'un survivant* (Paris: L'Harmattan, 2004).

Segamba, L., V. Ndikumasabo, C. Makinson and M. Ayad, *Demographic and Health Survey of Burundi, 1987* (Gitega and Columbia: Ministère de l'Intérieur Département de la Population and Institute for Resource Development/Westinghouse, 1988).

Siméant, J., 'Qu'a-t-on vu quand on ne voyait rien?', in M. Le Pape, J. Siméant and Cl. Vidal (eds), *Crises extrêmes. Face aux massacres, aux guerres civiles et aux génocides* (Paris: La Découverte, 2006).

Stearns, J.K., *Dancing in the Glory of Monsters: The Collapse of the Congo and the Great African War of Africa* (New York: PublicAffairs, 2011).

Sundin, J., 'Kigali's wound, through a doctor's eyes (experiences of a Red Cross doctor in Kigali, Rwanda)', *Harper's Magazine* (August 1994).

Terry, F., *Condemned to Repeat? The Paradox of Humanitarian Action* (Ithaca and London: Cornell University Press, 2002).

Toole, M.J. and R.J. Waldman, 'The public health aspects of complex emergencies and refugee situation', *Annual Review of Public Health*, 18 (1997), 283–312.

Turner, T., *The Congo Wars: Conflict, Myth & Reality* (London and New York: Zed Books, 2007).

Umuraza, C., *Une jeunesse rwandaise* (Paris: Karthala, 2008).

Umutesi, M.B., *Surviving the Slaughter: The Ordeal of a Rwandan Refugee in Zaire* (Madison: The University of Wisconsin Press, 2004) (Originally published in France as *Fuir ou mourir au Zaïre*, Paris: L'Harmattan, 2000).

Uvin, P., *Aiding Violence: The Development Enterprise in Rwanda* (West Hartford: Kumarian Press, 1998).

Vallaeys, A., *Médecins Sans Frontières. La biographie* (Paris: Fayard, 2004).

Verwimp, P., *Agricultural Policy, Crop Failure and the 'Ruriganiza' Famine (1989) in Southern Rwanda: A Prelude to Genocide?* (Leuven: Discussion paper series, Department of Economics, Katholieke Universiteit Leuven, 2002).

Vidal, Cl., 'Les humanitaires, témoins pour l'histoire', *Les Temps Modernes*, 627 (April–May–June 2004), 92–107.

Vidal, Cl., 'Le fait d'"entente en vue de commettre le génocide". Entre le judiciaire et l'historique au Rwanda', *L'Afrique des Grands Lacs: Annuaire 2014–2015* (Paris: L'Harmattan, 2015), 269–86.

Vidal, Cl. and J. Pinel, 'MSF "satellites": a strategy underlying different medical practices', in J.-H. Bradol and Cl. Vidal (eds), *Medical Innovations in Humanitarian Situations: The Work of Médecins Sans Frontières* (New York: MSF, 2011).

Vlassenroot, K., 'Citizenship, identity formation & conflict in South Kivu: the case of the Banyamulenge', *Review of African Political Economy*, 93–94 (2002), 499–516.

Willame, J.-C., *Banyarwanda et Banyamulenge. Violences ethniques et gestion de l'identitaire au Kivu* (Brussels and Paris: Cahiers Africains, Institut Africain, L'Harmattan, 1997).

Newspapers and magazines

Contact (MSF Belgium in-house magazine)
De Morgen
Foreign Policy
La Nouvelle Gazette
La Wallonie
Le Monde
Le Soir
Libération

Messages (MSF France in-house magazine)
Moscow Times
New York Times
Ouest-France
Philadelphia Inquirer
Washington Post

News agencies

AFP
Reuters
Voice Of America

Archives

Archives MSF, Paris
We consulted MSF's archives on the assistance programmes for Rwandan speaking people in Uganda, Zaire, Tanzania and Rwanda. Other than MSF documents, these archives also contain reports, press releases, minutes of meetings and communications of the United Nations, ICRC and other international humanitarian organisations. There is no inventory of these archives.

Websites and online resources

ICTR
http://41.220.139.198/Cases/tabid/77/Default.aspx?id=4&mnid=4
The Prosecutor v. Jean-Baptiste Gatete, Case No. ICTR-200-61-T, Jugement and sentence, 31 March 2011.
http://41.220.139.198/Cases/tabid/127/PID/2/default.aspx?id=4&mnid=2
http://41.220.139.198/Portals/0/Case%5CEnglish%5CGatete%5Cjudgement%5C110331.pdf
The Prosecutor v. Sylvestre Gacumbitsi, Case No. TPIR-2001-64-T, Judgment, 17 June 2004.
http://41.220.139.198/Portals/0/Case%5CEnglish%5CGacumbitsi%5CDecision%5C040617-judgement.pdf
ICRC www.icrc.org/en/resource-centre/result?t=Philippe+Gaillard
Lagarde F.
https://repositories.lib.utexas.edu/bitstream/handle/2152/15587/RWANDA_1990-2011Bibliographie_FL.pdf?sequence=4
www.univ-paris1.fr/fileadmin/BibliographieRwanda1990-2011/RWANDA_2012_Bibliographie.pdf
www.univ-paris1.fr/fileadmin/BibliographieRwanda1990-2011/Rwanda_2013_Bbibliographie_Sat_Jan_18.pdf
www.univ-paris1.fr/fileadmin/BibliographieRwanda1990-2011/RWANDA_2014_Bibliographie.pdf
MSF http://speakingout.msf.org/
UNDHA, IRIN, Great Lakes 1996, 1997
www.africa.upenn.edu/Hornet/undh96.html
www.africa.upenn.edu/Hornet/undh97.html

Index

Action by Churches Together (ACT) 108
Active Learning Network for Accountability
    and Performance in Humanitarian Action
    (ALNAP) 5
African Medical and Research Foundation
    (AMREF) 70
Akagera 14, 18
Amnesty 76, 78
Association Cooperazione Internazionale
    (COOPI) 70
Association des juristes démocrates 78
Association rwandaise pour la défense des
    droits de l'homme (ARDHO) 67
Association rwandaise pour la défense
    des droits de la personne et des libertés
    publiques (ADL) 83

Belgian Red Cross 20, 32
Benaco 43–4, 46–7, 55–7, 62, 64, 120
Biaro 114, 116–18, 120
Bidudu 17–18
Birambo 80
Birenga 23
Bugarura 17–18
Bugesera 16, 21–3, 26–7, 34, 36, 67, 69, 70, 81, 134
Bugnari 34
Bujumbura 7, 20, 28, 30, 34, 38, 108
Bukavu 7, 35, 37, 47–9, 50–1, 53, 57–8, 71,
    74, 103–5, 108–9, 110, 117, 135–6
Burenge 21–3
Busanze 83–4
Butare 7, 23–4, 27–8, 32–4, 36–7, 39, 66–8,
    70–1, 84–8, 90–2, 94–5, 97, 100, 118, 140

Butaro 18
Buyoga 17–18
Byumba 7, 15–18, 25–6, 35–7, 44, 66–7,
    70–1, 100

Caritas 20, 33, 83, 86–7, 92, 98, 110
Catholic Relief Services (CRS) 132
Centers for Disease Control and Prevention
    (CDC) 52
Central Hospital of Kigali (CHK) 24,
    27–8, 32, 70
Ceru 34
Chimanga 50–1
Common Causes 78
Compassion International 70
Concern 91
Cooperative for Assistance and Relief
    Everywhere (CARE) 45, 57, 70, 91
Cyabingo 17
Cyangugu 7, 32, 37, 42, 51, 67, 70–1, 117–18

Doctors of the World (MdM Médecins du
    Monde) 20, 95, 110, 118, 127

Équilibre 81

Feed the Children 81, 93

Gahara 21, 23
Gakurazo 83
Gashora 21, 23, 35
Gatare 34
Gatuna 18

German Red Cross 56
Gikoma 17–18
Gikongoro 25, 32–3, 37, 67, 70, 74–5, 81–5, 90, 93, 95, 100
Gisenyi 7, 16–17, 28, 31, 37, 67, 70–1, 102, 106, 118
Gishambashi 18
Gitarama 28, 32, 35–6, 67, 70, 82–3, 97–9, 100
Gitare 18–19, 36
Gituza 17–18
Goal 70, 81
Goma 7, 28, 35, 37, 39, 47–9, 52–3, 57–8, 61–4, 71, 74, 102, 105–6, 108, 128, 135

Hongo 50, 51
Human Rights Watch (HRW) 76
Huye 72, 87, 94

Inera 50–1
International Action against Hunger (AICF) 20, 23–4, 32, 47, 110
International Committee of the Red Cross (ICRC) 6, 24, 27–9, 30–3, 35–6, 38–9, 40, 42, 66–7, 70, 77, 82–3, 85–8, 91, 94, 95, 97–8, 100, 105, 109, 118, 122, 128, 132, 134–5
International Federation for Human Rights (FIDH) 16, 38, 78
International Federation of Red Cross and Red Crescent Societies (IFRC) 20, 120, 132
International Organization for Migration (IOM) 73, 86, 88

Kabgayi 28, 32, 83, 98
Kabira 50–1, 57–8, 135–6
Kahindo 48, 53
Kalehe 50–1
Kamanyola 50
Kampala 15
Karama 21, 23, 26–7
Kasese 108, 114–16
Kashusha 50–1
Katale 48–9, 50–3, 57, 64
Kayanza 33, 35, 71
Kibeho 33, 61, 82, 84–7, 89, 90–6, 100–1, 129
Kibumba 48–9, 53, 57, 105

Kibungo 23, 25, 28, 37, 44, 71, 120
Kibuye 17, 25, 37, 67, 70–1, 80–2, 100
Kigali 7, 9, 11, 16, 18–19, 20–9, 30–9, 40–1, 47, 61–2, 70, 77–9, 80–2, 84, 86–7, 89, 90–3, 96–7, 100, 105, 108, 117, 118, 122–3, 127–8, 134
Kigeme 90
Kinazi 81
King Faisal Hospital 31, 66, 70
Kinihira 17–18
Kinshasa 13, 16, 103, 121
Kirundo 7, 35, 71
Kisangani 107–24, 136
Kisaro 17
Kituku 48, 53
Kivumu 81
Kiziguro 17, 26

Lac Vert 48, 105
Liranga 123
Lubutu 108–10, 113
Lukolela 108, 122–3
Lula 114, 118–19
Lumasi 46–7, 54, 57, 63
Lutheran World Federation 70, 132

Mabanza 80
Masa 21–2
Mbandaka 103–4, 108, 119, 120–2
Mbarara 15
Medair 70
Medical Emergency Relief International (Merlin) 81, 91, 106
Mirama Hills 15
Mubuga 82
Mugambazi 17
Mugunga 48–9, 57, 102, 105–6
Mukingi 83
Mukingo 17
Mulindi 19, 24
Munigi 49
Murambi 18, 26, 44
Musebeya 81
Muvumba 15
Mwendo 80

Nakivale 15
Ndjoundou 123

Ngara 7, 35, 37, 43–7, 54, 56, 58, 64, 120, 135
Ngozi 35, 71
Nshili 83, 93
Nyacyonga 17–18
Nyakinama 17
Nyakizu 32, 91
Nyamagabe 82
Nyamata 36, 81
Nyanza 36, 71
Nyarushishi 32, 42
Nyungwe 87
Nzangwa 21–3, 27, 35

Obilo 113, 114
Office for the Coordination of Humanitarian
   Affairs (OCHA) 132
Office of US Foreign Disaster Assistance
   (OFDA) 132
Official Development Administration (ODA
   UK) 132
Overseas Development Institute (ODI) 5, 69,
   129, 132
Oxford Committee for Famine Relief (Oxfam)
   17, 20, 70, 81, 86–7, 107, 132

Regional Association for the Supply of
   Essential Medicines (ASRAMES) 106
Réseau Citoyens/Citizens' Network (RCN)
   79, 80, 97, 99
Rubengera 80
Rugamara 18–19
Ruhengeri 16–18, 23, 25, 35–7, 48, 67, 70,
   100, 106, 118, 127
Rukondo 82, 84
Runda 118
Runyinya 91
Rusine 17–18
Rusumo 44, 120
Rwandan Red Cross (RRC) 10, 14, 20–1, 27,
   29, 120
Rwandese Refugee Welfare Foundation
   (RRWF) 14

Saga 21, 34
Samaritan's Purse 70

Save the Children 81, 86, 119, 132
Shabunda 108, 117, 122
Solidarités 81
Steering Committee for Humanitarian
   Response (SCHR) 131–2

Tingi-Tingi 104, 107–13
Trocaire 81
Tumba 17–18

Ubundu 108, 113–16, 120
United Nations Assistance Mission for
   Rwanda (UNAMIR) 9, 72, 74–5, 80–2, 84,
   86–7, 89, 90, 93–4, 98
United Nations Children's Fund (UNICEF)
   22, 47, 70, 86–7, 99, 100, 109–10, 122, 128,
   132, 135
United Nations Department of Humanitarian
   Affairs (UNDHA) 69, 109, 132
United Nations High Commissioner for
   Human Rights (UNHCHR) 4, 86–7,
   91–2, 95
United Nations High Commissioner for
   Refugees (UNHCR) 4, 6, 10–12, 14, 20,
   43–4, 46–7, 49, 50, 52–9, 60–1, 63, 69,
   72–3, 76, 80, 83, 86–8, 95, 105–6, 108–9,
   110, 112, 114–19, 120–4, 126, 128
United Nations Rwanda Emergency Office
   (UNREO) 88
Unrepresented Nations and Peoples
   Organization (UNPO) 69
US Agency for International Development
   (USAID) 109
Uvira 7, 35, 64, 71, 104–5, 108, 110

Wendji 121
World Council of Churches 132
World Food Programme (WFP) 20, 21, 24,
   45, 50, 110, 111, 113, 117, 122–4, 132, 135
World Health Organization (WHO) 100, 132
World Relief 70
World Vision 70

Zairian Red Cross 113
ZOA 70